The Fetus as a Patient

Due to new developments in prenatal testing and therapy the fetus is increasingly visible, examinable and treatable in prenatal care. Accordingly, physicians tend to perceive the fetus as a patient and understand themselves as having certain professional duties towards it. However, it is far from clear what it means to speak of a patient in this connection.

This volume explores the usefulness and limitations of the concept of 'fetal patient' against the background of the recent seminal developments in prenatal or fetal medicine. It does so from an interdisciplinary and international perspective. Featuring internationally recognized experts in the field, the book discusses the normative implications of the concept of 'fetal patient' from a philosophical-theoretical as well as from a legal perspective. This includes its implications for the autonomy of the pregnant woman as well as its consequences for physician-patient-interactions in prenatal medicine.

Dagmar Schmitz is Assistant Professor of Medical Ethics and Theory at the Institute for History, Theory and Ethics in Medicine, RWTH Aachen University, Germany, and a member of the German Commission on Genetic Testing (GEKO). In her research, she is especially interested in ethical aspects of physician-patient-interactions and the beginning of life.

Angus Clarke is Clinical Professor at the Institute of Cancer and Genetics, Cardiff University, UK. He works as a clinical geneticist and teaches students of medicine and of genetic counselling. He undertakes research on the social and ethical aspects of human genetics and contributes to policy discussions on genetic services within UK and Europe.

Wybo Dondorp is Associate Professor of Biomedical Ethics, Research Schools CAPHRI and GROW, at Maastricht University, the Netherlands. His research interests include the ethics of reproductive medicine, genomics, and population screening. He is a member of the Health Council of the Netherlands and past coordinator of the Special Interest Group on Ethics of the International Society of Prenatal Diagnosis and Fetal Therapy (ISPD).

Biomedical Law and Ethics Library

Series Editor: Sheila A. M. McLean

About the Series Editor

Professor Sheila A.M. McLean is Professor Emerita of Law and Ethics in Medicine, School of Law, University of Glasgow, UK.

https://www.routledge.com/Biomedical-Law-and-Ethics-Library/book-series/CAV5

Scientific and clinical advances, social and political developments and the impact of healthcare on our lives raise profound ethical and legal questions. Medical law and ethics have become central to our understanding of these problems, and are important tools for the analysis and resolution of problems – real or imagined.

In this series, scholars at the forefront of biomedical law and ethics contribute to the debates in this area, with accessible, thought-provoking, and sometimes controversial, ideas. Each book in the series develops an independent hypothesis and argues cogently for a particular position. One of the major contributions of this series is the extent to which both law and ethics are utilised in the content of the books, and the shape of the series itself.

The books in this series are analytical, with a key target audience of lawyers, doctors, nurses, and the intelligent lay public.

Available titles:

The Legitimacy of Medical Treatment
What Role for the Medical Exception?
Sara Fovargue and Alexandra Mullock

End of Life Decision Making for Critically Impaired Infants
Resource Allocation and Difficult Decisions
Neera Bhatia

Revisiting the Regulation of Human Fertilisation and Embryology
Kirsty Horsey

The Voices and Rooms of European Bioethics
Richard Huxtable and Ruud ter Meulen

Autonomy and Pregnancy
A Comparative Analysis of Compelled Obstetric Intervention
Samantha Halliday

The Fetus as a Patient

A Contested Concept and its Normative Implications

Edited by Dagmar Schmitz, Angus Clarke and Wybo Dondorp

Routledge
Taylor & Francis Group
LONDON AND NEW YORK

First published 2018 by Routledge

2 Park Square, Milton Park, Abingdon, Oxfordshire OX14 4RN
52 Vanderbilt Avenue, New York, NY 10017

Routledge is an imprint of the Taylor & Francis Group, an informa business

First issued in paperback 2020

British Library Cataloguing-in-Publication Data
A catalogue record for this book is available from the British Library

Library of Congress Cataloguing-in-Publication Data
Names: Schmitz, Dagmar, 1971– | Clarke, Angus, 1954– editor. | Dondorp, Wybo J. editor.
Title: The fetus as a patient : a contested concept and its normative implications / [edited by] Dagmar Schmitz, Angus Clarke, Wybo Dondorp.
Description: Abingdon, Oxon ; New York, NY : Routledge, 2018. | Series: Biomedical law and ethics library | Includes bibliographical references and index.
Identifiers: LCCN 2017055107 | ISBN 9781138047488 (hardback)
Subjects: LCSH: Fetus—Diseases. | Medical ethics. | Fetus—Legal status, laws, etc.
Classification: LCC RG626 .F487 2018 | DDC 618.3/2—dc23
LC record available at https://lccn.loc.gov/2017055107

ISBN: 978-1-138-04748-8 (hbk)
ISBN: 978-0-367-59137-3 (pbk)

Typeset in Galliard
by Apex CoVantage, LLC

Contents

Notes on contributors viii
Acknowledgements x

PART I
Introduction 1

1 The fetus as a patient: a sustainable approach for clinical interactions in the field of new prenatal medicine? 3
DAGMAR SCHMITZ, ANGUS CLARKE, AND WYBO DONDORP

PART II
The fetus as a patient: a useful concept? 15

2 The disposable and protected fetus: contradictions in fetal status 17
LUCY FRITH

3 Which ethics for the fetus as patient? 28
CLAUDIA WIESEMANN

4 The ethical concept of the fetus as a patient: responses to its critics 40
LAURENCE B. MCCOLLOUGH AND FRANK A. CHERVENAK

5 Treating the fetus as a patient: possible implications for its moral status 50
KATRIN E. LÖRCH-MERKLE

PART III
The fetus as a patient: where does that leave the pregnant woman? 63

6 Insights from a perspective of cultural anthropology: a discourse analyses of representations of (genetic) reproductive medicine and the fetus in popular media 65
JANINA KRAUSE

7 The fetus as a patient: professional and patient discourse 78
HEATHER STRANGE

8 Means, ends, and the fetal patient 94
ANNA SMAJDOR

9 Caring for pregnant cancer patients 104
ALMA LINKEVICIUTE

PART IV
The fetus as a patient: challenges for clinical care pathways and interactions 115

10 Treatments and trials for the fetal patient: imposing the burdens of enthusiasm? 117
ANGUS CLARKE

11 Ethics of involving pregnant women in fetal therapy trials 133
E.J. (JOANNE) VERWEIJ

12 The 'normalization' of prenatal screening: prevention as prenatal beneficence 144
WYBO DONDORP AND GUIDO DE WERT

13 Beyond the fetal patient: the ethics of fetal treatment for Down syndrome 154
GUIDO DE WERT AND WYBO DONDORP

14 Prenatal therapy for differences of sexual development (DSD): fuzzy boundaries in the clinical discussion and the ethical debate 166
MATHIAS WIRTH AND MARC-ANTOINE MARQUIS

15 Perinatal palliative care as an option in prenatally diagnosed severe, life-limiting conditions of the fetus 181
KATHRIN KNOCHEL, FRANZISKA FLAIG, JULIA D. LOTZ, AND MONIKA FÜHRER

PART V
The fetus as a patient: legal perspective 195

16 The legal status of the fetus as a patient in Europe 197
ATINA KRAJEWSKA AND DIMITRIOS TSARAPATSANIS

Index 209

Contributors

Frank A. Chervenak is Given Foundation Professor and Chairman of Obstetrics and Gynecology, Weill Medical College of Cornell University, Ithaca, NY, USA.

Angus Clarke is Clinical Professor at the Institute of Cancer and Genetics, Cardiff University, UK.

Wybo Dondorp is Associate Professor of Biomedical Ethics, Research Schools CAPHRI and GROW, at Maastricht University, the Netherlands.

Franziska Flaig is a Medical Student at the Center of Pediatric Palliative Care, Hauner Children's Hospital, Ludwig-Maximilians-University Munich, Germany.

Lucy Frith is Reader in Bioethics and Social Science, in the Institute of Psychology, Health and Society, at the University of Liverpool, UK.

Monika Führer is a Professor of Pediatric Palliative Medicine and Head of the Center of Pediatric Palliative Care, Hauner Children's Hospital, Ludwig-Maximilians-University Munich, Germany.

Kathrin Knochel is a Physician at the Center of Pediatric Palliative Care, Hauner Children's Hospital, Ludwig-Maximilians-University Munich, Germany.

Atina Krajewska is a Senior Birmingham Fellow at the Birmingham Law School, University of Birmingham, UK, specializing in medical law and global health law.

Janina Krause is a PhD candidate at the Institute for Cultural Anthropology and European Ethnology at Goethe-University in Frankfurt am Main, Germany.

Alma Linkeviciute is a Bioethicist and Clinical Research Professional. Currently she works in the contract research (CRO) industry, specializing in Oncology Clinical Trials, She recently earned her PhD degree from the University of Milan, Italy.

Katrin E. Lörch-Merkle is a PhD candidate and a Part-time Lecturer in Practical Philosophy/Ethics, with a teaching focus mainly on Bio- and Medical Ethics at the Department of Philosophy at Eberhard Karls University Tübingen, Germany.

Julia D. Lotz is a Psychologist and Research Assistant at the Center of Pediatric Palliative Care, Hauner Children's Hospital, Ludwig-Maximilians-University Munich, Germany.

Laurence B. McCullough is Adjunct Professor of Ethics in Obstetrics and Gynecology, Weill Medical College of Cornell University, Ithaca, NY, USA, and Distinguished Emeritus Professor, Baylor College of Medicine, Houston, Texas, USA.

Marc-Antoine Marquis is a Canadian pediatrician and a Clinical Fellow within the Interprofessional Palliative Care Fellowship at Harvard University, USA.

Dagmar Schmitz is Assistant Professor of Medical Ethics and Theory at the Institute for History, Theory and Ethics in Medicine, RWTH Aachen University, Germany.

Anna Smajdor is an Associate Professor in Practical Philosophy at the Department of Philosophy, Classics, History of Art and Ideas at the University of Oslo, Norway.

Heather Strange is a Research Associate at Cardiff University's School of Medicine, Cardiff, UK, working within the fields of Medical Sociology, Science and Technology studies and Bio- and Medical Ethics.

Dimitrios Tsarapatsanis is a Lecturer at the School of Law, University of Sheffield, UK.

E.J. (Joanne) Verweij is a Resident in Gynecology at Leiden University Medical Center, the Netherlands.

Guido de Wert is Professor of Biomedical Ethics at the Department of Health Ethics and Society of Maastricht University, the Netherlands, Research Schools CAPHRI and GROW.

Claudia Wiesemann is Professor of History of Medicine and Medical Ethics and Head of the Department of Medical Ethics and History of Medicine at Göttingen University Medical Center, Germany, and member of the German Ethics Council.

Mathias Wirth is a Feodor Lynen Postdoc at the Yale Divinity School, New Haven, CT, USA. He is a member of the Affiliated Faculty and Staff of the Program for Biomedical Ethics at the Yale Medical School.

Acknowledgements

The editors would like to thank the German Federal Ministry of Education and Research and its ELSA Diagnostics program (funding code: 01GP1484) for generously funding the seminar "The fetus as a patient" which was held in Vaals (The Netherlands) in November 2015 and inspired the idea for this book project. Thanks also go to Vasilija Rolfes and Tim Ohnhäuser (both RWTH Aachen University) for their assistance in organizing the seminar. We are very grateful to all the participants of the seminar for their interest and insightful contributions many of which are now part of this collection (Chervenak, De Wert, Flaig, Frith, Knochel, Krause, Linkeviciute, Lörch-Merkle, McCullough, Smajdor, Strange, Wiesemann and Wirth). It is our great pleasure to also include contributions from other interested colleagues (Führer, Krajewska, Lotz, Marquis, Tsarapatsanis and Verweij).

We would like to thank the team at Routledge, in particular Alex Buckley, Philip Stirups and Alison Kirk, for their support and patience in the publishing process and Sheila MacLean for considering our project for publication in the Biomedical Law and Ethics Library. Finally, but not least, we are very grateful to Charlotte Frierson (RWTH Aachen University) for her continuous support in the editorial process of our project.

Part I

Introduction

1 The fetus as a patient: a sustainable approach for clinical interactions in the field of new prenatal medicine?

Dagmar Schmitz, Angus Clarke, and Wybo Dondorp

Pregnant women and physicians have not only a rather short common history but also one fraught with tension. The central category of medicine as a professional practice – the category of disease – triggers and justifies professional actions but does not seem appropriate for the vast majority of pregnancies. The state of pregnancy is not a state of disease, neither in a descriptive nor in an evaluative sense. Nevertheless, being pregnant nowadays for many women means being in need of or receiving health care, being a patient. Sophisticated clinical care pathways equipped with extensive sets of diagnostic tools have been established in order to monitor the progress of pregnancies and identify potential complications as early as possible. In many countries, a doctor (and not a midwife) is the key contact person for women during pregnancy. But not only have pregnant women been transformed into patients: increasingly, physicians are identifying the fetus as also being a patient requiring prenatal care. Fetuses themselves are subjected to diagnosis and to treatment. Their whole genome is analysed; they are anesthetized and operated on. Fetuses might even impress as

> prime *work objects* in medicine; they are challenging bodies that do not challenge clinicians socially. That is, fetuses cannot ask questions about their own illness or prognosis, nor can they disagree with a doctor's recommendation. (...) Fetal patients may well be considered the 'best' patients by medical workers.
>
> (Casper, 1998 p 214)

This volume will explore the normative implications of the concept of the fetal patient against the background of the recent seminal developments in prenatal and fetal medicine. In doing so, it will also draw attention to the clinical care pathways in prenatal medicine which started to evolve less than 200 years ago and now so powerfully shape our perception of pregnancy, childbirth and fetuses.

In this introduction, we will first give a sketch of the background to the issues discussed in the book, and then briefly introduce the separate chapters by linking them to different aspects of the debate about 'the fetus as a patient'.

Background

Medicalization is usually understood as a social 'process by which human problems come to be defined and treated as medical problems' (Sadler *et al.*, 2009). As a social practice, medicalization can have different functions and aims in addition to improving health and wellness, like for instance safeguarding the power and authority of physicians or satisfying a societal demand for technological solutions for certain problems. What happened to pregnancy and childbirth in many respects can be seen as a typical and strong example of a medicalization which has served various, in part critically evaluated, purposes (Johanson *et al.*, 2002). In its aftermath (but not exclusively caused by it), maternal and neonatal mortality rates decreased significantly. Whereas in the mid-seventeenth century approximately 10 per cent of all neonates died during or shortly after birth in England and Wales, this rate sunk to less than three per 1000 live births in 2014 (Office for National Statistics, 2017). In the same period, maternal mortality rates went down from 15 to 0.09 per 1000 births (Smith, 1993 p 1682). Given that many women had multiple pregnancies, the cumulative lifetime chance of a woman dying in childbirth was often between 5 and 10 per cent (Shorter, 1984 p 98 suggests 8 per cent from examining pre-1800 data from Germany, the USA and England). In some rural areas in the eighteenth century, maternal mortality remained as high as 2 per cent per pregnancy (e.g. in Brabant villages, in Belgium/Netherlands) when it was declining rapidly in cities with access to training for midwives and obstetricians (Shorter, 1984 p 99).

The pregnant woman as a patient

The beginning of the medicalization of childbirth dates back to the mid-eighteenth century (Loudon, 1993 p 1051). Until then and for 150 years thereafter, the phenomenon of giving birth belonged largely to the private and female sphere (with the occasional assistance of female midwives). During the course of the following century, however, the percentage of hospital births changed from 5 per cent (in 1900 in Europe and North America) to 95 per cent (in 2000) and, thus, the management of childbirth has moved nearly completely into the public (clinical), and often male, sphere (Baker and McCullough, 2009).

A similar shift took place in pregnancy management. Traditionally, the pregnant woman had been the unchallenged authority with regard to the unborn. She felt the first fetal movements (the quickening) which for centuries served as the first clear evidence of a pregnancy, and she had the power to share this new knowledge or keep it private. During the nineteenth and twentieth centuries and starting with fetal heart auscultation, the medical professions learned to assess the unborn life through various ways.

With the advent of ultrasound technology in obstetric care in the 1960s, the physician could finally visualize the fetus inside the womb. At around the same time, the photographer Lennard Nilsson famously portrayed fetuses in different stages of development outside the womb and, thus, created public images of the unborn life. Subsequently, the battle to save women's lives largely won, the focus of the obstetrician changed from maternal to perinatal mortality and acknowledged the physician's 'custodianship of the baby's future', as Ian Donald pointed out in his textbook on *Practical Obstetrical Problems* (Donald, 1964). We are now not only able to create 3D ultrasound images of the fetus. It is also possible to examine large parts of the fetal genome via cell-free DNA of placental origin in the blood of pregnant women, which raises hopes for a future 'fetal personalized medicine' (Bianchi, 2012). Previously unthinkable therapeutic actions like the prenatal therapy of certain chromosomal conditions or intrauterine surgery are coming into reach or are already established in specialized centers. Fetal medicine as a new medical subdiscipline is finally in full bloom and has an influence on many clinical interactions during and even independently of a pregnancy.

Is there a fetus?

Any medical encounter with a female, from menarche to menopause, has to consider the possibility she might be pregnant. The health care professional will need to ask, 'Might this woman's symptoms be caused by pregnancy?' And even if that is clearly not the case, then the possibility of pregnancy still has to become explicit if there is any question of performing an X-ray or prescribing a drug treatment. The fetus has an influence, even when absent!

Society also promotes fetal welfare in advance of any pregnancy, for example through implementing an active immunization programme for schoolchildren against rubella. This virus is generally harmless to children and adults but can cause severe damage to the embryo or fetus if a woman suffers a primary infection while pregnant. A more targeted programme to *prevent unhelpful* immunization – for the benefit of future Rhesus-positive infants born to Rhesus-negative women – is also provided through giving Rhesus antiserum to Rhesus-negative women after delivery or following miscarriage or an invasive procedure such as chorionic biopsy to minimize their chances of developing an actively unhelpful immunity against a possible future fetus.

A woman hoping to become pregnant will be advised to eat 'well' which might mean eating *less* if she is overweight, and to take supplements to ensure she has adequate folic acid intake, so that any embryo that develops will be protected from disorders of neural tube closure. And if she is on any dietary or pharmacological treatment, she will be advised that this should be optimized to allow for the pregnancy, especially with diet for phenylketonuria, anticonvulsant treatment for epilepsy, warfarin for anticoagulation or insulin treatment for diabetes mellitus, as fetal exposure to maternal hyperphenylalaninaemia, anticonvulsant drugs, warfarin or hyperglycaemia can be teratogenic and/or toxic. For the doctor, almost any medical encounter with a female adolescent or a young woman raises the question of pregnancy, even when the woman knows and declares that this is not possible.

Pregnancy and expectations of maternal behaviour

There is an even stronger societal expectation that a pregnant woman should avoid exposing her fetus to harmful influences. For instance, she should not smoke or consume alcohol, and should not take recreational or addictive drugs; indeed, fetal welfare may for many be a weightier deterrent to the consumption of such substances than the question of legality. These commitments are expected of a mother-to-be for the sake of her fetus as a future child, along with the expectation that she should be on a 'healthy' diet.

The importance of maternal nutrition is increasingly recognized as being for the long-term benefit of the future child and then adult, with higher risks of many common western disorders (hypertension, type 2 diabetes, stroke, coronary artery disease, etc.) if the woman is malnourished (through famine) or if the fetus is growth-retarded because of 'placental insufficiency', when the woman may be adequately nourished but the benefits are unable to reach the fetus (Lee, 2015). The malnutrition associated with gross inequalities within societies may contribute to poor fetal outcomes and so, indirectly, to the chronic health burdens of the next generation. These effects are mediated in part through epigenetic mechanisms, which may interact with physiological responses to inequity and deprivation, such as the hormonal effects of chronic stress. There are good grounds for supporting the nutrition and the education of girls and young women impacted by these societal processes as a way of reducing the burden of chronic disease in the future.

The question of enforcement of 'good maternal behaviour' is an issue in some jurisdictions, especially in the USA, where imprisonment can be used as a sanction for women whose lack of compliance with expected behaviour is too conspicuous. In European countries, the law would generally not allow such coercive measures, as it does not recognize the fetus as a bearer of legal rights (Dorscheidt, 2010). Moreover, after the 2004 *Vo v. France* ruling of the European Court of Human Rights, it is clear that Article 2 of the European Convention of Human Rights (stating that 'Everyone's right to life shall be protected by law') does not require member states to protect the life of the unborn.

Other recommendations for a pregnant woman are intended for the benefit of the maternal-fetal 'dyad', such as weight loss if the woman is obese, as this makes so much difference to the chances of an uncomplicated delivery (Mutsaerts *et al.*, 2014). More broadly, psycho-physiological studies indicate that the fetus becomes responsive to, and presumably aware of, stimulation through multiple sensory modalities. For example, the fetus learns to recognize different voices and distinguish different languages (Karmiloff and Karmiloff-Smith, 2001); enthusiasts claim benefits from exposing the fetus to Mozart.

Fetal surveillance: from enabling 'reproductive choice' to allowing therapeutic interventions

At the same time as we take steps to support the healthy development of the fetus, there are two types of surveillance to which the fetus is subject. First is the monitoring of the pregnancy to identify opportunities for helpful interventions that will promote the joint welfare of the pregnant woman and the fetus. This includes checks on the woman's blood pressure, her weight, her haemoglobin and her general health.

The second type of surveillance addresses the question of whether there are any specific problems with the growth and development of the fetus, as assessed by maternal blood tests (giving information about the chance of the fetus being affected by chromosomal abnormalities such as Down's syndrome) and fetal ultrasound scans (checking principally for structural malformations). This second type of surveillance has usually, in the past, amounted to the question of whether *this particular* fetus is 'good enough' to be accepted and nurtured, or whether it would be better to end the pregnancy. Clearly these two types of surveillance are very different and, from the perspective of the fetus, diametrically opposed in purpose (Dondorp *et al.*, 2015).

In the past, establishing the diagnosis of a genetic disorder in the fetus led to few options other than the decision whether to continue or to terminate the pregnancy. Given that a firm diagnosis required fetal tissue, and all methods of obtaining fetal tissue were invasive and carry a risk of miscarriage, it can be seen that those parents who were willing to accept the investigation would also, usually, be likely to decide to terminate the pregnancy if affected. It would be difficult to regard a fetus subject to such investigation as a patient, as one would not usually seek 'to terminate a patient'. However, with the development of non-invasive prenatal testing (NIPT) of various types, this situation may be changing (Bianchi, 2012). Such tests examine the cell-free DNA in the maternal blood, about 5–10 per cent of which is derived from the chorion (the outer fetal membrane, effectively the placenta) from about 8–9 weeks' gestation. This gives information about the genetic constitution of the fetus. Thus, relatively simple and perfectly safe maternal blood tests can indicate an increased chance of the fetus being affected by a chromosomal trisomy, such as Down's syndrome, and can be diagnostic of a variety of other disorders. The performance of such tests (especially their sensitivity and their positive predictive value) depend critically upon precisely what assay is being performed under what circumstances, and generalizations should be avoided (Nuffield Council on Bioethics, 2017).

If a couple is known in advance to be at risk of an inherited disorder in their future children, then it will often be possible to arrange for NIPT from 9–10 weeks in a pregnancy, to see if the fetus will be affected. This result may be diagnostic, as when the disorder is a dominant condition transmissible from the father, but in other circumstances it may not be so highly accurate – the positive predictive value may be significantly below 100 per cent – so that an invasive test to confirm the NIPT result may then be warranted, if important decisions are to be made on the findings (Norton *et al.*, 2015).

Currently, where NIPT is provided in the context of prenatal screening, this is with the aim of enabling pregnant women (and their partners) to make a well-informed choice between terminating an affected pregnancy or preparing for the birth of a child with special needs (Dondorp *et al.*, 2015). However, the same technological developments that have led to a considerable improvement of prenatal screening with this aim, will also contribute to developing positively therapeutic interventions with the aim of improving pregnancy outcomes. This entails a blurring of the distinction between the two types of fetal investigation (Jorgensen *et al.*, 2014).

The novel feature of prenatal testing is that *in utero* therapeutic interventions are becoming available for some potentially serious disorders. With no hazard from the diagnostic procedure, which is a simple maternal blood sample, those who would not wish to terminate an affected fetus may still want NIPT so as either to prepare themselves for an(other) affected child or, sometimes, to see whether intrauterine treatments may be available. It is becoming possible to regard a fetus investigated in this way as a patient, who will potentially benefit from experimental treatments or, if the condition is an early-lethal and untreatable disorder, perinatal palliative care.

Treating the fetus

With ever improving fetal imaging tools, used both on indication and as a form of screening, obstetrics has changed into perinatology or maternal-fetal medicine, with the latter phrasing meant to acknowledge that all forms of fetal treatment still have to pass through the body of the pregnant woman, thus turning her into a patient for the sake of treating the fetus (Nuffield Council on Bioethics, 2006).

The main forms of prenatal treatment consist of 1) drugs administered to the pregnant woman that are meant to reach the fetus via the placenta and 2) direct interventions in the womb (Deprest *et al.*, 2011). Examples of the former include betamethasone to improve fetal lung development in fetuses at risk of premature birth, and medication for fetal cardiac arrhythmias. Currently, direct interventions most often involve minimally invasive procedures using needles (as in blood transfusions for fetal haemolytic disease) or endoscopic surgical tools (as in the use of lasers to separate the circulations of twins threatened by twin-to-twin transfusion syndrome). In these procedures, the womb itself remains closed, which has important benefits in terms of lower risks for the woman and lower risks of procedure-induced prematurity as compared with 'open fetal surgery' where the womb is opened in order to allow access to the fetus and then closed again after the procedure, hoping that the pregnancy will hold and continue without complications (Casper, 1998 p 182–9). For pregnant women, open fetal surgery means a major operation, the need to take contraction-inhibiting drugs and delivery by a caesarean section, as well as complication risks extending to further pregnancies. In the pioneering days of fetal surgery, such high risk open interventions were done as 'ultima ratio' procedures meant to save the life of fetuses with life-threatening conditions (Lyerly and Mahowald, 2001). Open fetal surgery has since been largely abandoned, both in response to trials showing a less than favourable balance of benefits and harms for specific applications, and because of improving results of postnatal and minimally invasive alternatives (Oepkes, 2008).

An exception to this trend is open fetal surgery for spina bifida, where a multicentre randomized controlled trial (RCT) has clearly established the value of this approach over postnatal surgery in terms of a reduced need for a hydrocephalus shunt by the age of 12 months and significantly improved mental and motor function scores at 30 months of age (Adzick *et al.*, 2011). However, the trial also confirms high rates both of serious maternal complications and of preterm birth. Although minimally invasive endoscopic surgery would theoretically seem to promise lower complication risks, a recent meta-analysis did not support this (Araujo Junior *et al.*, 2016). Follow-up research remains important to compare the long-term effects of prenatal and postnatal surgery both on the child's health and wellbeing, and on the future reproductive health of the mother.

General criteria for offering fetal treatment specify that the diagnosis of the condition must be certain, the natural history of the disorder must be clearly understood, and there must be no equally effective postnatal therapy available (Deprest *et al.*, 2011). These criteria are crucial as without clear benefits that may not also be obtained postnatally, there can be no justification for imposing burdens and risks upon the pregnant woman. The 'no equally effective postnatal treatment' criterion can be met in two types of cases, reflecting two different reasons for offering fetal treatment: 1) lethal conditions that without in utero interventions lead to high rates of fetal or perinatal mortality, and 2) non-lethal conditions where prenatal treatment leads to better health and quality-of-life outcomes for the future child than can be expected without treatment or with postnatal intervention (Dondorp and de Wert, 2018).

Most applications of fetal treatment are still experimental. Given small numbers, funding problems and challenges of recruitment for RCTs, evidence-based fetal therapy is still very much an ideal (Rodrigues *et al.*, 2011).There is a dearth of long-term follow-up data on the health of children born after such treatment (Gebb *et al.*, 2015). More research into the (reproductive) health and psychosocial wellbeing of women who underwent prenatal treatment is also needed.

The book

The fetus is increasingly visible, examinable and also treatable in prenatal care, as anticipated in the very term 'fetal medicine', an expanding obstetric subspecialty. Accordingly, physicians often perceive the fetus as a patient and understand themselves as having certain professional duties towards the fetus. Unlike with other patients, however, it is far from clear what professional duties in the case of fetuses would involve. Do physicians owe fetuses anything? Is the concept of the fetal patient a theoretically consistent and practically sustainable framework for clinical interactions in prenatal medicine? If so, how can possible conflicts in professional obligations towards pregnant women and towards their fetuses be solved? This volume tries comprehensively to address these and many other open questions surrounding the concept of the fetal patient and the new fetal medicine from four different perspectives.

The fetus as a patient: a useful concept?

The philosophical debate about what we generally owe embryos and fetuses and on which grounds, the debate about their moral status, seems to be never-ending and highly controversial. This is what distinguishes fetuses from most of the patients in health care institutions, who are regarded as having a full moral status which significantly shapes our professional duties towards them. Most guidelines, recommendations and laws seem to imply that a human embryo or fetus has some but not the full moral status. But there is no consensus about the grounds on which this lesser degree of moral status can be based. The first question then is how this relates to the professional duties of physicians towards fetuses in prenatal medicine. Can we determine what we owe fetuses in prenatal medicine without having a clear understanding of what we owe fetuses in general?

Lucy Frith examines the changing status of the fetus and argues that the fetus now occupies two possibly contradictory positions in medicine and society: the 'disposable fetus' of prenatal testing and the 'protected fetus' of the personhood movement. Both of these discourses conceptualize the fetus as a separate being and potentially compromise the autonomy of the pregnant woman. *Claudia Wiesemann* in the following chapter emphasizes that exactly this notion of separability can lead ethical evaluations in prenatal medicine astray, because these conflicts cannot be analysed in terms of the distinct individual rights of mother and fetus. She argues that physical connectedness is of the utmost importance for moral relationships and favours a relational ethical perspective on conflicts in prenatal medicine.

Laurence B. McCullough and Frank A. Chervenak are well-known for arguing that being a patient from an ethical perspective can be framed as having a dependent moral status which results in beneficence-based obligations of the physician. They state this is true regardless of whether the fetal patient can also be accorded the independent moral status of a person and so theirs is a pragmatic approach to the ethical conflicts in prenatal medicine. In this volume, they respond to the main lines of critique of their approach by questioning the privileged status of being morally independent. *Katrin Lörch-Merkle*, in contrast, tries to show that the concept of the fetal patient not only arrives with implicit assumptions about an independent moral status of the fetus but may also undermine the rights and interests of the future child.

The fetus as a patient: where does that leave the pregnant woman?

Those who understand fetuses as individual patients, will have to deal with possible conflicts in relation to the rights and interests of the pregnant woman – the other potential patient in prenatal care. As outlined earlier, the concept of patienthood is not readily applicable to pregnant women, and pregnancy is not usually a state of disease. A large part of prenatal medicine aims at informing the reproductive choices of pregnant women and couples. Consequently, interactions between physicians and pregnant women are mainly evaluated with respect to the principle of reproductive autonomy and not in terms of beneficence. How then does the concept of the fetal patient affect the concept of the reproductive autonomy of the pregnant woman, and how is this concept represented, perceived and justified? The second part of the volume focuses on these questions and starts with *Janina Krause*. She analyses from an anthropological point of view the images and metaphors of fetuses especially in medical contexts as they are created in discourses of popular media and how they shape public perspectives on pregnancy and motherhood. This view is complemented by an analysis of patient- and expert-discourses in the context of the new NIPT technologies in the following chapter. Here, *Heather Strange* shows that the specific figuring of the fetus as a patient is a highly contested one in connection with prenatal testing, where the results potentially affect the continued existence of the fetus. But it is not only how we understand the reproductive autonomy of pregnant women in the context of prenatal testing that seems to be at odds with the idea of a fetal patient. *Anna Smajdor* argues that *any* kind of prenatal treatment aimed to benefit the fetus may be ethically problematic, because it potentially entails treating the pregnant woman as a mere means to benefit the fetus. Informed consent procedures might not be sufficient to prevent pregnant women from being treated (or treating themselves) as a mere means or ensure that they are free from social coercion. Also in situations where the health of the pregnant woman is primarily affected and the status of patienthood is easily applicable to her, the main ethical focus of clinical interactions is still not beneficence-, but autonomy-based, as *Alma Linkeviciute* highlights for cases of maternal cancer during pregnancy. Counselling services for the pregnant woman with a special emphasis on ethical counselling and relationships in these difficult decision-making processes could empower women and, thus, ensure free and informed choices also for the benefit of the fetus.

The fetus as a patient: challenges for clinical care pathways and interactions

It is evident that concepts of (health care) professional duties towards the fetus vary significantly in relation to the underlying understanding of the moral status of the fetus as a patient. Every account bears its own difficulties not only with regard to the theoretical basis but also to the consequences for clinical care pathways. The following section of this volume analyses different types of clinical care pathways and how they relate to concepts of the fetus as a patient in prenatal medicine. *Angus Clarke* starts by focusing on experimental treatments for the fetus. In the rapidly evolving discipline of fetal medicine, many new therapeutic approaches to inherited disorders are developed for prenatal use and are of still unclear effectiveness. So pregnant women may sometimes face the choice between consenting to treat an affected fetus with an uncertain outcome or avoiding the birth of an affected child. Possible challenges that will need to be addressed by a coherent normative framework for experimental treatments in fetal medicine are outlined in this chapter. In the next chapter, *Joanne Verweij* uses the example of stem-cell therapy for osteoporosis imperfecta (OI) as a case for discussing some of these challenges. She highlights the difficulty of the multiple, and potentially conflicting, professional roles of the researcher and the physician in clinical trials. To avoid inducing therapeutic misconceptions and false hope, clinical research pathways have to be developed which minimize these risks for pregnant women involved in these trials and clarify the roles of the involved professional agents.

Wybo Dondorp and Guido de Wert then discuss another consequence of the increasing availability of prenatal treatments in relation to clinical care pathways. The main aim of prenatal screening might shift from ensuring autonomous decision-making in pregnancy to the prevention of diseases which will come along with important consequences for the accompanying normative framework. In the case of trisomy 21, seminal new developments now suggest that prenatal treatments intended to improve the cognitive outcome of affected persons will become clinically available in the near future. *Guido de Wert and Wybo Dondorp* explore some critical appraisals of this therapeutic approach from different perspectives and emphasize that the interests of the future child could provide a fruitful alternative to concepts of the fetal patient.

Mathias Wirth and Marc-Antoine Marquis then focus on a seemingly established clinical care pathway for a prenatal treatment of an inherited disorder and describe the ethical and clinical complexities of prenatally administering dexamethasone to the pregnant woman in suspected cases of congenital adrenal hyperplasia affecting the fetus. To understand these fetuses as patients triggers a clinical action, although the medical and ethical justifications for this action are in many cases unclear and might actually harm the interests of the future child.

Finally, *Kathrin Knochel* and colleagues draw attention to the new clinical care pathways of perinatal palliative medicine and the fetus as a patient in this context. They show how treating the fetus (and then the newborn child) as a patient in palliative care could be part of a more holistic approach to support pregnant women and couples as they become the parents of a fetus who has been given the diagnosis of a life-limiting disease and who then becomes a child with a perinatally- or neonatally-lethal disorder.

The fetus as a patient: legal perspective

The volume ends with an overview of the legal status of the fetus in Europe, with a view to exploring the possibility of medically treating the human fetus as a distinct patient at later stages of pregnancy. *Atina Krajewska and Dimitrios Tsarapatsanis* first examine the legal status of the fetus in different national legislations, then against the background of the relevant case law of the European Court of Human Rights. The implications for clinical interactions in prenatal medicine are highlighted.

Concluding remarks

The chapters in this volume indicate both the great academic interest in the fetus as a topic of enquiry and the growth in biomedical activity in developing treatments for the fetus. These combine to ensure that the topic is of growing relevance to practitioners as well as biomedical researchers and scholars in the humanities. We therefore hope that this volume will be of interest to those in all three groups and that it will promote further reflection, constructive discussion and practical progress.

References

Adzick, N. S., Thom, E. A., Spong, C. Y., Brock, J. W., III Burrows, P. K., Johnson, M. P., Howell, L. J., Farrell, J. A., Dabrowiak, M. E., Sutton, L. N., Gupta, N., Tulipan, N. B., D'Alton, M. E., Farmer, D. L. and Moms Investigators, M. 2011. A randomized trial of prenatal versus postnatal repair of myelomeningocele. *N Engl J Med*, 364, 993–1004.

Araujo Junior, E., Eggink, A. J., Van Den Dobbelsteen, J., Martins, W. P. and Oepkes, D. 2016. Procedure-related complications of open vs. endoscopic fetal surgery for treatment of spina bifida in an era of intrauterine myelomeningocele repair: systematic review and meta-analysis. *Ultrasound Obstet Gynecol*, 48, 151–60.

Baker, R. B. and Mccullough, L. B. 2009. Medical ethics through the life cycle in Europe and the Americas. *In:* Baker, R. B. and Mccullough, L. B. (eds.) *The Cambridge World History of Medical Ethics*. Cambridge and New York: Cambridge University Press.

Bianchi, D. W. 2012. From prenatal genomic diagnosis to fetal personalized medicine: progress and challenges. *Nat Med*, 18, 1041–51.

Casper, M. J. 1998. *The making of the Unborn Patient. A Social Anatomy of Fetal Surgery*, New Brunswick, NJ and London, Rutgers University Press.

Deprest, J., Toelen, J., Debyser, Z., Rodrigues, C., Devlieger, R., De Catte, L., Lewi, L., Van Mieghem, T., Naulaers, G., Vandevelde, M., Claus, F. and Dierickx, K. 2011. The fetal patient – ethical aspects of fetal therapy. *Facts Views Vis Obgyn*, 3, 221–7.

Donald, I. 1964. *Practical Obstetrical Problems*, London: Lloyd-Luke.

Dondorp, W. and De Wert, G. 2018. Ethical issues in maternal-fetal medicine (in press). *In:* Rodeck, C. H. and Whittle, M. J. (eds.) *Fetal Medicine: Basic Science and Clinical Practice*. London: Elsevier.

Dondorp, W., De Wert, G., Bombard, Y., Bianchi, D. W., Bergmann, C., Borry, P., Chitty, L. S., Fellmann, F., Forzano, F., Hall, A., Henneman, L., Howard, H. C., Lucassen, A., Ormond, K., Peterlin, B., Radojkovic, D., Rogowski, W., Soller, M., Tibben, A., Tranebjaerg, L., Van El, C. G., Cornel, M. C., European Society of Human, G. and American Society of Human, G. 2015. Non-invasive prenatal testing for aneuploidy and beyond: challenges of responsible innovation in prenatal screening. *Eur J Hum Genet*, 23, 1438–50.

Dorscheidt, J. H. 2010. Developments in legal and medical practice regarding the unborn child and the need to expand prenatal legal protection. *Eur J Health Law*, 17, 433–54.

Gebb, J., Dar, P., Rosner, M. and Evans, M. I. 2015. Long-term neurologic outcomes after common fetal interventions. *Am J Obstet Gynecol*, 212, 527 e1–9.

Johanson, R., Newburn, M. and Macfarlane, A. 2002. Has the medicalisation of childbirth gone too far? *BMJ*, 324, 892–5.

Jorgensen, J. M., Hedley, P. L., Gjerris, M. and Christiansen, M. 2014. Including ethical considerations in models for first-trimester screening for pre-eclampsia. *Reprod Biomed Online*, 28, 638–43.

Karmiloff, K. and Karmiloff-Smith, A. 2001. Speech perception in and out of the womb. *Pathways to Language*. Cambridge, MA and London England: Harvard University Press.

Lee, H. S. 2015. Impact of maternal diet on the epigenome during in utero life and the developmental programming of diseases in childhood and adulthood. *Nutrients*, 7, 9492–507.

Loudon, I. 1993. Childbirth. *In:* Bynum, W. F. and Porter, R. (eds.) *Companion Encyclopedia of the History of Medicine*. London and New York: Routledge.

Lyerly, A. D. and Mahowald, M. B. 2001. Maternal-fetal surgery: the fallacy of abstraction and the problem of equipoise. *Health Care Anal*, 9, 151–65.

Mutsaerts, M. A., Groen, H., Buiter-Van Der Meer, A., Sijtsma, A., Sauer, P. J., Land, J. A., Mol, B. W., Corpeleijn, E. and Hoek, A. 2014. Effects of paternal and maternal lifestyle factors on pregnancy complications and perinatal outcome. A population-based birth-cohort study: the GECKO Drenthe cohort. *Hum Reprod*, 29, 824–34.

Norton, M. E., Jacobsson, B., Swamy, G. K., Laurent, L. C., Ranzini, A. C., Brar, H., Tomlinson, M. W., Pereira, L., Spitz, J. L., Hollemon, D., Cuckle, H., Musci, T. J. and Wapner, R. J. 2015. Cell-free DNA analysis for noninvasive examination of trisomy. *N Engl J Med*, 372, 1589–97.

Nuffield Council on Bioethics 2006. *Critical Care Decisions in Fetal and Neonatal Medicine: Ethical Issues*. London: Nuffield Council on Bioethics.

Nuffield Council on Bioethics 2017. *Non-Invasive Prenatal Diagnosis*. Report of a Working Party. London: Nuffield Council on Bioethics.

Oepkes, D. 2008. *Fetal Therapy. Update on the Current Level of Knowledge*. The Hague: Health Council of the Netherlands.

Office For National Statistics 2017. *Live Births, Neonatal and Post Neonatal Deaths by Selected Causes Mentioned on Death Certificate, England and Wales, 2001 to 2015* [Online]. Available: www.ons.gov.uk/peoplepopulationandcommunity/birthsdeathsandmarriages/deaths/adhocs/006955livebirthsneonataland postneonataldeathsbyselectedcausesmentionedondeathcertificateenglandand wales2001to2015 [Accessed 0509 2017].

Rodrigues, H. C., Deprest, J. and Berg, P. P. vam den 2011. When referring physicians and researchers disagree on equipoise: the TOTAL trial experience. *Prenat Diagn*, 31, 589–94.

Sadler, J. Z., Jotterand, F., Lee, S. C. and Inrig, S. 2009. Can medicalization be good? Situating medicalization within bioethics. *Theor Med Bioeth*, 30, 411–25.

Shorter, E. 1984. *A History of Women's Bodies*, Harmondsworth: Penguin Books.

Smith, R. M. 1993. Demography and medicine. *In:* Bynum, W. F. and Porter, R. (eds.) *Companion Encyclopedia of the History of Medicine*. London and New York: Routledge.

Part II

The fetus as a patient: a useful concept?

2 The disposable and protected fetus: contradictions in fetal status

Lucy Frith

Introduction

The moral status of the fetus is one of the most contested areas of bioethics debate, and prolife and prochoice positions on abortion have polarised US politics in the modern era (Wilson, 2012). I will argue that there are two apparently contradictory views of the fetus: the 'disposable fetus' of prenatal testing and the 'protected fetus' of the personhood movements. The 'disposable fetus' is an entity that undergoes prenatal testing and if found defective (in some way) can be aborted. The 'protected fetus' has a number of forms, but in essence it positions the fetus as an entity with its own rights and interests that impose duties on others, generally, the pregnant woman. At one extreme, there is the 'personhood movement', with organisations like Personhood USA, and One of US in Europe, who campaign to have laws across the globe changed to recognise that personhood, and hence legal status, begins at fertilisation. While not necessarily committed to a view of the fetus having full moral status, there is also a growing focus in health and popular literature on how to ensure the welfare of your fetus in utero (Abate, 2013).

The chapter will first outline these two positions and then explore how they share some key features – they are both premised on the conceptualisation of the fetus as a separate being from the mother and they both are based on attributing certain types of interest to the fetus.

I will conclude by illustrating some of the problems raised by the conceptualisation of the fetus as a being with interests and how this affects women.

The disposable fetus

The ability to see, monitor, and safely abort the fetus has radically changed our view of this entity. As Epstein notes, 'in early modern Europe, women controlled information, experience, and beliefs concerning reproduction, and women held authority over it' (Epstein, 1995: 139). William Blackstone in his comments on the laws of England in 1765 states that life, 'begins in the contemplation of law as soon as an infant is able to stir in the mother's womb' (quoted in Epstein). This quickening, the movement of the fetus inside the woman was held, even by the

Church, to mark a morally significant point, after which abortion was not allowed and a woman could not 'go to the gallows'. Quickening could only be felt by the women herself, it was a point essentially mediated by the woman.

The use of ultrasound in obstetrics in the mid-1950s can be defined as a starting point for the ability to externally monitor the fetus. Ian Donald, a Scottish obstetrician, was the first to introduce diagnostic ultrasound to obstetrics and gynaecology in the late 1950s (Donald *et al.*, 1958). With these developments in technology by the mid-1960s, the use of ultrasound in obstetric practice was growing. It is reported that by 1966 28 per cent of obstetric patients in Donald's Glasgow centre were receiving ultrasound (Oakley, 1986). One of Donald's team, Stuart Campbell, brought the technology to England in 1968 (Campbell, 2010). In Campbell's hospital by the early 1970s about half of women were given an ultrasound and by 1978 it was normal for most women.

In the UK, the use of ultrasound in pregnancy moved from being a diagnostic test for pregnancies at risk to a general screening tool – all pregnancies were now subject to surveillance in this way. This was a gradual process. In the late 1980s such screening was still not routine and only offered to women in recognised risk groups (Luck, 1992), and ultrasound did not become routine in practice till the late 1990s. By the early 2000s an ultrasound at 18–20 weeks was being recommended in the UK for all women (NCCWH, 2003). Although there were campaigns by AIMs and the National Childbirth Trust against the use of this technology, Jean Robinson, from AIMS noted, campaigning against ultrasound was not easy as it was popular with women in the way other interventions such as induction were not (McIntosh, 2013). Recent developments in 3 D ultrasound, a three-dimensional image of the fetus, and 4 D that shows movement, allow an even greater ability to 'see' the fetus in a form that looks much more like a 'baby' than 2 D scans do. These scans are often called 'souvenir' or 'boutique scans' and are generally not recommended by the medical profession (FDA). In sum, in the UK, almost all women now undergo some form of prenatal testing. Current public concerns over screening in pregnancy are now about lack of access to the newest techniques rather than concerns over too much screening (Guardian, 2009).

This ability to perform such surveillance and screening, leads to the conceptualisation of the fetus as something separate from the woman. As Ettore notes, 'within the discourse of reproductive medicine, the "producer" (the pregnant woman) and the "product" (fetus) are detached prenatally by the use of technologies' (2007: 2). Pregnancy is now determined by technology, the pregnancy test, and then 'seeing' the fetus at a dating scan at 8–12 weeks. The mother is no longer the custodian of foetal experience; this can now be observed directly. With this direct access to the baby, obstetrics became more concerned with the baby rather than maternal health, as Donald noted in his textbook, *Practical Obstetric Problems*, 'In place of maternal mortality, perinatal mortality has now become the yardstick by which we review our work. This is at least a sound beginning which acknowledges our custodianship of the baby's future' (Donald, 1964).

Editions of the Myles midwifery textbook published in the early 1970s included a new section on perinatal health reflecting this new emphasis on the fetus (Myles, 1971). In sum, the fetus and pregnant woman have become separated, arguably by the ability of medical technologies to 'see' and monitor the fetus (Lupton, 2013).

One consequence of this is the ability to 'treat' or 'manage' fetal abnormalities – the fetus is disposable – it can be terminated. In this way, the 'disposable fetus' is an entity that undergoes prenatal testing and if found defective (in some way) can be aborted; as Barbara Katz Rothman (1993) has noted, any pregnancy is a 'tentative pregnancy' until proven otherwise.

The protected fetus

With the construction of the pregnant woman and the fetus as separate entities, another version of the fetus is privileged – the 'protected fetus'. This is the increasing positioning of the fetus as an entity with its own rights and interests that imposes duties on others, generally, on the pregnant woman, and sometimes receives legal protection.[1] In this chapter I want to consider two main forms of the protected fetus: those found in the personhood movements in the US, and the rise in concepts of fetal welfare and fetal mothering.

Fetal personhood movements

At one extreme, there is the 'personhood movement' in the United States, with organisations like Personhood USA, who campaign to have laws across the globe changed to recognise that the fetus has personhood. This is the 'strong personhood' position, that the fetus has a moral status akin to a fully functioning adult and hence should have legal status. A key belief here is that morally significant life begins at conception. This is symbolised by the fingerprint:

> The fingerprint is the symbol of a unique human being, one that has never existed before and will never exist again. Paradoxically, fingerprints appear on a preborn child at the precise moment that most abortions take place. It is as if God himself wanted to ensure that none of his children are ever forgotten. The fingerprint inspires Personhood to make an imprint on our culture in defence of life.
>
> (personhood.com)

One of the consequences of this kind of belief is that at least 23 states in the US have fetal homicide laws that apply to the earliest stages of pregnancy ('any state of gestation,' 'conception,' 'fertilisation' or 'post-fertilisation') (NCSL). There have also been personhood laws in Oklahoma and Virginia and a recent law in Georgia (ASRM, 2012). For example in Alabama, the 'Ala. Code 13A-6–1' (2006) defines 'person', for the purpose of criminal homicide or assaults, to include an unborn child in utero at any stage of development, regardless of viability. Personhood Bills and Ballots have been introduced in the following states: Arkansas, Iowa, Indiana, Kansas, Missouri; Montana, New Hampshire; Virginia; North Carolina; South Carolina; Tennessee, Texas, Washington (Resolve).[2]

Fetal mothering

The second element of the protected fetus is the concept of fetal mothering, while not necessarily committed to a view of the fetus having full moral status, there is a growing focus in the realm of healthcare advice and popular literature on how to ensure the welfare of your fetus in utero. It has been argued that the fetus has become subject to the same kind of intensive mothering practices that women have been exhorted to adopt for existing children.

There has been a rise in an 'intensive motherhood narrative', alongside intensive parenting (helicopter parents, tiger mothers, etc.), and this has been charted by the work of authors such as Hays, who argued that the 'good' mother is one who intensively mothers. 'The ideology of intensive mothering is a general model that advises mothers to expend a tremendous amount of time, energy and money in raising their children' (Hays, 1996: x). The importance of prioritising the child is a key part of this 'good' mother ideology. As Hays says, intensive mothering includes the 'logic of unselfish nurturing' (Hays, 1996: x). For example, part of this trend is to view motherhood as something that should be all-consuming: 'Working mothers were no longer heroines, symbols of the new and healthy freedoms won by Mother's Lib. They were villains, selfish and unnatural. If a woman "chose" to work, she was doing so at the "expense" of her child' (Warner, 2006: 91). This has become extended not just to existing children but to those in the womb. As Abate notes:

> Expectant mothers commonly face an array of parental responsibilities long before their baby is actually born. From securing various items like diapers and clothing to ensuring the baby's proper development by eating well and getting sufficient rest, the work of motherhood far predates the newborn's arrival.
>
> (2013: 332)

For example, there is a new and growing genre of 'fetus fiction', which became a library heading in 2008. An example of this is the picture book called Ma! *There's Nothing to Do Here!* Abate states:

> The picture book adds – however unintentionally or inadvertently to the tremendous social pressures placed on parents in general and new mothers in particular during the twenty-first century. Pregnant women have long been seen as responsible for ensuring the physical, intellectual and cognitive development of their baby. To aid in this process, in fact, women are commonly urged to abide by various exhortations, from eating a nutritious diet

> and getting sufficient rest to taking prenatal vitamins and avoiding drinking and smoking. *Ma! There's Nothing to Do Here!* adds another, equal-parts absurdist and alarming, item to this ever growing list of responsibilities for pregnant mothers: ensuring that their fetus is properly amused or sufficiently entertained.
>
> (Abate, 2013: 328)

That entertaining the fetus is something a woman might contemplate is evidenced by the growth in products designed to stimulate the fetus in utero. For example the BabyPod is a small speaker that pregnant women inserts into their vagina and plays music to the fetus. 'Babypod is a device that stimulates before birth through music. With BabyPod, babies learn to vocalise from the womb' (BabyPod). Thus, the focus on pregnant women's behaviour both legally in the US and in health, media and general pregnancy advice, reflects the view that the woman should extend her 'good' mothering to before birth.

Exploring these contradictions

In these two domains, the disposable and the protected fetus, the fetus arguably occupies two contradictory and competing positions. On the one hand, it is an entity that can be disposed of; and on the other it is a being that has interests or/and rights and therefore needs protection. Although these two views of the fetus appear to be contradictory, they both garner strength and can be justified by the separation of the fetus and the pregnant woman. The development of screening and monitoring has led to the ability to conceptualise the fetus as a separate being from the mother. As Lupton notes, the 'intensification of focus on unborn entities and their welfare is predominantly due to the creation and introduction of technologies that are able to create, visualise, medically test and screen unborn bodies' (2013: 3). This separation leads to the positioning of the fetus and the woman as two separate beings, and as separate beings they can or could come into conflict.[3] It is this separation of the fetus from the pregnant woman that links these two positions. It must be noted that the separation of the fetus and the pregnant woman is not a neutral phenomenon, and of course, not a completely new one either, as Epstein observes.

> Although the move toward criminalizing the conduct of pregnant women is radically new in United States jurisprudence, it harks back to an ancient tradition of searching for explanations for birth mishaps in the minds and bodies of pregnant women, a tradition that reached its peak during the eighteenth century.
>
> (1995: 145)

What has changed, as noted above, is the ability to manipulate the fetus – to see and monitor it and to safely[4] abort it if necessary. This means there is potential for some form of external control over the fetus: it can be regulated and mediated by the medical profession, and this was not possible before the advent of these medical advances.

Arguably, a possible consequence of this fetal separation is a growing conception of the fetus as a being that can have interests, and this is a further element that links these two views. As Mills notes, this separation has ethical implications:

> I suggest that the impact of ultrasound images on ethical intuitions derives in part from the way in which such images work upon and through the sympathetic imagination. In this, ultrasound images hail or call the foetus into being as a subject toward which we bear a social relationship and, by virtue of that, such images also work to establish a particularly ethical relationship.
>
> (2011: 102)

While the two views of the fetus have radically different implications (i.e. the protected fetus, in terms of the strong personhood movements would never be subject to an abortion), both views incorporate a concept of fetal interests – but they differ in how these are seen to be attaching to the fetus. In the case of the disposable fetus – the fetus has interests in its future – but these are currently weak interests; whereas, for the protected fetus – the fetus has interests in its future – and these are conceptualised as strong interests. As noted above, the protected fetus can have a number of forms. The personhood movement would see the fetus's interests as currently strong and akin to an adult, whereas those who might advocate 'intensively' mothering their fetus do not have to be committed to seeing the fetus as person.

I have argued that both disposable and protected fetus can imply some conception of fetal interests. Leaving aside the 'strong personhood' position, what might these weaker interests look like?

Jeff McMahan (2006) argues that it is morally more reprehensible to harm a fetus prenatally than to abort a fetus. He states that the fetus can have future interests that will become manifest when it becomes a person, and that although the fetus' current interests are weak (i.e. it has a weak interest in staying alive), actions that damage the fetus' future interests (in McMahan's example prenatal injury) will damage interests held by the person the fetus will become. McMahan's argument proceeds by outlining assumptions about the fetus and future interests that he says are generally held. One such assumption, that he reports as held in most moral belief systems, is that we accept that current actions should be constrained by 'respect for future interests – that is, interests that do not exist now, and indeed whose bearers may not exist now, but that will exist in the future'. He argues that we have a belief that it would be wrong to plant a bomb programmed to detonate in 150 years that could harm the interests of people who do not exist now. The fetus's current interests are weak, so it is not wrong to frustrate these current interests. But it is wrong to inflict some kind of prenatal injury on the fetus that will harm future interests it might have, as the interests of the future child are strong (conditional on it being born). This is because if the fetus has such an injury inflicted and comes to be born, this injury will frustrate (to use McMahan's terminology) the many future interests this person will have throughout their life. 'Prenatal injury frustrates future interests, which may be the interests of a person and also quite strong' (McMahan, 2006: 632). The fetus lacks capacity for consciousness. Its intrinsic nature is significantly different from an adult's and it does not deserve respect in the Kantian sense: 'Fetuses have interests and can be harmed but lack rights and cannot be wronged' (McMahan, 2006: 627). Marquis (1989) argues that these interests tell against aborting the fetus, as it is future interests that are important, rather than interests based on the current state of sentience, or lack of.[5] Killing a fetus frustrates its interests in a 'valuable future', just like killing an adult does. Steinbock (2006: 32) adopts a different perspective and argues that based on Feinberg's conception of interests, the fetus is not an entity that can be said to have interests, she says, 'I deny that when I was a fetus, I had an interest or stake in my valuable future. I think that when I was a mindless fetus, I had no interests at all'.

These accounts have been subject to debate and criticism, and in this chapter I do not have space to adequately address all the permutations of these debates. Further, there have been detailed debates over the moral status of the fetus and the implications this has for abortion (for example, Warren, 1973) and accounts that start from the premise that the fetus is a person, and then argue that due to the special relationship between the fetus and the pregnant woman abortion is still permissible, such as Judith Jarvis Thompson's famous article (1971).[6]

I do not want to relive this debate or seek to justify a particular position on the status of the fetus and, correspondingly, on what is and is not an appropriate treatment of the fetus. As Mackenzie notes: 'the morality of abortion is not simply or even primarily about questions concerning personhood and foetal status but more fundamentally is about women's self-determination' (1992: 55). In conclusion to this chapter, I want to consider some of the practical implications of allowing the fetus' interests – arguably in any form.

Conclusion

My overriding contention is that allowing fetal interests is a 'foot in the door' so to speak, to giving the fetus priority over the woman. This is an empirical rather than a philosophical claim. Those who want to give the fetus some form of interests would argue that their conclusion does not lead to privileging of the fetus over the woman – that there is nothing logically implied in their positions – and that is correct. However, how these debates play out in practice need to be considered.[7] I argue that the ability to 'see' the fetus as a separate being can lead to conceptions of fetal interests and this can lead or create harms to women, primarily by restricting their autonomy and justifying this on the basis of some form of fetal interests.

While it might be argued that the disposable fetus is not a threat to a woman's autonomy, many authors have noted the implications of prenatal screening regimes for women and how this can compromise women's free choices in this area. For instance, authors such as Donovan (2006) and Ettore (2007) argue that such initiatives frame women's choices in a way that is not always to their benefit and threatens their ability to freely give consent to prenatal testing.

It is also argued that fetal screening is not premised on offering abortions for abnormalities, but on extending reproductive choice, but therapeutic logic suggests that if a test for a condition is offered and the condition is found, the solution, apart from doing nothing, is to terminate the pregnancy. Women have the choice not to terminate and, in the UK, no one is forced against their own will, but a termination is the only option in terms of active management. It is estimated, for example, that 92 per cent of women who receive a positive Down's test (i.e. amniocentesis or CVS) go on to terminate the pregnancy (NHS Choices).

According to Barbara Duden (1983) pregnancy is now a disembodied experience and women are restricted to the visual and the medical rather than feeling the experience themselves. Donovan (2006) for example has questioned whether it is possible for women to experience pregnancy as normal in our new model of disembodied medically mediated, risky pregnancies that need regular surveillance. The vast majority of women in the UK have some form of prenatal testing, 90 per cent had a dating scan and 98.5 per cent reported having a 20-week anomaly scan, 85 per cent report having had a scan by 13 weeks or earlier (NPEU: 2010). Thus, the growing ability to test and monitor the fetus has led, in the UK, to almost all women undergoing some form of prenatal testing.

In the US, where fetal personhood is more widely held (see p. 000), such conceptualisations (which are underpinned by a strong personhood position) have led to women being imprisoned on the grounds that they are harming their fetus. Such prosecutions are possible under legislation, 'Often known as "fetal assault", 'chemical endangerment' or 'personhood' laws, these measures have been used to arrest and prosecute women who experience pregnancy complications and conditions such as drug dependence' (Amnesty, 2017: 7). Amnesty International argues that laws like this are a serious threat to women's human and reproductive rights.

In the UK, the fetus does not have the same kind of legal status. While as noted, criminalisation for drug and alcohol abuse has occurred in the US, to date, the UK has not sought to make mothers-to-be criminally responsible for behaviour that might endanger their fetus. In *S v. St George's NHS Trust* (1997), the Court of Appeal made it plain that pregnant women retain the same autonomy over their bodies as any other person. They can refuse medical treatment regardless of the danger to themselves or their child. The law has long recognised that traditional legal principles are ill suited to pregnancy. As Lord Mustill said in A G's Reference (No. 3 of 994) [1998] AC 245, 255 6: 'To apply to such an organism the principles of a law evolved in relation to autonomous beings is bound to mislead.' Accordingly, neither the common law nor the legislature has imposed a duty of care on pregnant women to safeguard the fetus. 'There is a compelling public interest in safeguarding pregnant women and their foetuses from the detrimental effects of criminalisation' (Court of Appeal, 2014). Defining birth as the key point of moral significance therefore, arguably, safeguards the pregnant woman from a number of human rights abuses.[8]

Hence, the conceptualisation of the fetus as a separate being, that can have interests, and possibly corresponding rights, can pit the woman against her fetus in an adversarial way. It could involve forcing treatment on competent adults i.e. the pregnant woman as noted above. It can also involve an intrusion into the women's personal life and her decisions that competent adults are not usually subject to. This compromising of the woman's autonomy, seeing it as legitimate to police, restrict, or coerce her in the interests of the fetus, are dangerous developments. Whatever one's views of the moral status of the fetus, the costs to women's autonomy and position in society is too great, to allow the forcing of woman to act in certain ways towards their fetus. Due to the unique position of the fetus (within the woman's body) any intervention or observation has to be done through her. While it may be morally desirable that women act in ways that are beneficial to their fetus, this should not be legally enforceable. Ultimately, a woman should have the right to choose whether she aborts the fetus or carries it to term, and how she acts during the pregnancy.

References

Abate, M. (2013) A womb with a political view, children's literature. *Education*, 44, 326–343.

Amnesty International (2017) *Criminalizing Pregnancy: policing pregnant women who use drugs in the US.* www.amnesty.org/en/documents/amr51/6203/2017/en/

Appeal No: C3/2014/0775. www.bpas.org/media/1184/bpas-birthrights-cp-v-cica-intervention.pdf

ASRM, (2012) ASRM communicates formal opposition on personhood measures in Oklahoma and Virginia. *ASRM Bulletin*, 14.

Babypod website www.babypod.net/en/

Campbell, S. (2010) Early sonographic prenatal diagnosis. *Prenatal Diagnosis*, 30, 613–615.

Court of Appeal (2014) Appeal No: C3/2014/0775. www.bpas.org/media/1184/bpas-birthrights-cp-v-cica-intervention.pdf

Donald, I (1964) *Practical Obstetric Problems.* 3rd edition. London: Lloyd-Luke.

www.personhood.com/about

Donald, I, Macvicar, J, and Brown, TG. (1958) Investigation of abdominal masses by pulsed ultrasound. *The Lancet*, 7, 1188–1195.

Donovan, S (2006) The impact of a culture of prenatal screening on women's experiences of pregnancy. *Health Sociology Review*, 15 (5), 397–405.

Duden, B (1983) *Disembodying Women: Perspectives on Pregnancy and the Unborn.* Cambridge, MA; Harvard University Press.

Epstein, J (1995) The pregnant imagination, fetal Rights, and women's bodies: a historical inquiry. *Yale Journal of Law & the Humanities*, 7 (1).

Ettore, E (2007) Prenatal screening: impact on normal pregnancies. *Encyclopedia of Life Sciences*, doi: 10.1002/9780470015902.a0005645

FDA, Ultrasound imaging. www.fda.gov/radiation-emittingproducts/radiationemitting-productsandprocedures/medicalimaging/ucm115357.htm [accessed 30 June 2017].

Fovargue, S and Miola, J (2010) The legal status of the fetus. *Clinical Ethics.* 5, 122–124.
Guardian, The. *NHS failure on Down's screening kills healthy babies*, 16 May, 2009.
Hays, S (1996). *The Cultural Contradictions of Motherhood.* New Haven, CT: Yale University Press.
Kamm, F (1992) *Creation and Abortion: A Study In Moral and Legal Philosophy.* New York: Oxford University Press.
Luck, C (1992) Value of routine ultrasound scanning at 19 weeks. *BMJ 1992*, 304, 1474–1478.
Lupton, D (2013) *The Social Worlds of the Unborn.* Basingstoke, Palgrave Macmillan.
Mackenzie, C (1992) Abortion and embodiment. *Australian Journal of Philosophy*, 70 (2), 136–155.
Marquis, D (1989) Why abortion if immoral. *Journal of Philosophy.* 86 (4), 183–202.
McIntosh, T (2013) *A Social History of Maternity and Childbirth.* London, Routledge.
McMahan, J. (2006) Paradoxes of abortion and prenatal injury. *Ethics*, 116, 625–655.
Mills, C (2011) Futures of reproduction. *International Library of Ethics, Law, and the New Medicine 49.* New York: Springer Science.
Myles, M (1971) *A Textbook for Midwives*, 7th edn. Edinburgh: E & F Livingston Ltd.
National Collaborating Centre for Women's Health (NCCWH) (2003) *Antenatal care: routine care for the healthy pregnant women.* http://cpd.screening.nhs.uk/choicestoolbox/docs/antenatal-care.pdf
NCSL www.ncsl.org/research/health/fetal-homicide-state-laws.aspx [accessed 30 June 2017]
NHS Choices, Down's Syndrome Q & A, www.nhs.uk/news/2008/11November/Pages/DownssyndromeQA.aspx
NICE (2010) Antenatal Care: Guidance 62.
National Perinatal Epidemiology Unit (2010) *Delivered with Care: A National Survey of Women's Experiences of Maternity Care in 2010*, www.npeu.ox.ac.uk/downloads/files/reports/Maternity-Survey-Report-2010.pdf
Oakley, A (1986) The history of ultrasonography, *Birth*, 13, 8–13.
Resolve, www.resolve.org/get-involved/the-center-for-infertility-justice/personhood-legislation/ (accessed 30 June 2017)
Rothman, B (1993) *The Tentative Pregnancy.* New York: Penguin.
Steinbock, B. (2006) The morality of killing human embryos. *Journal of Law, Medicine & Ethics*, 34, 26–34.
Thompson, J-J (1971) A defense of abortion. *Philosophy and Public Affairs*, 1 (1), 47–66.
Warner, J. (2006) *Perfect Madness: Motherhood in the Age of Anxiety.* New York: Riverhead Books.
Warren, M. (1973) On the moral and legal status of abortion. *The Monist.* 57, 43–62.
Wilson, A. (2012) Review of 'God's own party: the making of the Christian right' by Daniel K. Williams. *Politics, Religion & Ideology*, 13 (1), 134–135.

Notes

1 For example, cases of women being prosecuted for injuring their foetuses, see discussion p. 000.
2 The status of the fetus has not occupied the same political space in the UK, and women's decisions about childbirth are protected by the law.

3 See Mills (2011) for an overview of the feminist literature in this area.
4 Safely, in terms of as safe as any invasive medical procedure is.
5 It should be noted that Marquis takes a different view of fetal interests than McMahan.
6 More recently, Frances Kamm (1992) has developed an argument for abortion while maintaining the fetus is a person.
7 See Lupton (2013) for a detailed sociological consideration of the implications of constructions of the fetus as a distinct entity.
8 Although it should be noted that English law does offer the fetus some protection, see Fovargue and Miiola (2010).

3 Which ethics for the fetus as patient?

Claudia Wiesemann

In ethics, there is rarely a situation more vexing than pregnancy. Ethical theory is grounded on the fact that the subject of ethical deliberation, the moral agent, is an individual human being with individual human rights and responsibilities.[1] The pregnant woman is such a human individual; yet, at the same time, she is more than that, for in her womb she bears another human being who might also be considered an individual. In consequence, challenging ethical conflicts arise between her and the fetus that is part of her. Is it possible to frame these pregnancy conflicts in terms of conflicting individual moral rights? A special conflict arises when the fetus requires an operation for a serious health condition, but the pregnant woman is not willing to undergo surgery. Though fetal surgery is still experimental (Wenstrom *et al.*, 2014), it raises instructive ethical questions regarding the moral status of the fetus. The fetus displays many of the characteristics of human individuality and, thus, may seem to deserve equal moral consideration. Yet, this would imply a direct interference with the pregnant woman's body and her individual rights. Should both be treated as patients, as Chervenak *et al.* and McCullough and Chervenak suggest (Chervenak *et al.*, 2004; McCullough and Chervenak, 2008), and if so, then how exactly? Would it be appropriate to simply balance the benefits and harms involved, as is customary in similar dilemmas?

Luckily, such cases are rare since the large majority of pregnant women are ready to endure whatever is best for their unborn children. But precisely because so much is at stake when an individual's liberty and bodily integrity are in danger of being compromised, the rare cases in which the interests of mother and fetus clash demand considerable thought. A challenging question is whether the conflict between mother and fetus can be framed as one between two equally morally relevant individual subjects.

This issue might, on first view, look worn out. Much of the abortion debate has raged over the question whether the fetus has a right to life, which must be defended against the pregnant woman's conflicting interests (for an overview, see Karnein, 2012.). Some ethicists vigorously defend the position that it does; others are willing to accord to fetuses only gradually increasing moral rights. To this lengthy and tedious debate, moral conflicts in fetal surgery might add something new and refreshing. They are about questions pertaining not to the fetus's right to life but to the mother's responsibility to provide healthcare to her unborn child. Pregnant women who consider refusing fetal surgery do not usually want to be rid of the child. On the contrary, they desire to have it. And if they do refuse to have surgery that might be important for the child, they do not mean to deny its right to life. Because of the positive stance that a pregnant woman generally takes towards her child, one might be inclined simply to override her refusal. After all, does she not want to give birth to a healthy child? But things are not that easy.

In the abortion debate, numerous arguments have been put forward, none of which I need to repeat here. Suffice it to say that the subject of fetal surgery brings into the spotlight one issue that has been only scarcely considered until now, namely, how to decide when two individuals' fundamental moral claims to bodily integrity clash. Normally, one human individual's right to physical integrity can be maintained without compromising that of another. Thus, in everyday life, such a moral conflict is virtually non-existent because human individuals are not connected closely enough for it to be able to arise. But that is not the case in pregnancy, where one human individual is a physical part of the other. Pregnancy is a unique form of the physical existence of two morally relevant humans where one abides and grows inside the other (Young, 1990). This unique constellation provokes instructive questions about what it means to be a human individual and what that implies for moral standing. How much individuality is necessary to be an individual human moral subject with individual moral rights? Should mother and fetus be treated differently, given the fact that one dwells within the body of the other? What, at any rate, constitutes the *individual body* of a morally relevant *individual subject*? And how does this impact on pregnancy conflicts?

I will answer these questions in three steps. First, I shall discuss what it is to be a human individual. For that purpose, I shall examine different criteria of individuality and discuss their relevance for pregnancy conflicts. Second, I shall assess their significance for moral standing and show why a certain criterion of individuality, namely, physical individuation, is most relevant for this ethical debate. Finally, I shall outline the major implications of these observations for framing ethical conflicts in fetal surgery.

What does it mean to be a human individual?

'Individuality' can have several meanings. It can be understood as genetic, biological, psychological, numerical, and physical individuality (Hucklenbroich, 2003). A human being can, for example, be considered an individual because he or she has a unique *genetic* make-up unlike those of other human individuals. The genes that code for our individual phenotypes render us distinct from each other. With its individual genome and resulting individual phenotype, the fetus is a genetic individual. Even when there is a genetic twin, epigenetic effects and new (post-conception) mutations make him or her a unique individual in comparison to all other genetic subjects. In a *biological* sense, 'individuality' can be understood as being a member of a kind, e.g., one example of the species *Homo sapiens*. Species are groups of organisms that share certain traits, such as a common ancestry. Since the fetus shares the traits that are typical for the group of organisms we call 'humans', it is a true member of that group. Understood in a *psychological* sense, 'individuality' refers to the psychological events – perceptions, thoughts and memories – human beings experience through the course of their lifetimes. By the time the nervous system begins to develop, it can be assumed that fetuses have mental experiences and start developing individual personalities, which makes them to individuals in the psychological sense, too.

Yet, the term is less easily applicable when it comes to numerical and physical individuality. Some think the fetus is already *numerically* individual early in embryonic development, from around the second week onwards, when twinning can no longer occur (Ford, 1988). But even then, the fetus dwells within another human individual, the pregnant woman. In the numerical sense, it is impossible to separate the fetus from the mother: both are one and two at the same time. This intertwined form of existence becomes even more intriguing when individuality is judged with regard to the *physical* existence of the fetus, i.e., in terms of its spatial position and material characteristics. Physically, the fetus is spatially and materially part of the mother's body. It has not yet been individuated from her to become a spatially and materially separate organism, whereas the pregnant woman, at least before pregnancy, has been an individual in the physical sense, from the time she was born.

Thus, the fetus is not physically individuated. But why not exactly? Barry Smith and Berit Brogaard have denied that the fetus is a true part of the mother's organism and, therefore, held that it is an independent subject (Smith and Brogaard, 2003). Does it not just sit within the woman's body, as in a hole, without being *functionally integrated* into her organism? According to Smith and Brogaard, the embryo is equivalent to, for example, a cherry stone, which can seem, falsely, to be part of a human body, for the stone, if swallowed, resides within the eater's body but only in a spatial sense. It will pass through the intestines without being assimilated and be excreted more or less unchanged. The uterus, so Smith and Brogaard hold, is comparable to the digestive and the respiratory tracts. They are just inner extensions of the outer environment, and material from that environment, like cherry stones, a fly we accidentally inhale, and semen, can enter the body via these tracts.[2] Yet, these materials do not become a true part of the organism. They are expelled, as when we cough out the fly, or excreted, like a cherry stone, without turning into true organismic material. Smith and Brogaard argue that the fetus is such an entity that is part of the woman's body only spatially, not materially or functionally, since it sits in her genital tract and is thus only located in an inner extension of the outer environment.

Yet, unlike a cherry stone or fly, the fetus is connected to the mother by the umbilical cord and the placenta, an organ that develops from both embryonic and uterine tissue. The placenta is an organic structure shared by mother and fetus and a material bridge between the two, enabling the transport of nutrients, hormones, and, to some extent, also cells, toxic substances, and microbes. For the nine months of pregnancy, the fetus is thereby connected to the mother's organism and becomes a functional part of it, depending on her to provide it the means of existence, which the mother's organism is ready to offer. Without the mother breathing and eating, the fetus would not survive and, thus, not be able to grow. It depends on the mother's organism to process oxygen and food in a form that it can absorb, for sugar and fat have to be metabolized to be of use to the fetus. This renders the fetus not just a spatial but also a true functional part of the pregnant woman. In this regard, it cannot be considered a physical individual until after it is born and starts breathing, eating, and metabolizing oxygen and nutrients on its own, no longer depending on another organism for these vital functions.

To sum up, the fetus can be considered a genetic, a biological, and, to some extent, a psychological individual. Yet, its numerical individuality is doubtful. And it is not an individual in the physical sense; rather, it is a spatial, material, and functional part of another human individual on whom it wholly depends for maintaining its existence (Wiesemann, 2006: 60–81). Physical individuation occurs only when the fetus is expelled from the mother's organism and performs all the functions necessary to maintain itself on its own. Though the new-born will still be dependent on others for nourishment and shelter, its continued existence will no longer be contingent upon one particular and irreplaceable organism as it was when it dwelt within the mother's womb.

The significance of physical individuation for moral status

Physical individuation is not just interesting from a biological point of view; it is also of particular ethical relevance. Yet, in ethical discourses there is a strong tendency to overlook the fact that the fetus is a true physical part of another human being's body. Ethicists write about the fetus as if it were a human being and a moral subject in its own right.[3] This view was popularized by a whole genre of visualizing the unborn, epitomized by the Swedish photographer Lennart Nilsson's fascinating and suggestive pictures of the embryo (Duden, 1994).[4] In these images, the fetus is always alone and unconnected to any structure that might involve another human being, the amnion nothing more than an open space where the fetus sits, the umbilical cord barely visible, if at all, with nothing human at its other end. This iconographic tradition – the fetus as 'astronaut in space' – highlights the fetus's supposed independence in virtually all respects: spatially, materially, and functionally. Ironically, Nilsson had to resort to aborted fetuses to be able to depict them as the isolated individuals that appear in his photographs (Newman, 1996: 16–17). This iconography continues to influence not only how we imagine the unborn but also the ways we speak about them. In moral conflicts, it suggests envisioning the fetus as an independent moral subject despite the physical premises of its existence.[5] Admittedly, this attitude towards the fetus follows a long-standing, influential, and noble tendency in ethical theory to dismiss physical difference as irrelevant to moral deliberation. According to this tradition, human beings are acknowledged to have moral standing irrespective of their sex, age, skin colour, and any other physical characteristics. Thus, it seems only logical for the moral discourse on pregnancy conflicts to disregard the physical features of the pregnant woman and her fetus and treat both as equal and essentially unrelated moral subjects.

However, some physical properties are highly relevant for the concept of the moral subject. They are relevant not just in the case of pregnancy but whenever they occur in human relationships. The concept of the moral subject that we tacitly assume when we talk about basic moral requirements implies physical independence from other moral subjects. More precisely, negative rights to freedom and non-interference make sense only when the moral subject who has these rights is physically unconnected to another moral subject claiming the same entitlements. We do not pay much attention to this implication because, normally, born human beings are physical individuals. Yet, the tacit assumption can be made explicit by examining those rare cases when human beings remain physically connected after birth, as, for example, when conjoined twins cannot be surgically separated (Barilan, 2002; Barilan, 2003).

Abigail and Brittany Hensel are a well-known pair of conjoined twins who starred in their own reality series, on the British TV channel TLC, documenting their lives and the particular challenges they have to master.[6] Abigail and Brittany are two distinct personalities with two heads, hearts and spines, but they have only two arms and two legs and share the whole lower part of their body; so, they have to coordinate their movements when they want to do something or go somewhere. Conjoined twins are well suited to direct our attention to some of the implicit preconceptions of ethical theory. Imagine, for example, that in a sudden state of fury one twin shoots a stranger. Criminal homicide is usually punished by imprisonment or, in some countries, execution. But how are such legal sanctions to be applied in the case of conjoined twins? One would inevitably have to sanction the innocent twin, too. The state would have to intrude on the freedom of one twin in order to punish the transgression of the other.

This thought experiment reveals what we tacitly assume of moral agents and their moral responsibility, namely, that the responsible person is not just a moral individual but also a physical one, someone who enjoys a distinct, physically separate form of bodily existence, who can be protected against unwanted intrusions and prevented from committing them. As freedom from wrongful interference usually presupposes physical independence, it is largely meaningless for conjoined twins.[7] One twin must endure what the other decides that he or she will do, and it would not make sense to try to prevent that by appealing to a right to non-interference. If one wants to drink too much alcohol, the other will get drunk, too. If one must undergo surgery, the other has to be anaesthetized, too. And if one commits suicide, the other will die, too. In short, demanding respect for one twin's negative rights means violating the other's. To cope with this fundamental conflict, conjoined twins have to develop a moral system of their own, which must be much more relational than anything we know, and the fact that such a way of life is possible is a constant source of fascination for those of us whose bodies are separated, by nature, from each other.

There are striking similarities between Abigail and Brittany Hensel, and mother and fetus. Mother and fetus, too, are so closely physically connected that, in general, interfering with one of them also interferes with the other. The fetus can only be a patient when the mother is one, too. Operating on the fetus would require cutting through the mother's womb. And, vice versa, a drug for treating the mother's ailment can also enter the fetus's bloodstream (Oduncu *et al.*, 2003). These are good reasons why mother and fetus should not be treated as independent moral subjects whose rights should be weighed one against the other. Since the physical precondition of the basic entitlement of moral subjects, the right to non-interference, cannot be met, moral conflicts in pregnancy must be articulated in terms that employ concepts specially tailored to such an exceptional form of relational existence.

There are also differences between conjoined twins and mother and fetus that have to be acknowledged in moral deliberation. Mother and fetus are not equally physically dependent on each other. The mother can care for and nourish herself; the fetus cannot. She can go wherever she wants; the fetus cannot. She can survive without the fetus; before the age of viability, the fetus cannot and for a long time after has a high risk of dying if separated. If the mother dies, the fetus is very likely to die, too, but not the other way around. In short, the mother is already a fully individuated human subject, someone who can usually claim full moral standing; the fetus is not. This lopsided dependency indicates that if one has to decide between competing interests, the mother's may have greater weight than those of the fetus.

Other dissimilarities are relevant, too. The duration of fetal physical dependency is limited. Unlike Abigail and Brittany, mother and fetus are connected to each other only for the nine months of pregnancy. Moreover, the fact that mother and fetus are physically bound to each other is the result of the behaviour of one of them and, thus, the pregnant woman bears responsibility for their situation, if the pregnancy was not caused by rape. If she consented to unprotected sexual intercourse, then she has consented, at least implicitly, to the possibility of having to share her body with another human being for a certain period of time. One might be tempted to assume that if a woman willingly enters into a situation like pregnancy, in which the need for certain sacrifices comes naturally, she has the obligation to make many, if not all, of the sacrifices that are needed. This assumption is all too tempting since taking care of a child involves sacrificing much of one's life for the sake of someone else. But, even if a woman deliberately sought to have a child, and many women become pregnant without ever planning to do so, it does not follow that she consented to every form of intrusion into her body for the sake of the fetus. Although we might reasonably assume that she implicitly agreed to taking care of her baby during pregnancy, e.g., by maintaining a healthy diet and having regular check-ups, this does not automatically extend to demanding intrusions, such as surgery, into her body and personal life. At any rate, most women who consider having a child are not familiar with most of the interventions that are now possible, and even if they know about fetal surgery, they will not have anticipated such a situation for themselves, let alone deliberated about the pros and cons and the consequences for their health and life. In fact, if every woman were required to give her full and informed consent to all medical interventions for all possible pregnancy complications before having unprotected intercourse, we would soon run out of babies.

Ethical principles for pregnancy interventions

Ethical principles for pregnancy interventions should be geared to the particular physical relationship of mother and fetus. The right to freedom from unwanted interference, for example, says that everyone should be able to pursue their own idea of happiness and the good life and not be prevented from doing so as long as they do not harm anyone else (Mill, 1865). At first sight, the application of this principle to pregnancy conflicts appears simple and straightforward. Since the mother would harm the fetus if she does not consent to a necessary surgical intervention, she would violate the principle and, in consequence, her freedom from unwanted interference should not be sustained. However, this justification is fundamentally misleading. As I have shown, such a principle makes sense only on the assumption that it is possible to pursue one's own conception of happiness and the good life without harming others because the pursuit requires nothing more than that others leave one alone and one leaves them alone. The simplicity of that rule is the reason why the principle of non-interference is considered a universal and basic ethical principle, especially in a world of strangers. Yet, to have such universal scope and to be of such universal value, the principle of non-interference must not habitually impose onerous duties, such as having to accept bodily intrusions for the sake of someone else. It should be easy to adhere to, even though every now and then one might find it difficult to tolerate, say, the conception of the good life that a particularly eccentric neighbour is determined to pursue. In contrast, in a world in which every human being is physically connected to someone else, a principle of non-interference would create awkward and sometimes even paradoxical situations and, thus, would not have been laid down in the first place.[8]

When interference is unavoidable given physical connectedness, as in pregnancy, non-interference cannot be a basic ethical principle. Most importantly, one should not, in consequence, proceed in case of conflict to a second-line solution such as balancing the benefits and harms involved.[9] Even the most straightforward utilitarian would exempt some fundamental principles, most notably liberty principles, from being the subject of such a trade-off. In pregnancy conflicts, it is necessary to look for appropriate fundamental moral principles to govern the interaction of mother and fetus.[10] The physical integrity of the pregnant woman, for example, may be such an important moral value that it should not be subjected to a maximization of utility.

From the example of Abigail and Brittany Hensel, we learn that an ethical theory developed for human beings who are not physically individuated from others has to be truly relational. In the case of conjoined twins, the siblings are on equal terms since both entered life at the same time, under the same conditions, and are equally dependent on each other. It is not so in the case of pregnancy. The pregnant woman is a fully individuated human subject sharing her body with a fetus who is completely dependent on her. The relation of the mother to her fetus is a unidirectional one of *care* and *responsibility*. And care is a relational practice. In a caring relationship, the carer is devoted to fostering the growth and flourishing of another human being (Gilligan, 1998; Held, 2006), and responsibility is the attitude of the carer. A responsible carer is committed to figuring out the most appropriate measures to further the aims of the other's growth and flourishing.

In a relationship of responsible care, much depends on what can usually and reasonably be expected from the carer. Before answering this question, one should take a closer look at the types of relationship characterized by care and responsibility. Such relationships are dialectic, i.e., they further two different but interdependent aims. In a mature caring relationship, as Carol Gilligan explains, the carer should be capable of balancing care for the other and care for herself. Caring does not require sacrificing oneself, and the carer is not expected to exhaust herself in fulfilling her commitment to the other (Gilligan, 1998). Rather, responsible care for others can only be fully realized by taking responsibility for oneself and one's own fundamental needs since only a person who is flourishing herself can foster uncompromised flourishing in others. In pregnancy, this holds true in an elemental sense since the pregnant woman can nurture a baby only when she is healthy herself. After all, a woman bearing a child faces the highest possible risk: she might die from being pregnant or giving birth, thereby not only losing her own life but also risking the life of the child. Hence, caring responsibly for the child and for herself are necessarily intertwined and are essential elements of a parental relationship, especially in pregnancy, when the mother's and fetus's bodies are so closely connected. They are all the more important since being a parent means caring for another person for a very long period of time, usually for a lifetime. High personal risks and a lifelong, all-embracing, personal commitment make parenthood a unique form of human relationship, more demanding than any other relationship we know. It is therefore one of the most intriguing tasks of parenthood to continue to find the right balance of self-care and care for others, especially when caring for more than one child.

One has to understand the profound significance of this lifelong responsibility, which has its beginnings in the first months of pregnancy, in order to realize the daunting task the pregnant woman is ready to shoulder. Quite literally, her life is at stake. Life with a child is a long, complex, all-encompassing and risky endeavour. If it is also the most rewarding personal experience in life, it is so because of the total physical, emotional, and social commitment that parents take on (Wiesemann, 2016). Both parents are responsible for maintaining this caring relationship; however, before birth, due to her close physical connection with the fetus, the gestational mother occupies a unique moral position. Since society should appreciate the exceptional commitment the pregnant woman is ready to take on, and fundamentally depends for its continued existence on the willingness of many women to do so, it should acknowledge and respect their individual responsibility for decisions in ethical conflicts about fetal therapy. The deeper reason is not only that the pregnant woman, unlike the fetus, is already a fully individuated moral subject with the right to non-interference and bodily integrity. Nor is it that deciding against the woman's preference usually entails violating her physical integrity, which is a serious wrong in itself. It is that failing to acknowledge her prerogative also entails overriding her well-grounded decisional latitude in finding the right balance of responsible care for herself and the fetus. Physicians, ethicists, and judges who, in the end, neither have to bear the physical risks nor face up to the potentially lifelong social and emotional consequences of their judgment are not more qualified to make such decisions than the mother herself.

Hence, the pregnant woman should be acknowledged as the most qualified expert in making such complex decisions.[11] Nevertheless, healthcare workers also bear responsibility for the well-being of mother and child, though they have to keep in mind, as Lyerly *et al.* hold, that 'the paradigmatic patient is an entity physically individuated and fully separate from others' (Lyerly *et al.*, 2008: 43). At any rate, those who argue in favour of treating the fetus like a patient have yet to tackle the moral problems resulting from its lack of individuation. The fetus may be considered a patient in the sense that healthcare workers are responsible for its well-being, under the general condition that its status as physically and, thus, also morally dependent is taken into account. If possible, mother and fetus should be treated as a unit of moral relevance. Yet, in a conflict the mother, as the fully individuated moral subject, should have the prerogative to decide. Most importantly, healthcare workers should provide the mother with the best information available to help her decide. They should seek alternatives to bodily intrusion or, if no such options are feasible, reduce the risks of intervention to her and her baby as much as possible. If the risks are known to be low, the benefit to the fetus is high and very likely, then explicit recommendation of an intervention should also be considered in order to reduce the pregnant woman's burden of decision-making.

Conclusion

Ethical conflicts in pregnancy are traditionally analysed in terms of the individual rights of mother and fetus. I have argued that a relational perspective is better suited to the moral significance of pregnancy and parenthood. To this end, I have shown that physical connectedness, as in pregnancy, is of the utmost importance for moral relationships. Standard approaches based on freedom from unwanted interference face serious difficulties when the human beings involved are not physically individuated from each other. The example of conjoined twins illustrates why, in these exceptional situations, the very basis of this approach is false. A concept of responsible care is much more appropriate to grasp ethical conflicts in pregnancy. The mother's responsible care is necessarily a dialectic practice comprising care for her unborn child as well as for herself. Facing risks to her life and envisioning a lifelong responsibility for another human being, the mother has the duty, and the right, to find an appropriate balance between the interests of the child and her self-interests. Healthcare workers should support her as much as possible in this complex and utmost challenging task.

References

Annas, G.J. (1982) Forced cesareans: the most unkindest cut of all. *Hastings Center Report*, 12 (3), 16–17, 45.

Annas, G.J. (1988) She's going to die: the case of Angela C. *Hastings Center Report*, 18 (1), 23–25.

Barilan, Y.M. (2002) Head-counting vs. heart-counting. An examination of the recent case of the conjoined twins from Malta. *Perspectives in Biology and Medicine*, 45 (4), 593–605.

Barilan, Y.M. (2003) One or two: an examination of the recent case of conjoined twins from Malta. *Journal of Medicine and Philosophy*, 28 (1), 27–44.

Casper, M.J. (1998) *The Making of the Unborn Patient. A Social Anatomy of Fetal Surgery*. New Brunswick, NJ: Rutgers University Press.

Chervenak, F.A. and McCullough, L.B. (1993) Clinical management of brain death during pregnancy. *Journal of Clinical Ethics*, 4 (4), 349–350.

Chervenak, F.A., McCullough, L.B., Knapp, R.C., Caputo, T.A., and Barber, H.R.K. (2004) A clinically comprehensive ethical framework for offering and recommending cancer treatment before and during pregnancy. *Cancer.* 100, 215–222.

Dörries, A. (2014) *Fetomaternale Operationen: ethische Aspekte bei der Einführung innovativer Verfahren*. In: Steger, F., Ehm, S. and Tchirikov, M. (eds.) *Pränatale Diagnostik und Therapie in Ethik, Medizin und Recht*. Heidelberg, Springer, pp. 58–66.

Duden, B. (1994) *Der Frauenleib als öffentlicher Ort. Vom Mißbrauch des Begriffs Leben*. Munich: Deutscher Taschenbuchverlag.

Ford, N.M. (1988) *When did I Begin. Conception of the Human Individual in History, Philosophy and science*. Cambridge: Cambridge University Press.

Frader, J.E. (1993) Have we lost our senses? Problems with maintaining brain-dead bodies carrying fetuses. *Journal of Clinical Ethics*, 4 (4), 347–348.

Gilligan, C. (1998) *In A Different Voice. Psychological Theory and Women's Development*. Cambridge, MA: Harvard University Press.

Gillon, R. (2001) Imposed separation of conjoined twins – moral hubris by the English courts? *Journal of Medical Ethics*, 27 (1), 3–4.

Glover, J.J. (1993) Incubators and organ donors. *Journal of Clinical Ethics*, 4 (4), 342–347.

Held, V. (2006) *The Ethics of Care: Personal, Political, and Global*. Oxford, Oxford University Press.

Hucklenbroich, P. (2003) *Individuation, Kontinuität und Potential. Zum Paradigmastreit in der Theorie der Reproduktion*. In: Siep, L. and Quante, M. (eds.) *Der Umgang mit dem beginnenden menschlichen Leben. Ethische, medizintheoretische und rechtliche Probleme aus niederländischer und deutscher Perspektive*. Münster: Lit, pp. 37–57.

Jordan, J.M. III. (1988) Incubating for the state: the precarious autonomy of persistently vegetative and brain-dead pregnant women. *Georgia Law Review*, 22, 1103–1165.

Karnein, A. (2012) *A Theory of Unborn Life. From Abortion to Genetic Manipulation*. New York, Oxford University Press.

Lyerly, A.D., Little, M.O., and Faden, R.R. (2008) A critique of the 'fetus as patient'. *American Journal of Bioethics*, 8 (7), 42–44.
Mattingly, S.S. (1992) The maternal-fetal dyad. Exploring the two-patient obstetric Model. *Hastings Cent Rep*, 22 (1), 13–18.
McCullough, L.B. and Chervenak, F.A. (2008) A critical analysis of the concept and discourse of 'unborn child'. *American Journal of Bioethics*, 8 (7), 34–39.
Mill, J.S. (1865) *On Liberty*. London: Longman, Green, Longman, Roberts & Green.
Miskhin, B. (1988) But she's not an 'inanimate container ... '. *Hastings Center Report*, 18 (3), 40–41.
Mulholland, K.A. (1987) A time to be born and a time to die. A pregnant woman's right to die with dignity. *Indiana Law Review*, 20, 859–878.
Newman, K. (1996) *Fetal Positions Individualism, Science, Visuality*. Stanford, CA: Stanford University Press.
Oduncu, F.S., Kimmig R., Hepp H., and Emmerich B. (2003) Cancer in pregnancy: maternal-fetal conflict. *Journal of Cancer Research and Clinical Oncology*, 129 (3), 133–146.
Petchesky R.P. (1987) *Foetal Images: the Power of Visual Culture in the Politics of Reproduction*. In: Stanworth, M. (ed.) *Reproductive Technologies. Gender, Motherhood and Medicine*. Minneapolis, MN, University of Minnesota Press, pp. 57–80.
Rodrigues, H.C., van den Berg, P.P., and Düwell, M. (2013) Dotting the I's and crossing the T's: Autonomy and/or beneficence? The 'fetus as a patient' in maternal-fetal surgery. *Journal of Medical Ethics*, 39 (4), 219–223.
Smajdor, A. (2011) Ethical challenges in fetal surgery. *Journal of Medical Ethics*, 37 (2), 88–91.
Smith, B. and Brogaard, B. (2003) Sixteen days. *Journal of Medicine and Philosophy*, 28 (1), 45–78.
Thomson, J.J. (1971) A defense of abortion. *Philosophy and Public Affairs*, 1, 37–66.
Warren, M.A. (1989) The moral significance of birth. *Hypatia*, 4, 46–65.
Wenstrom, C.D. and Carr S.R. (2014) Fetal surgery, principles, indications, and evidence. *Obstetrics and Gynecology*, 24 (4), 817–835.
Whitbeck, C. (1983) The moral implications of regarding women as people: new perspectives on pregnancy and personhood. In: Bondeson, W.B. and Spicker, S.F. (eds.) *Abortion and the Status of the Fetus*. Dordrecht: Reidel, pp. 247–272.
Wiesemann, C. (2006) *Von der Verantwortung, ein Kind zu bekommen. Eine Ethik der Elternschaft*. Munich: C. H. Beck.
Wiesemann, C. (2016) *Moral Equality, Bioethics, and the Child*. New York: Springer.
Young, I.M. (1990) *Pregnant Embodiment. Subjectivity and Alienation*. In: Young, I.M. (ed.) *Throwing Like a Girl and Other Essays in Feminist Philosophy and Social Theory*. Bloomington, IN: Indiana University Press, pp. 160–174.

Notes

1 I am grateful to Greg Sax, Wybo Dondorp, Angus Clark, and Charlotte Frierson for their helpful remarks on first drafts of the chapter.
2 The common function of the respiratory, digestive, and genital tracts can be deduced from a common anatomical feature: they are all lined with a cell layer, the mucosa that functions as both a barrier and a gateway to the inner organism.
3 Some notable exceptions being Whitbeck, 1983, Warren, 1989, Young, 1990, Mattingly, 1992.

4 Karen Newman (1996: 67) sees the individuality of the fetus as constructed through historical discourses: 'The autonomous human child represented in midwifery manuals, obstetrical atlases, anatomical sculpture, modern medical dictionaries, and new medical specialties is independent of the woman's body, whole and undivided, always male, and virtually never dissected, opened, wounded, or permeable; it is the image *par excellence* of rights-bearing Enlightenment Man ferociously rendered in the fabled state of nature.' See also Petchesky, 1987.

5 Mattingly 1992, Casper 1998, and Anna Smajdor (2011) discuss how ultrasound technology has made the embryo visible and created an 'urge to intervene'.

6 Abby and Britanny www.tlc.com/tv-shows/abby-and-brittany/. See also https://en.wikipedia.org/wiki/Abby_and_Brittany_Hensel (accessed 4 May 2017).

7 In 2001, the English Court of Appeal had to decide about the surgical separation of Mary and Jodie, conjoined twins of a Maltese couple, by which one twin (Mary) would inevitably die. The Court resorted to giving Jodie the status of the only relevant moral subject by ruling that Mary was a 'parasite' who sucked the life blood out of her twin sister (cf. Gillon, 2001).

8 Judith Jarvis Thomson (1971) has drawn our attention to this fact. In her paper on abortion, she develops the example of a person who is kidnapped and attached to the circulatory system of a famous violinist.

9 Chervenak *et al.* (2004), adopted such an approach for those cases when the fetus has attained viability. Later, two of the co-authors of this paper revised their position, stating, "the viable fetus should not be understood as a separate patient" (McCullough and Chervenak., 2008: 38). For criticism, see Lyerly *et al.*, 2008; Rodrigues *et al.*, (2013).

10 Similar topics were discussed in the ethical debates on forced cesareans (Annas, 1982; Annas 1988; Mishkin, 1988) and on brain death and pregnancy (Mulholland, 1987; Jordan, 1988; Glover, 1993; Frader, 1993, Chervenak and McCullough, 1993).

11 Similarly, Anna Smajdor (2011) argues against a reversion to paternalism by withholding information about the option of fetal surgery. Dörries (2014) points out that fetal surgery is still experimental and requires not only informed consent but also systematic evaluation through clinical trials.

4 The ethical concept of the fetus as a patient: responses to its critics

Laurence B. McCollough and Frank A. Chervenak

Introduction

Thinking of the fetus as a patient, for purposes of clinical care (Harrison *et al.*, 2001; Moise, 2014), innovation (an experiment conducted for the benefit of an individual patient) (Chervenak and McCullough, 2002), or research (an experiment conducted to create generalizable knowledge) (Chervenak and McCullough, 2002), introduces the moral discourse of being a patient into maternal-fetal, perinatal, and neonatal medicine and healthcare (Chervenak and McCullough 2002). Professionally responsible management of this momentous change requires close attention to the ethical concept of the fetus as a patient, which we have explicated by appealing to the concept of dependent moral status (McCullough and Chervenak, 1994; Chervenak and McCullough, 2014). The purpose of this chapter is to respond to the critics of this approach, who share the commitment to independent moral status as the best, or indeed only, way to understand moral status.

Our response occurs along two main lines. First, we respond to our critics by critically appraising the privileged status of independent moral status. Our goal will be to illustrate the grave philosophical perils of the concept of independent moral status. Second, we respond to our critics by showing that there are no metaphysical requirements, such as being a person, for a human being to become a patient and therefore for the fetus to become a patient. Being a patient is therefore not a matter of having independent moral status as a person but of having dependent moral status, i.e., the moral status generated by a social role that others create. We conclude by identifying the chief advantage of the non-metaphysical, pragmatic concept of the fetus as a patient, its clinical comprehensiveness.

The perils of independent moral status

Moral status means that others have a moral obligation to an entity. Moral status is distinct from legal status, in which the obligations created by moral status are enforced by the state. The justifications of moral status may be distinguished into two groups. One line of justification appeals to constitutive properties of the entity, which is known as independent moral status. This is the dominant approach in the obstetric ethics literature. Indeed, that independent moral status is the only philosophically reliable way to think about moral status is taken for granted. Mahowald (2006), for example, criticizes our approach by alleging that the fetus is a separate patient. If it were, she continues, its moral status would create ethical obligations independently of the pregnant woman. Strong (1997) argues that the moral status of the fetus comes in degrees, resulting in ethical obligations to the fetus that are systematically secondary to ethical obligations to the pregnant woman. These are degrees of independent moral status. A second line of justification appeals to the social role occupied by the entity, which is known as dependent moral status. Put another way, independent moral status is self-generated, while dependent moral status is generated by others, especially when they commit themselves to create and sustain social roles (McCullough and Chervenak, 1994; Chervenak and McCullough, 2014).

Inasmuch as independent moral status originates in constitutive properties of an entity, independent moral status is necessarily a metaphysical concept. Because the constitutive properties of an entity generate moral obligations to it, such an entity's moral status is not a function of the constitutive properties of any other entity or what others might think about an entity ('extrinsic denominations' in an older discourse of metaphysics, especially Leibniz's (McCullough, 1996)). This is the meaning of 'independent' in independent moral status.

In the history of Western philosophy, the concept of independent moral status was developed to replace the status of being one of God's creatures, as a consequence of which one's moral status was inviolate (because God's creative act, once willed, reflected His perfection), with a moral status that was (equally) inviolate. Such moral status requires the firmest possible foundations, a kind of metaphysical perfection, which a creator God provides. This shift from a theological to secular metaphysics of moral status reaches its most sophisticated expression in the moral philosophy of Immanuel Kant (1964): each person is a member of the kingdom of ends and therefore cannot ever be treated as a means merely. (Notice how the phrase, "of ends" replaces "of God on earth.") Kantian bioethics and medical ethics treat moral status as the independent moral status of persons: rational, self-conscious entities that can distinguish themselves for all other entities and give themselves value (Kant 1964). The constitutive properties of rationality and self-consciousness generate independent moral status because all other rational, self-conscious entities must acknowledge these constitutive properties. This line of reasoning deploys the logic of discovery (in Kant, the transcendental logic of discovery; hence the use of 'deduction' in the *Critique of Pure Reason*) and not of invention. The result of discovery is unbiased and universal, thus supplying the firmest possible foundations for independent moral status. This logic of discovery is deployed in the quest for certainty in moral philosophy (Gracia, 2010), a quest fulfilled when one can establish the metaphysical foundations of independent moral status.

From the perspective of independent moral status thus understood, dependent moral status lacks secure foundations. After all, social roles are not discovered but invented. Unlike the metaphysical necessity delivered by adherence to the logic of discovery (including the transcendental logic of discovery), the logic of invention displays no necessity, much less metaphysical necessity. Indeed, dependent moral status is moral status without metaphysical foundations. Dependent moral status is therefore not metaphysical but pragmatic in the sense of this word from William James' pragmatism: dependent moral status is made true by the commitments of persons to create and sustain social roles. Foundationalists in moral philosophy become very nervous at this point and reject dependent moral status as unreliable, confident in the reliability of metaphysically foundationalist independent moral status (Engelhardt, 1995).

Foundationalists' confidence in the security of independent moral status is misplaced because accounts of independent moral status founder. First, the identification of independent moral status relies on claims for the logic of discovery that do not withstand close scrutiny from the perspective of the far more modest claims for the logic of discovery made by Baconian scientists, epitomized in the moral sense natural philosophy of the Scottish Enlightenment. For these philosophers, David Hume (2000) chief among them, reason is the weaker of the two human capacities by which we come to understand the world (McCullough, 1998). Reason is simply incapable of the deliverances of a logic of discovery directed to the revelation of necessary truths; reason is just a calculating machine for matching means to ends. The ends are not generated by reason, but by the other constituent component of human nature, instinct. Reason (with a capital R) detached from observational experience results in speculative metaphysics, which is philosophically worthless at best and a philosophical menace at worst. From the perspective of the contemporary science of behavioral psychology, Hume's modest assessment of human reason may be much closer to our scientific understanding of the limits of human reasoning than Kant's expansive understanding of reason. Put another way, it is doubtful that Reason exists but not that reason exists. The philosophical methods for identifying the constitutive properties of an entity that generate its independent moral status are not as secure as proponents of independent moral status must assume.

Second, the clinical applicability of independent moral status is limited by the clinical reality of neurological development and of neurologic anomalies, diseases, and injuries. Some human beings are not yet entities with independent moral status, i.e., persons. This category includes fetuses and, for some philosophers, infants (Tooley, 1972). Some human beings will never generate independent moral status because, as a result of catastrophic brain anomalies such as anencephaly or severe or profound cognitive disability (McCullough, 1984), they will never have the constitutive properties of rationality and self-consciousness. Some human beings who have gained and exhibited independent moral can lose it, as a result of catastrophic brain injury or as a result of progressive, degenerative brain diseases such as advanced dementias. Temporary, iatrogenic loss of independent moral status also occurs, e.g., as a result of general anesthesia.

Philosophers have put forward a variety of metaphysical work-arounds for this problem of clinical inadequacy e.g., the concept of a social person (Engelhardt 1986). But that is all that they are. Once the constitutive properties that generate independent moral status are lost, independent moral status is lost. Independent moral status is a binomial concept. The work-arounds are not metaphysical but created to manage the problem of clinical inadequacy. The logic of invention has been bootlegged into the philosophical argument, a methodological move that is forbidden to foundationalists.

Third, proponents of independent moral status equivocate on the meaning of "person," which is supposed to designate entities with independent moral status. One meaning is Kantian, the individual as self-legislating law giver living in the kingdom of ends (Kant, 1964). The second is Millian, the individual as free from substantial control or coercion by others (Mill, 1974), which has influenced bioethics (Beauchamp and Childress, 2013). Only the Kantian sense of "person" qualifies for independent moral status.

The appeal to the concept of independent moral status as the basis for a philosophical account of the moral status of the fetus is replete with philosophical peril. Philosophically privileged independent moral status in the work of our critics does not withstand close scrutiny.

The pragmatic ethical concept of being a patient

Dependent moral status: a pragmatic concept

Dependent moral status does not appeal to Reason deployed in the logic of discovery of necessary truths, including necessary transcendental truths. Dependent moral status dispenses with metaphysics and embraces Jamesian pragmatism: dependent moral status is invented in the invention of social roles. This will do nicely, if one quests for reliability rather than certainty in moral reasoning (Gracia, 2010). Dependent moral status is sustained when human beings make a sustained commitment to them and thus make dependent moral status true. Dependent moral status becomes a function of sustained social roles, because social roles define moral obligations to the entities in each social role. The concept of dependent moral status thus makes no appeal to constitutive properties and sidesteps altogether the need for Reason and its metaphysical and transcendental deliverances. As a consequence, necessity is jettisoned but clinical comprehensiveness is gained, as will become clear in the explication of the ethical concept of being a patient. Reliability of moral judgment is also gained.

The ethical concept of being a patient

The ethical concept of the human being as a patient was introduced into the history of Western (and global) medical ethics by the Scottish physician and moral scientist, John Gregory (1724–1773) (Gregory, 1772; McCullough, 1998). Before Gregory, the word "patient" was not in common use in the history of Western medical ethics. In the Latin literature that preceded the publication of Gregory's *Lectures on the Duties and Qualifications of a Physician* in 1772 *aegrotus* or "the sick one" was used. Friedrich Hoffmann's *Medicus Politicus* (1738), which Gregory would have studied while he was a student at Leyden in the 1740s, sets forth an ethics for the contractual relationship between the physician and the individual contracting for his services. The latter, either the wealthy who could afford the physician's fees or the prince employing the physician to care for the prince's subjects, had power over the physician, leading Hoffmann to articulate the concept of the politic physician who acted on prudence. Prudence is the virtue that schools us in the discipline of identifying our legitimate self-interests and acting to protect and foster them. Hoffmann adopted a concept of enlightened self-interest, in which the legitimate self-interests of the physician are defined by the interests of the sick individual.

Gregory was concerned about the power of physicians over the sick poor in the Royal Infirmary of Edinburgh and the potential for abuse of the sick poor, especially as subjects of research. As a moral scientist, he could not accept the potentially predatory nature of a contractual relationship. Indeed, Gregory railed against commerce as predatory on virtue. In response, he created a medical ethics based on what, he argued, are the virtues of sympathy (as described in Hume's *Treatise*) (McCullough, 1999) and he reformed medicine into a profession (McCullough, 1998).

Gregory's ethical concept of medicine as a profession comprises three fundamental commitments (McCullough, 2006). First, physicians should become and remain scientifically and clinically competent, practicing medicine to standards of intellectual excellence. This entailed critically assessing and then improving medical practice on the basis of what Bacon called "experience," the careful observation of natural and controlled clinical experiments and the use of the results to improve practice (McCullough, 1998). This was a nascent form of what we now know as evidence-based medicine. This commitment is expressed in the intellectual virtue of candor: to be open to correction of one's clinical judgment and practice, from whatever quarter suggestions may come, including from patients and other practitioners, who should not be regarded as competitors but colleagues. Second, physicians should use their scientific and clinical competence to protect the health and life of the patient as their primary concern and motivation, keeping self-interest systematically secondary. This commitment is expressed in the twin moral virtues of sympathy: tenderness (a direct engagement with the patient) and steadiness (remaining in control of one's engagement and not becoming either hardhearted or out of control). This is not empathy or detached concern but real caring, an engaged concern. Third, physicians as a group should reject the "corporation spirit," i.e., the group-self-interest of a guild in economic, social, and political power, in favor of the interests of patients and society, a concept that Percival later captured when he conceptualized the profession of medicine as a "public trust" (Percival, 1803: 52) (McCullough, 2006).

Making these three commitments transforms self-interested, guild-oriented practitioners into professional physicians in the ethical sense of "professional." Making and sustaining these three commitments creates the social role of being a patient. Making and sustaining these three commitments thereby transforms the sick, who previously had contractual relationships with practitioners, into patients, who are in the professional relationship with physicians (Gregory, 1772; McCullough, 1998).

The ethical concept of being a patient can now be set out: a human being becomes a patient when that individual presents to a physician (or other healthcare professional) and there exist clinical interventions that are reliably expected to benefit that individual clinically (McCullough and Chervenak, 1994; Chervenak and McCullough, 2014). Becoming a patient means that one can count on the protection of one's life and health by the physician; the professional physician is trustworthy. Being a patient is an invented social role sustained by the three commitments of physicians to professionalism in medicine.

We emphasize that Gregory's concept of human beings as patients does not require that one must have independent moral status, or be a person, in order to be a patient, in either of the two main ethical senses of "person." William Ruddick and William Wilcox (1982) challenge the view that being a person is a necessary condition for being a patient, by separating the ethical concept of being a patient from the ethical concept of being a person. They consider the proposition, "If someone is a patient, he or she is a person" (Ruddick and Wilcox, 1982: 13), which proposition, they say, is "clearly false" (Ruddick and Wilcox, 1982: 13). They reach this conclusion on the basis of the observation that some human patients are not persons, e.g., anencephalic infants. On such an account, we add, patients in permanent vegetative state and patients who are neurologically devastated from submersion injury or severe head trauma, i.e., who have irreversibly lost interactive capacity, are no longer persons. Infants are not persons, in either the Kantian or Millian sense, but infants in neonatal intensive care units are surely pediatric patients. Patients with dementias so advanced that their identity seems to have been obliterated are at best doubtfully persons and perhaps no longer persons, but they are nonetheless patients when in the care of geriatricians. Ruddick and Wilcox (1982) also note that non-human animals can be patients by being presented to a veterinary healthcare professional. The discourse of being patient in veterinary medicine, a discourse that has been common for decades, is non-metaphysical. Ruddick and Wilcox point out, for example, that "monkeys recovering from experimental implantation of intracranial shunts" are patients, even though they are not persons (Ruddick and Wilcox, 1982: 13).

The ethical concept of the fetus as a patient

Fetuses become patients when they are presented to a healthcare professional and there exist clinical interventions that are reliably expected to benefit clinically the fetus and the future child that it can become. Such *clinical links* between the fetus and its later becoming a child are crucial for the ethical concept of the fetus as a patient (McCullough and Chervenak, 1994; Chervenak and McCullough, 2014).

Can the previable fetus (Chervenak, McCullough, and Levene, 2007) be understood to be a patient independently of the autonomy of the pregnant woman? An affirmative answer would require showing that the fetus has independent moral status or is a person in the philosophical sense of the term. The ethical concept of the fetus as a patient, like the ethical concept of being a patient generally, has no such requirement. Moreover, the now millennia-old debate about the independent moral status of the fetus makes it plain that there is no answer that is authoritative (Callahan and Callahan, 1984). There is no theological perspective that all the world's religions could accept from which to answer in the affirmative, or in the negative for that matter (not to mention that theological debates are actually about dependent moral status – as God's creature – and not about independent moral status). There is also no philosophical perspective that has shown itself to be authoritative, despite centuries of effort. There is thus no authoritative view in ethics generally, whether philosophical or theological, about whether the fetus has independent moral status. Whether the fetus has full moral status of some kind and therefore should be regarded as a patient is not independent of the pregnant woman's autonomy: this is a matter for her to decide for herself. Respect for the woman's autonomy to reach the moral judgment about whether the previable fetus is a patient is at the heart of obstetric ethics (McCullough and Chervenak, 1994; Chervenak and McCullough, 2014).

We emphasize that the fetal patient not is a *separate* patient, as Mahowald (2006), for example, has claimed against us. If the fetus were to be understood as a separate patient, clinical ethical judgment about beneficence-based obligations could be accomplished without any reference to the pregnant woman and clinical ethical judgment would have to take into account only the net clinical benefit of intervention on the fetus. On our account of the ethical concept of the fetus as a patient, beneficence-based obligations to the fetal patient are *only one component* of the physician's or investigator's clinical ethical judgment. As such, beneficence-based obligations to the fetal patient must *in all cases* be balanced against both beneficence-based and autonomy-based obligations to the pregnant patient. The professional relationship between the physician and a fetal patient does *not* make beneficence-based obligations to the fetal patient the physician's sole ethical consideration: beneficence-based and autonomy-based obligations to the pregnant patient must *in all cases* be identified and then balanced against beneficence-based obligations to the fetal patient (Chervenak and McCullough, 1985; McCullough and Chervenak, 1994; Chervenak and McCullough, 2014). Criticism of our account based on the claim that we are committed to the concept of the fetus as a separate patient fails. This response underscores the principal advantage the ethical concept of the fetus as a patient: it makes no appeal to the discourses of personhood, fetal rights, and the unborn child (McCullough and Chervenak, 2008). The result is a clinically comprehensive concept of dependent moral status, in sharp contrast to the clinically limited scope of independent moral status.

The beneficence-based account of the ethical concept of being a patient and its application to the fetus, when it is a patient, has an important ethical implication: all patients are patients without regard to the constitutive properties of independent moral status, rationality, and self-consciousness. Clinically, becoming a patient is not a function of the degree of cognitive developmental capacity or function. An individual human being's developmental capacity and function – from absent, to emerging, to intact, to temporarily lost, to declining, to irreversibly lost – makes no difference to whether that individual is a patient. Our approach thus differs from metaphysical accounts of critics who hold that the fetus gains independent moral status in increments or by degree during pregnancy (Strong, 1997). The ethical concept of the fetus as a patient does not mean that beneficence-based obligations to it would automatically have precedence in obstetric ethics. Only obligations based on independent moral status are candidates for having such precedence, a problem for our critics but not for us.

Mahowald's complaint that our ethical framework "offers no clues on how to prioritize these obligations in cases of conflict" (Mahowald, 2006: 39) is ambiguous. Her claim might mean that we do not *a priori* lexically order one of the obligations over all of the others. Mahowald does do so: autonomy-based obligations to the pregnant woman are lexically ordered first. This results in maternal rights-based reductionism and absolutism, which we reject as defective (Chervenak, McCullough, and Brent, 2011).

Conclusion

Critics of our account of the ethical concept of the fetus as a patient share a commitment – usually implicit – to the concept of independent moral status. Further, they privilege independent moral status as the sole philosophically secure account of moral status. We have responded by arguing that, far from being the secure philosophical foundation that critics of our account assume, the concept of independent moral status is philosophically imperiled and therefore insecure. Our account escapes these perils because it is based on the concept of dependent moral status. The result is an ethical concept of the fetus as a patient that is pragmatic, non-metaphysical, and clinically comprehensive. The fetus has dependent, not independent, moral status when it becomes a patient. This status is very powerful, because it is a function of the three commitments that define medicine as a profession that protects all patients. The dependent moral status of fetus as a patient is therefore more durable than independent moral status, which can be gained and lost or never gained at all.

The ethical concepts of the fetus as a patient and of the pregnant woman as a patient are *both* essential components of obstetric ethics. The ethical concepts of the fetus as a patient and of the pregnant woman as a patient are beneficence-based and derive from the ethical concept of being a patient that was introduced into the history of Western medical ethics by Dr. Gregory. When the pregnant woman has the capacity to participate in decision-making about obstetric care, then she is autonomous; she has independent moral status, which originates from elsewhere than the ethical concept of being a patient. Pregnant women, including adolescent pregnant women, have independent moral status, which means that their moral status is independent of any and every social role that they occupy, including becoming a patient. But their independent moral status in and of itself does not make them patients; the professional commitments of physicians do this important clinical work. The ethical concept of the fetus as a patient withstands close scrutiny by its critics. Moreover, as a pragmatic, non-metaphysical, clinically comprehensive concept it is superior to accounts of obstetric ethics that are based on the philosophically imperiled concept of independent moral status.

References

Beauchamp, T.L. and Childress, J.F. (2013) *Principles of Biomedical Ethics*. 7th ed. New York, Oxford University Press.

Callahan, S. and Callahan, D. (eds). (1984) *Abortion: Understanding Differences*. New York, Plenum Press.

Chervenak, F.A. and McCullough, L.B. (1985) Perinatal Ethics: A Practical Method of Analysis of Obligations to Mother and Fetus. *Obstetrics and Gynecology*, 66 (3), 442–446.

Chervenak, F.A. and McCullough, L.B. (2002) A Comprehensive Ethical Framework for Fetal Research and its Application to Fetal Surgery for Spina Bifida. *American Journal of Obstetrics and Gynecology*, 187 (1), 10–14.

Chervenak, F.A., McCullough, L.B., and Levene, M.I. (2007) An Ethically Justified Clinically Comprehensive Approach to Periviability: Gynaecological, Obstetric, Perinatal, and Neonatal dimensions. *Journal of Obstetrics and Gynaecology*, 27 (1), 3–7.

Chervenak, F.A., McCullough, L.B., and Brent, R.L. (2011) The Professional Responsibility Model of Obstetric Ethics: Avoiding the Perils of Clashing Rights. *American Journal of Obstetrics and Gynecology*, 205 (4), 315.el–5.

Chervenak, F.A. and McCullough, L.B. (2014). *The Professional Responsibility Model of Perinatal Ethics*. Berlin, Walter de Gruyter.

Engelhardt, H.T., Jr. (1986) *The Foundations of Bioethics*. New York, Oxford University Press.

Engelhardt, H.T., Jr. (1995) *The Foundations of Bioethics*, 2nd ed. New York, Oxford University Press.

Gracia, D. (2010) Philosophy: Ancient and Contemporary Approaches. In: J. Sugarman and D.P. Sulmasy (eds), *Methods in Medical Ethics*, 2nd ed. Washington, DC, Georgetown University Press, pp. 55–71.

Gregory, J. (1772) *Lectures on the Duties and Qualifications of a Physician*. London, W. Strahan and T. Cadell. Reprinted in L.B. McCullough (ed), *John Gregory's Writings on Medical Ethics and Philosophy of Medicine*. Dordrecht, Kluwer Academic Publishers, 1998, pp. 161–245.

Harrison, M.A., Evans, M.I., Adzick, N.S., and Holzgreve, W. (2001) *The Unborn Patient: The Art and Science of Fetal Therapy*, 3rd. ed. Philadelphia, PA, W.B. Saunders Company.

Hoffmann, Friedrich. (1738) *Medicus politicus; sive, regulae prudentiae secundum quas medicus juvenis studia sua & vitae rationem dirigere debet*. Leiden, Philip Bonk.

Hume, D. (2000) *A Treatise of Human Nature*, ed. Norton, D.F., and M.J. Norton. New York, Oxford University Press.

Kant, I. (1964). *Groundwork of the Metaphysics of Morals*, trans. Paton, H.J.. New York, Harper Torchbooks.

Mahowald, M.B. (2006) *Bioethics and Women: Across the Lifespan*. New York, Oxford University Press.

McCullough, L.B. (1984) The World Gained and the World Lost: Ethical Dimensions of labeling the Mentally Retarded. In: Kopelman L, and Moskop J (eds), *Ethics and Mental Retardation*. Dordrecht, D. Reidel, pp. 99–118.

McCullough, L.B. (1996) *Leibniz on Individuals and Individuation: The Persistence of Premodern Ideas in Modern Philosophy*. Dordrecht, Kluwer.

McCullough, L.B. (1998) *John Gregory and the Invention of Professional Medical Ethics and the Profession of Medicine*. Dordrecht: Kluwer.

McCullough, L.B. (1999) Hume's Influence on John Gregory and the History of Medical Ethics. *Journal of Medicine and Philosophy*, 24 (4), 376–395.

McCullough, L.B. (2006) The Ethical Concept of Medicine as a Profession: Its Origins in Modern Medical Ethics and Implications for Physicians. In: N. Kenny, and W. Shelton (eds), *Lost Virtue: Professional Character Development in Medical Education*. New York, Elsevier, pp. 17–27.

McCullough, L.B, and Chervenak, F.A. (1994) *Ethics in Obstetrics and Gynecology*. New York, Oxford University Press.

McCullough, L.B., and Chervenak, F.A. (2008) A Critical Analysis of the Concept and Discourse of 'Unborn Child'. *American Journal of Bioethics*, 8 (7), 34–39.

Mill, J.S. (1974) *On liberty*, ed. and intro. Himmelfarb, G. New York, Penguin Books.

Moise, K. (2014) The History of Fetal Therapy. *American Journal of Perinatology*, 31 (7), 557–566.

Percival, T. (1803) *Medical Ethics: Or a Code of Institutes and Precepts, Adapted to the Professional Conduct of Physicians and Surgeons*. London, J. Johnson & R. Bickerstaff.

Ruddick, W.F. and Wilcox, W. (1982) Operating on the Fetus. *The Hastings Center Report*, 12 (5), 10–14.

Strong, C. (1997) *Ethics in Reproductive Medicine: A New Framework*. New Haven, CT, Yale University Press.

Tooley, M. (1972) Abortion and Infanticide. *Philosophy and Public Affairs*, 2 (1), 37–65.

5 Treating the fetus as a patient: possible implications for its moral status

Katrin E. Lörch-Merkle

Owing to the rapidity of biomedical development and the increase in therapeutic options, 'reasoning about the fetus (remains) a complex, often vexing, challenge' (Lyerly, Little & Faden, 2008: 42) up to today. Furthermore, a satisfactory answer is still a desideratum, considering the fetus as a patient is set to become an even more vital factor, and it plays a central role conceptually as well as clinically.

In this chapter I address the concept of 'the fetus as a patient' and thus the question, whether this term could be useful for normative frameworks for clinical interactions in the field of the new prenatal medicine. According to Laurence McCullough and Frank Chervenak, Roy Petrie, whom they consider to have been a founder of modern maternal-fetal medicine, has been the pioneer in the clinical application of this ethical concept. Based on their previous work, they sought a thoroughly pragmatic, non-metaphysical analysis to elucidate the theory of the fetus as a patient as such and the implications of this concept for maternal-fetal medicine.

Even though the initial study of McCullough and Chervenak dates back about 20 years, it has lost none of its importance. In a considerable body of literature, they have approached this problem consistently over the years. In the end they 'conclude[d] that the ethical concept of the fetus as a patient should replace the discourse of "unborn child" when that phrase is used normatively' (McCullough & Chervenak, 2008: 34). Hence, revisiting their 'critical analysis', this chapter discusses the consistency and adequacy of this approach as a whole and aims furthermore to outline the possible implications for the fetus's moral status and the underlying concept of the person.

This chapter is divided into three sections and structured as outlined below.

As a first step, I approach the concept of the patient (as a person) as such by some introductory remarks. The second section briefly introduces McCullough and Chervenak's 'critical analysis of the concept and the discourse of the "unborn child"' and Brown's subsequent critique of this concept (Brown, 2008: 47–49). My aim here is especially to discuss the resulting difficulties of their solution of a replacement of this discourse by instead using the ethical concept of the fetus as a patient and its moral status. In a third and final part, my conclusions are drawn whilst outlining that some possible consequences of the concept of the fetus as a patient might lead into a normative asymmetry.

Introduction

According to the Cologne Manifesto *The Right of Otherness* from the 1990s (Kölner Manifest, 1994), (invasive) prenatal diagnosis has for a long time been seen as predominantly of benefit to third parties, namely for parents or society as a whole. With its primary focus on diagnosis and not therapeutic options (and a persisting lack of therapeutic knowledge and possibilities) only seldom might it have served the unborn child itself. Hence, it is very much on the boundary of the medical task to cure. Nowadays, in contrast, more and more obstetricians and gynaecologists emphasize the benefit for both the fetus and the mother due to medical advances and the resulting options in prenatal screening and diagnosis. The rapid advancements that we can see, both in fetal therapy and surgery, have allowed the wish to diagnose often to become a reality, and sometimes also the wish to treat and cure the fetus. This of course leads to an increasingly common view of the fetus as a patient. The fundamental question here is whether this new 'view' of the fetus might have deeper implications. And, if so, what type of implications these may be. When talking about patients in a broader and more general sense, we usually do this in a somewhat 'personalistic' kind of view. This means that we typically regard a patient as being a person, and as such possessing 'exclusive superior moral status'. Even though this might be a highly ambivalent concept in philosophy due its underlying ontologies, it is 'generally assumed to have a central place in morality' (DeGrazia, 1997: 301).

Hence, in the first instance I would like to shed some light on personhood in general. Normally society 'treat[s] humanity as the deciding mark of personhood, no doubt because the terms are locally coextensive or almost coextensive', which means a kind of congruence, in an analytical or logical sense, as Daniel Denett has already pointed out (Dennet, 1976).

Thus, human beings are the only persons we recognize (so far, in this time and place). And *vice versa*, we do recognize almost all human beings as persons, even though – especially in a medical setting – we can easily imagine conditions that exclude them from being actual persons (e.g. mentally defective human beings, human beings declared insane by licensed psychiatrists). And – for sure – we also can picture and specify several unmistakable conditions for being a person.

According to Dennet, a metaphysical notion of a person is a necessary condition of personhood. This metaphysical notion, 'roughly, the notion of an intelligent, conscious, feeling agent' (ibid.: 176) is intertwined with a moral notion that he distinguishes as a second condition of personhood, 'roughly, the notion of an agent who is accountable, who has both rights and responsibilities' (ibid.). As he initially seems to be uncertain whether both notions coincide or whether 'it is merely that being a person in the metaphysical sense is a necessary but not sufficient condition of being a person in the moral sense', Denett finally concludes that both notions namely 'are not separate and distinct concepts but just two different and unstable resting points on the same continuum' (ibid.: 176, 193), whereby the moral notion could (only) function as a regulative, normative ideal, which could factually never be fulfilled.

Even though he denies that they are sufficient to ensure that any actual entity is a person, as the concept remains 'inescapably normative', he emphasizes that it is still not obsolete in as much as we cannot cease to regard others – and, even more so, ourselves – as persons. And he nevertheless considers 'six familiar themes' as at least necessary (metaphysical) conditions for personhood.

- First (and most obvious), that persons are rational beings. And as we would add, as such autonomous beings. However, emphasizing rationality should not misappropriate the fact, that humans are also emotional beings. The intertwining of both these spheres is for certain one of the special attributes of the *conditio humana*.
- Second, that persons are beings to which states of consciousness are attributed (or psychological, mental or intentional predicates, are ascribed).
- Third, whether something counts as a person or not depends in some way on an attitude taken toward it, a stance adopted with respect to it. Which is of high impact for the clinical application, as we might say.
- Fourth, the object toward which this personal stance is taken must be capable of reciprocating in some way. In other words, being a person means to treat others as persons and therefore treating them morally.
- Fifth, persons must be capable of verbal communication.
- Sixth: persons are distinguishable from other entities by being conscious in some special way, namely a property, we often call self-conscious (ibid.: 177ff.).

David DeGrazia, is another who wonders, whether the concept of personhood, which plays such a central role in morality in so far as it is used to justify the exclusive or radically superior status of persons, could 'carry such heavy normative freight' (DeGrazia, 1997: 301). His approach could be seen as an alternative to Dennet's, because he instead emphasizes that 'Personhood is associated with a cluster of more specific properties' (namely, among others, autonomy, rationality, self-awareness or moral agency). Interestingly enough, DeGrazia thinks that not all of these properties are strictly necessary for being a person, but that it is also not sufficient to have just one of these properties. As we can easily imagine, human beings lacking autonomy (like e.g. infants or humans with moderate mental retardation) still appear to us as persons. There also 'might be autonomous beings who have no conception of morality and who are therefore not moral agents' and consequently lacking traits commonly tied to personhood (ibid.: 303). In that sense, autonomy does not seem a necessary condition for personhood, whether it is sufficient is even more uncertain. A person is someone who has enough of these properties, where 'enough' takes account both of how many of these properties are instantiated and of the degree to which each is instantiated: a being with the capacity for sufficiently complex forms of consciousness (each of the properties representing a form of consciousness).

He opines that personhood remains 'a vague concept insofar it is not analyzable into necessary and sufficient conditions'[1] and hence morally unsuitable 'in contexts where who qualifies is genuinely debatable [...]' (DeGrazia, 1997: 301).

But whether we are likely to pursue rather a traditional or a more analytic and as such pluralistic view, regarding personhood as a *cluster* concept (ibid.: 306), they all have in common to rely on diverse conditions. Even though it entails not only descriptive but also prescriptive or moral content – hence the reason for its vagueness – it 'allows us to identify paradigm person, and, beyond such easy cases, other beings who are sufficiently similar to warrant inclusion under the concept' (cf. ibid.: 320). There is no need – also for reasons of space – to go into further detail in the philosophy of the person here.

It seems obvious that these conditions are valid in the clinical context and medical ethics as well, for example, in the doctor-patient-relationship. But there is at least one expectation of high significance: we often do have situations in this realm (let us consider e.g. cases of severe illness, accidents and so on) that lead to a special form of first contact. Such circumstances, wherein patients – and in this context severely impaired persons, because of having lost temporarily or permanently at least one or several/all conditions of personhood – are treated as if actually being a person in the complete sense, necessitates particular handling and social interaction.

Even though it cannot be assured whether this is a good definition, we would like to call it, say, something like 'treatment-as-if-a-full-person'.

So why is this the case, and why do we (or almost all of us) have the strong belief, that acting in such a way is not only acceptable but even required? Well, we cannot deny that we do have and should have a certain attitude towards those who used to be persons or whom we expect in the future to become persons, not only in daily life but even more so in medical contexts, but with that, acknowledging their special moral status.

In his instructive, even inspiring, paper, Hauskeller has proved that this attitude is grounded in a concept of human dignity, not as *dignitas* but instead as *bonitas*. According to him, respect is the sentiment or disposition with which we tend to respond to the perception of dignitas, whereas bonitas on the other hand invites a different emotional response, which is better expressed as awe than as respect. Even though both can be defined or designated as, 'basic moral dispositions (...), awe can be described as immediate value-experience, in the sense that the value of the object is discovered in and through the experience itself'. It is this concept of awe that is directed toward others in their vulnerability,[2] and therefore is highly attractive in the realm of clinical ethics. But for it to be readily transferred also towards embryos, as Hauskeller himself emphasizes, the 'awe' would have to be demonstrated first in this setting.

But even if one would agree that moral value can be 'discovered' through experience and emotion, the reflection on the moral status of the fetus, especially of the fetus as a patient, remains a complex and difficult endeavour. It is quite understandable that not only those who provide practical care for fetuses and hence feel a special responsibility for them, but also those who theorize about fetuses should seek an adequate terminology to designate this entity.

McCullough and Chervenak's idea of the fetus as a patient – a pragmatic and non-metaphysic approach?

About 20 years ago, Laurence McCullough and Frank Chervenak elaborated on the concept of the fetus as a patient. In their article, they carefully construed concepts and discourses of the unborn child in connection with the abortion debate and shown, that none of them offers an adequate or even more critical account of it. They provide their own critical analysis in three stages. In a first stage, they distinguish between normative and descriptive uses in order to describe fetuses; in the second they stress the normative content of the concept of the unborn child (and its failure in establishing the independent moral status of fetuses and their rights) and in a third and last step, they argue that the normative content of 'unborn child' is that of dependent beneficence-based moral status. As a consequence, they demand the replacement of this narrative in favour of the concept of the fetus as a patient, which they see fit as a pragmatic, non-metaphysical approach to clinical application.

The authors demonstrate furthermore, that the term is used by opponents of abortion not only descriptively but also normatively, to assert the moral status of fetuses as well as of (pre-) embryos and with that a legal status. For if moral status means: 'that human beings have obligations towards an entity, to protect and promote its interests' (McCullough & Chervenak, 2008: 35), legal status means that state power should be used to enforce such obligations. They identify a 'strategic ambiguity in the form of using a historical, familiar and uncontroversial descriptive use of 'unborn child', by that course of action bootlegging in the *normative* meaning' and hence 'failing the intellectual requirements of justifying' it (ibid.: 35ff.).

According to the authors, 'dependent moral status' only implies that human beings have obligations to protect an entity's interests because of its social role that has been created and structured for that purpose. Attempts at public discourse, in contrast, often aim to assert an independent moral status based on rights and with that more or less relying on the concept of person or personhood.

This implicit recourse to that concept unveils the societal need for a higher-level based orientation but is nevertheless also leading to positions in disputes that McCullough and Chervenak consider to be irreconcilable and theoretically inconsistent. Denying an independent, i.e. rights-based, moral status for the fetus or embryo, they instead strongly argue for a beneficence-grounded, dependent moral status. Furthermore they assert that the ethical concept of the 'fetus as a patient' is philosophically coherent and should be used in a clinically relevant manner, whereas 'fetal patients' are simply seen as a special case of the general moral category of being a patient.[3]

To draw a short interim-conclusion according to McCullough and Chervenak, the concept of the fetus as a patient proves to be qualified to avoid the ambiguity of the term 'unborn child', insofar as it emphasizes the beneficence-based, rather than the rights-based, nature of the obligations towards this early stage of life, thereby stressing its dependent status. The authors point out that, whereas persons do have rights, patients may not always or necessarily do so. Even though they deny an independent moral status for the fetus, they emphasize that it can be a fitting object of beneficence. In this context, it has to be carefully examined what the concept of fetal patienthood could contribute to avoid bringing on board larger questions over reproductive decision-making and, in a more theoretical sense, whether – as Brown argues in his critique, 'the proposed principle-based framework inherently assigns and relies on such a status' (Brown, 2008: 48) despite this rejection of an independent moral status for the fetus.

As mentioned above, the authors themselves emphasize that fetal patients should count simply as a special category of patients. One of the conditions for becoming a patient is the existence of 'clinical interventions that are reliably expected to clinically benefit the child and, later, the person that the fetus is expected to become.' (McCullough & Chervenak, 2008: 37). The clinical application of this concept therefore is dependent on the existence of an exact link between an embryo or fetus and its later becoming a child and a person. This may give the impression that the use of the concept of the fetal patient instead of the phrase unborn child in the realm of application, is bearing the same burden of proof as the responsibility to protect and to promote its interests (as a later person) remains exactly the same. Furthermore, the authors claim that their concept of the fetus as a patient is – in comparison to the concept of the unborn child – not only a pragmatic but also a non-metaphysical approach.

Mindful of the abortion debate, maybe this approach truly is more pragmatic insofar as it is a social concept and therefore the basis of the reasoning is highly descriptive; at least at first glance, see e.g. the explanations of viability of the fetus which in the US are considered as really helpful and ethically true (Chervenak & McCullough, 1996). Interestingly enough, they are once again the subject of discussion concerning the right of abortion within the debate on 'Trumpcare' and turn out still to be unsolved.[4]

Nonetheless, this discussion mainly focuses on the relationship between three different qualities of principle-based obligations: the beneficence-based obligation toward the fetus, and both the beneficence-based obligation and the autonomy-based obligation toward the pregnant woman and hence the future mother. As 'there is no basis for saying that a fetus has a perspective on its interests, [t] here can therefore be no autonomy-based obligations to any fetus' (Chervenak & McCullough, 1996: 116). This triad could pose new problems as there is an analogy to the Beauchamp/Childress principlism (Beauchamp & Childress, 2009), which comes without an internal hierarchy among the principles, so that the balance between principles must be established each time, according to highly complex but coherent reasoning.

Not being a physician (and thus not having any clinical obligations and responsibilities at all) I do not want to be so presumptuous as to evaluate the resulting difficulties. But I would dare to say, being quite sure, that there will be many of them. Besides, I am also unable to see how, and how effectively, this concept may be employed to strengthen the position of the fetus as a patient against the pregnant woman's reproductive autonomy.

However, as McCullough and Chervenak stress exactly that point, I aim to return to the previously mentioned, more theoretical and, let us say, higher-level problem, namely that the proposed principle-based framework inherently assigns and relies on such a special status and therefore has a strong metaphysical foundation. As Brown demonstrates, both the concept of the patient, and in addition the assertion that we have 'beneficence-based obligations' towards patients, smuggle in normative meaning, and is for that reason bootlegging itself (Brown, 2008: 48).

These considerations of an underlying concept of (independent) moral status as a patient, are necessarily based on the concept of personhood. And that in turn almost leads to the considerations of a dependent status as patient. With this course of reasoning Brown's reproach about begging the question becomes clear, in as far as this assumption of the aforementioned (an independent moral status as a patient, based on personhood) is a necessary condition of the following (a dependent moral status), which was meant to replace the previous. Because of this fundamental theoretical problem, McCullough's and Chervenak's model is not only philosophically flawed but might also impact substantially on the pregnant woman and exert a powerful societal influence, as it may be used to constrain women's right to autonomously control what happens to their bodies.

From theory to praxis – even more snags in the realm of clinical application?

The discourse of fetal patienthood could pose further problems concerning the realm of clinical application. In their 'critique of the fetus as a patient', Lyerly, Little, and Faden (2008) have already pointed out that one of the resulting problems could be a tendency to think of the fetus as separate from the pregnant woman, and thereby to disregard the physical and social relationship they have, or, in contrast, due to an overunification, possibly even perceiving the pregnant woman as a patient herself. Nevertheless, in respect of the pregnant woman, the 'issues of bodily dominion' with deeply intertwined physiologies and all the implications for health, life and bodily integrity must still be of overriding interest during pregnancy and also birth, even when the fetus has full moral status, as Little argues (2008). At least, being a patient implies a normative status and, with this, concrete expectations for healthcare, given that we consider physicians and healthcare professionals as having a strong duty towards their individual patients. In this regard, the concept of the fetus as a patient not only presupposes its specific moral status but is rather likely to strengthen it, even against the pregnant woman.

Interestingly enough, McCullough and Chervenak particularly highlight this point: despite the overriding beneficence- and autonomy-based obligations towards the pregnant woman, the concept of the fetus as a patient allows and hence ethically legitimizes 'directive counselling, i.e. recommending a form of management, for fetal benefit'.[5] Nevertheless, we should be fully aware that 'fetuses, though they are members of our species, and perhaps newborns, are not [yet] persons because they have none of the properties associated with personhood' (DeGrazia, 1997: 308). (For this reason, approaches in the sense of an inclusion-theory in the philosophy of the person (Kipke, 2001) are not likely to persuade us.) But what fetuses do have is the potentiality to achieve the relevant properties and hence to become a person, and as such they have a certain moral status. This is in accordance with what a great many people do believe in, namely 'a graduated view of embryonic and fetal status'.[6]

However, this is presumably only one side of the coin. Unlike in cases concerning adult patients, in paediatrics we have a triadic relationship between child parents and doctor. All therapeutic measures and treatments should be orientated towards the child's welfare, while the basic ethical conflict is between the duty to save lives and the duty not to do harm, which may be summarized as the duty not to cause more harm than benefit. Assuming that analogy between paediatrics and prenatal medicine is appropriate here, we should carefully examine whether the view of the fetus as a patient might not also undermine its moral status as an entity that is of a natural inevitability, and [has its own] dignity as being an end in itself in the Hauskellerian perspective. Because that view emphasizes its dependent status, it might lead to medical interventions that disturb fetal development with regard to the suffering patient at a later time.

Or, as Jason Eberl tries to explain it according to classical natural law theory:

> a being's moral status is related to the set of intrinsic capacities it possesses and the inherent value in allowing such capacities to develop into full actualization. [...] Hence there is a fundamental value in allowing an embryo or fetus to develop from a state of being *potentially* self-conscious, rational and autonomous to a state of being *actually* such.
>
> (Eberl, 2008: 45)

As McCullough and Chervenak develop their concept against the background of clinical practice, they define the starting point for morality in this realm as 'the obligation to protect and to promote the interests of the patient [and as such in] "two perspectives in terms of which [they] can be understood: that of the physician and that of the patient"' (Chervenak & McCullough, 1996: 115).

Proceeding from the assumption that we are far away from 'closure on a single authoritative account of the independent moral status of the fetus' (ibid.: 117) they plead for at least a dependent moral status as sufficient to count as a patient and thus the underlying assumption that,

> the fetus is a patient when the fetus is presented for medical interventions, whether diagnostic or therapeutic, that reasonably can be expected to result in a greater balance of goods over harms for the person the fetus can later become during early childhood.
>
> (ibid.: 117)

They therefore require a link between the fetus now and the child later, who will achieve independent status.

McCullough and Chervenak argue that one such link could be *viability*, which is to be understood as an extrinsic factor grounded in both biological and technological factors and not as an intrinsic property of the fetus. As it exists as a mere 'function of biomedical and technological capacities' (ibid.: 117), viability varies in different parts of the world dependent on skills and capabilities.

Once having reached the stage of viability and together with the further condition that it must be able to profit from medical care, the fetus has become a patient and consequently directive counselling for fetal benefit is ethically justified according to McCullough and Chervenak. It should depend on the presence and severity of anomalies and involves e.g. recommending obstetric management or recommending against or for termination of pregnancy (cf. ibid.: 117ff.).

Being based solely on these extrinsic factors (on the one hand gestational age, and on the other hand skills and capacities) the word 'patient' could be used merely as a technical term. But in that case, divested of its former substance, it could easily degenerate into a purely arbitrary factor. If decisions of fetal life and death depend solely on such extrinsic factors, the intrinsic property of moral status would be completely undermined.

If, furthermore, the concept of the fetus as a patient is only used in such a manner as to anticipate the later patient as one whose suffering and harm should be avoided on any account, then this approach may even demonstrate a normative asymmetry, in that it may even lead to the non-existence of that very same future patient.

Conversely, and as a logical consequence, 'the pre-viable fetus [is] presented to the physician solely as a function of the pregnant woman's autonomy' (ibid.: 118). As a result of that reasoning, the authors claim that there exist no rights-based obligations towards the fetus at all. If this were true, the moral status of the fetus could be even further flattened from a legal perspective.

If we would assume that fetuses are to be regarded as persons in full sense, Eberl has a fair point to criticize this very deduction against this background, by pointing out,

> that the question then becomes what our ethical attitude should be towards an entity which may be reasonably argued to have the moral status of a person, when a conclusive rational demonstration of its status as such is not immediately forthcoming.
>
> (Eberl, 2008: 44)

But even if we only try to defend a gradualist account of the moral status of the fetus on the basis of a certain form of the argument from potential, we should keep in mind that certain interpretations of the concept are more likely to weaken the status of the fetus rather than to strengthen it.

To draw a conclusion

We should be aware that the 'moral status' of the fetus is still the subject of discussion in moral philosophy and is still at least an ambiguous concept. Surely none of the approaches that rely on an underlying philosophical concept of the person (all the same if patient, child or something else) was designed with the fetus in mind.

With their concept of the fetal patient McCullough and Chervenak wanted to deliver a pragmatic and non-metaphysical approach for obstetric counselling. As the clinical application of this concept is dependent on the existence of precisely this link between an embryo or fetus and its later becoming a child and then a person, the authors argue that one potential link between an embryo or fetus could be viability, as an extrinsic factor and not as an intrinsic property of the fetus as such. If the concept of the 'patient' then were used 'merely as a technical term stipulated to mean an object of some unspecified beneficence-based medical obligation' it might be helpful in clinical practice but at the price of being philosophically flawed. Moreover, if the term 'unborn child' could be reduced to a technical term in the same manner, it could also be rendered morally acceptable (neutral) and need not then be replaced.

This may give the impression, by means of a contradiction in addition, that the use of the concept of the 'fetal patient' instead of the phrase 'unborn child' in the realm of clinical application, is bearing the same (theoretical) burden of proof as the responsibility to protect and to promote its interests (as a later person) remains exactly the same.

Even though 'viability' as a concrete and extrinsic criterion for fetal patienthood might not be that bad for practical use, we should also bear in mind that it is at least arbitrary and as a result, could weaken the fetus's moral status.

In this chapter we have outlined some of the possible consequences of talking about the fetus as a patient and the fetus's specific moral status. In using such a strong ethical concept in the realm of clinical application, we should try to become fully aware, not only of its more or less theoretical problems and the implications we have to handle (like the metaphysical foundation and eventually the resulting normative asymmetries) but also and to an even greater extent, of its practical consequences for not only the fetus but also for the pregnant woman, her family, and society as a whole. For that reason, I want to stress how important it is to uncover the underlying theories and presuppositions, and to make our own assumptions and beliefs even more explicit.

References

Beauchamp, T. L. & Childress, J. F. (2009) *Principles of Biomedical Ethics*. 6th ed. New York: Oxford University Press.

Brown, S. D. (2008) The 'Fetus as Patient': A Critique. *The American Journal of Bioethics*, 7, 47–49.

Chervenak, F. A. & McCullough, L. B. (1996) The Fetus as a Patient: An Essential Ethical Concept for Maternal-Fetal Medicine. *Journal of Maternal-Fetal Medicine*, 5(3), 115–119.

Dennet, Daniel (1976) *Conditions of Personhood*. Berkeley and Los Angeles: University of California Press, pp. 175–179, 193.

DeGrazia, D. (1997) Great Apes, Dolphins, and the Concept of Personhood. *The Southern Journal of Philosophy*, 35, 301–320, 301.

Eberl, J. T. (2008) The Moral Status of 'Unborn Children' Without Rights. *The American Journal of Bioethics*, 7(8), 44–45, 45.

Hauskeller, M. (2012) *Believing in the Dignity of Human Embryos*. Equinox Online, pp. 53–65. Available at www.ncbi.nlm.nih.gov/pubmed/23350217

Kipke, R. (2001)Mensch und Person.Der Begriff der Person in der Bioethik und die Frage nach dem Lebensrecht aller Menschen, Berlin.

Kölner Manifest (1994) 'Vom Recht auf Anderssein', published in Neuer-Miebach. T. &Tarneden, R. (eds.), *Vom Recht auf Anderssein. Anfragen an pränatale Diagnostik und humangenetische Beratung*, Marburg: Lebenshilfe-Verl., Düsseldorf: Verl. Selbstbestimmtes Leben, 148–149.

Little, M. O. (2008) Abortion and the margins of personhood. *Rutgers Law Journal*, 39 (331), 331–348, p. 345.

Lyerly, A. D., Little, M. O. & Faden, R. R. (2008) A Critique of the 'Fetus as Patient'. *The American Journal of Bioethics*, 7, 42–44.

McCullough, L. B. & Chervenak, F. A. (2008) A Critical Analysis of the Concept and Discourse of the 'Unborn Child'. *American Journal of Bioethics*, 8 (7), 34–39.

Parfit, D. (1984) *Reasons and Persons*. Oxford: Oxford University Press.

Vahabzadeh (2017) Back to knitting needles. Is equality possible without the right of abortion? The dispute abbout Trumpcare and right-wing populist positions in Europe indicate an unsolved problem, SZ, 27 March, 9.

Notes

1 Hence the assumption, that personhood is a determinate matter, more specifically, that 'for any X, the claim that X is a person is either or false' goes wrong. He instead emphasizes that the vagueness of personhood entails 'that even complete factual knowledge would not permit a decision (non arbitrarily) in every case whether a being is a person', cf. De Grazia (1997: 305).

2 'We do respond to something that is there and that we feel is worthy of protection. Our decision depends on how we feel about the matter, or more precisely how we relate to the entities in question' (Hauskeller, 2012: 65).

3 The fetus becomes a patient when 1) it is presented to the physician or other healthcare professional, and 2) there exist clinical interventions that are reliably expected to clinically benefit the child and later, the person, that the fetus is expected to become (McCullough and Chervanak, 2008: 37).

4 Cf. for example the article in the German newspaper *Süddeutsche Zeitung* in which Vahabzadeh refers to the US rules on abortion whereupon termination of pregnancy is allowed until the fetus is viable outside the mother's womb (Vahabzadeh, 2017). Zurück zur Stricknadel. Kann es Gleichberechtigung ohne das Recht auf Abtreibung geben? Der Streit um Trumpcare und rechtspopulistische Positionen in Europa verweisen auf ein ungelöstes Problem [Back to knitting needles. Is equality possible without the right of abortion? The dispute abbout Trumpcare and right-wing populist positions in Europe indicate

an unsolved problem], SZ, 27 March, 9. In 1973, this regulation was arbitrarily fixed of 28 week of pregnancy (see *Roe vs. Wade*) Later it has been reduced of 24 weeks.

5 'In the United States the Authors believe, viability presently occurs at approximately 24 weeks of gestational age (Chervenak & McCullough, 1996: 117).

6 'Even at early stages of pregnancy, developing human life has an important value worthy of respect; its status grows as it does, as a gradually increasing unit, at some point late in pregnancy, the fetus is deserving of the very strong moral protection due newborns' (Little, 2008: 332).

Part III

The fetus as a patient: where does that leave the pregnant woman?

6 Insights from a perspective of cultural anthropology: a discourse analyses of representations of (genetic) reproductive medicine and the fetus in popular media

Janina Krause

This chapter gives a cultural anthropological perspective on how popular media – specifically, the *Bild-Zeitung* – describes reproductive medicine and the fetus. What images of the body and of women appear when popular discourses access medical knowledge, or what appears as being medical knowledge?

While ethical experts discuss whether the fetus should be seen as a patient, which would come along with certain duties on the side of physicians, popular media has already found another answer and locates the duties solely on the side of the pregnant woman. Within the popular discourse the fetus is described as separated from the maternal body and imagined as an independent social and bodily entity. This concept of the fetus has massive influence on how the female body and female (reproductive) autonomy are pictured. Women appear to be the ones who have to take – privately and individually – responsibility for the wellbeing of the fetus. In contrast the role of technology and scientific research as well as the role of the physician and medical treatment is hardly criticised. Against this background, I understand the popular representations of the fetus as a snapshot of a process of normalisation that tries to establish a new understanding of reproductive autonomy, that pretends to respect the freedom of decision making, but has actually lost its feminist content of an autonomous female body.

I have reached this conclusion by investigating articles of the online edition of *Bild* in a discourse theoretical manner. I extracted what figures of speech and linguistic strategies *Bild* uses to make the character of the fetus tangible.

Theoretical background: discourse and metaphors

The term *discourse* is often understood as debate or discussion. In this chapter, though, I will explicitly refer to the term of discourse and its theory as defined by Michel Foucault. His discourse theory states that language is not a reflection of reality, but a tool to create it. Foucault's discourse is a social and cultural practice, which generates knowledge, objects and the subjects it talks about. To analyse the discourse means to uncover its inner structure and order (Foucault, 1997).

Therefore I investigated popular articles on reproductive medicine and the fetus, to examine what language and patterns of language they are based upon. This contribution focusses on bringing out the cultural and historical dimensions of these patterns understood as strategies of making a certain character of the fetus tangible.

In this context it makes sense to not just ask what statements are repeated and how they are organised but it is worth adding the field of metaphors to the discourse analysis. Usually metaphors are known to be used mostly in lyrical texts, while scientific texts do without them. To assume scientific language and concepts do not include figures of speech reflects the opposition of nature and culture that takes part in shaping social order since its appearance during modernity. The scientific standard, in particular experimental science, is known for its objectivity and practicality. But actually even scientific texts are stuffed with metaphors.

Yet since the 1980s representatives of science and technology studies declared that they had overcome the demarcation between nature and culture and acknowledged that they cannot be separated (Haraway, 1991; Latour, 2002).[1] To name something nature can be a practice to make it inviolable. Regarding these circumstances, the opposition of nature and culture is not valued as a given fact but as a tool to create social order. I assume that patterns of social order inscribe themselves in scientific and popular scientific texts. Accordingly, the analysed articles and the scientific concepts they report about refer to and suggest a certain kind of social order.

Against this theoretical background, I tried to find out how women emerge and are portrayed when popular media report on the fetus and reproductive technologies.

Bild on (genetic) reproductive medicine and the fetus

Bild is one of the most popular newspapers in Germany. It was first published in 1952 by the publisher Axel-Springer-Verlag in Berlin and refers to itself as the biggest European daily newspaper. Although *Bild* is occasionally accused in public of questionable journalistic methods, it is still rated as a 'solid part of German daily life'[2] (Voss, 1999: 19). *Bild* regularly publishes articles on scientific topics. Popular science tries to extract what they report on from the specific scientific vocabulary and still follow the scientific power of definition. The popular scientific discourse has creative and fictional parts but must still be based on scientific evidence. Popular science can be seen as a discursive space, in which the power of scientific definition can take up a big part (Sarasin, 2003).

Siegfried Jäger describes *Bild* as a 'machine of discourse, a type of major regulator that contributes to making circumstances normal which basically are not normal, but cruel, inhuman and daunting. [...] *Bild* maintains a pro-biopolitical course through concealing the negative sides of biopolitics, and emphasising what is seen as positive.' (Jäger, 1997: 63). Popular media like *Bild* represent a level of discourse picking up matters from scientific discourses and making them suitable for everyday life (Jäger, 1997: 5). Under these circumstances, and referring to Angela McRobbie, the analysed popular representations are understood as technologies of governance (Villa & McRobbie, 2010).

Metaphors of the body

As mentioned above *Bild* takes a position in the centre of a discourse that Foucault called biopolitics. Biopolitics include all techniques and methods to regulate the population and to optimise its health. It is this power that organises our society by having an impact on every single body. Whereas the pre-modern body used to clash with the authority of the state while being punished, biopower has tried to optimise the body by letting the subject realise that taking care of itself is an existential value. This change of positions between power and body – focusing on healthcare – marks the origin of the life sciences (Foucault, 1983). But what does the subject and its body look like, appearing within the knowledge of those powerful instances and the popularisation of their knowledge?

Bodies in popular media are described through two certain metaphors, which deserve closer attention because they provide models and figures of thought not only forming body images but also reflecting back to act on the processes of social order. In fact political entities are often imagined as corporeal entities[3], accordingly body metaphors can be understood as 'soft tools'[4] to create political and social order (Koschorke *et al.*, 2007: 5).

While describing the human body, popular media use terms like 'energy supply' (Bockholt, 2008), 'energy use', 'function', and 'production'[5] (Sell, 2014). These terms point to description of industrial processes or machines. The use of this machine metaphor refers back to the changes initiated by industrialisation: 'The new technologies of the industrial age led to a different image of the body. A thermodynamic machine was not only an analogy of the body, but the body basically became identical.'[6] (Rabinbach, 1998: 295). The body has been imagined as a machine since the seventeenth century but also persists as a body, whose power can be increased, and whose qualities can be used to full capacity. In his book *The Selfish Gene*, that was first published in 1976 and that was honoured in 2016 by the *Guardian* as the best non-fiction book, the evolutionary biologist Richard Dawkins suggests to 'treat the individual as a survival machine built by a short-lived confederation of long-lived genes' (Dawkins, 2006: 44). The concept of the body as a machine fits seamlessly into popular representations of genetics. Additionally, the quote points to the second central metaphor that structures our image of the body, but surpasses the language of industrialisation: the idea of the body as an information-processing system. Within the texts of *Bild* the body is furthermore described as 'a result of a constantly running genetic program that can be turned on or turned off' (Altmann, 2007). This metaphorical core of genetics consisting of text and readability has a huge historical dimension[7] and transfers certain qualities onto the human body.

Bild uses expressions like 'identifying genes', or the gene as 'information that is copied' (Bild, 2009). These ideas of the body as information, sign, and text, influence our understanding of disease. If living matter is regarded as a code or as information, disease becomes a hereditary mistake (Lemke, 2006).

Donna Haraway argues that there has been a significant shift during the past decades concerning how bodies appear within scientific knowledge. What used to be an organism became an issue of genetic code and access to information. Biotechnology is writing technology per se. While the organism is disappearing, biotic components – sort of information-processing systems – are left over (Haraway, 1991).

Reporting about reproductive medicine is grounded increasingly on the machine metaphor. *Bild* uses phrases like 'produce embryos, remove cells, develop stem cells, and plant mini-embryos into the uterus' (Bild, n.d.a). As the term *reproductive medicine* itself demonstrates, a terminology of production processes is used. The uterus is pictured as the central place of production which the expert can cultivate. The female body, mainly consisting of a uterus and egg cells, is fragmented into useful separated components. Referring to Marilyn Strathern, reproductive medicine speaks the language of industrial patriarchy (Strathern, 1992).

Representations of women and the fetus

The so called 'Erlanger Baby'[8] for instance illustrates the consequences that might derive from a biotechnological body concept in extreme cases. Related Stories – narratives on *dead and comatose mothers* – form one of several subcategories (further subcategories printed in italics below) of reports on the fetus. This topic – using dead or comatose pregnant women as incubators – is one of the few that make *Bild* take up a critical position, recommending everybody's right to die in dignity (*Bild*, 2014a). However, when concerning *abortion and miscarriage*, *Bild* presents the female body as a threat to the fetus and uses the medical rhetoric to enforce its ambivalent position. The body concepts of modern reproductive technologies have been bashed by feminist researchers since their ascendance during the 80s – not only in the field of science and technology studies. The cultural anthropologist Brigitta Hauser-Schäublin puts it like this: 'The tendency to present the fetus as an individual person who needs an intrauterine care system (instead of a woman carrying a growing being) leads to cases like the Erlanger Baby' (Hauser-Schäublin, 1995: 171).

To rank *Bild*'s ethical position it can be concluded that *Bild* argues explicitly pro dying in dignity and implicitly against abortion. *Bild* reports for instance on 'The War against Girls in Asia' and describes that 'female fetuses get systematically killed inside the mother's womb' (Bild, 2015b; 2017). Another article reports on a pregnant woman, who was abandoned by the 'unborn baby's daddy' (Jost, 2012) and thought about abortion out of rage. While women's potential reasons to seek an abortion are not discussed, *Bild* identifies abortion as murdering the fetus. Furthermore *Bild* names one exception that might legitimate abortion: if the fetus is evidently suffering a disease. 'With a heavy heart, the mother agreed to the abortion of the sick fetus' (*Bild*, 2011). The feminist achievement that women's bodies belong to themselves – especially when it comes to abortion – seems to be exchanged for the idea that a woman's body belongs to the fetus.

This tendency is particularly apparent within articles that describe *fetal life in the uterus.* In such articles, ultrasound pictures present the fetus as an individual.

The observer can retrace its ability to dream or to smile. 'Hannah opens her little mouth wide and points her index finger. Her mummy is Manuela Pietsch (33) from Magdeburg' says an image caption of an ultrasound picture. The unborn Hannah, who can be recognised clearly – quite the contrary to her mother – is imagined as an independent being with social and emotional qualities. Technologies of visualisation, in particular, have offered a view on this individual and separated it/her from the mother's body. In the course of biotechnological development, the single physical body of the pregnant woman and her expected child has been transformed – as we have seen before – into a fetus and an intrauterine care system that holds a higher or lower risk for the fetus (Duden, 1991) – as we are about to see.

But not only has the recently established technology of ultrasound scanning played an important role in the discourse of the fetus; *Bild* also reports on *technological innovations in reproductive medicine* (like procedures being used in states that have more liberal rights on this matter than Germany) and the controversial discussion of 2010 on a law on preimplantation genetic diagnosis (PGD) in Germany. Occasionally, *Bild* quotes representatives from medical ethics, although the newspaper takes an extremely technophilic position. Since the beginning of the cultural industry, the characters of the mad scientist, as well as of the mad-man-monster, have both shaped popular narrations on science, and might reveal a tension between science and laymen. The best-known examples of such characters might be found in Shelley's *Frankenstein*, where the mad scientist uses his specific knowledge to conduct dubious and menacing research (Tanner, 2009; Sarasin, 2003). Within a few articles on reproductive technologies – for instance about a researcher, who cloned himself – the expert is imagined as a mad scientist. However, if it comes to physicians taking care of women through pregnancy, a mad scientist does not appear. Physicians are hardly mentioned in popular representations on the fetus. This can be rated as another strategy in designing a new understanding of women's autonomy, because with the physician's absence there is only the pregnant woman left to make decisions.

For instance this can be observed in articles on non-invasive-prenatal-testing (NIPT). The following image has the commentary, 'Riskless medical check-up for pregnant women. New blood test tracks Down syndrome'. This phrase lets NIPT appear as a technology that a) meets the individual needs of pregnant women, b) provides the choice of safety through information, and c) depicts Down syndrome as something that must be 'tracked down' and taken care of privately by the pregnant woman. Particularly, informing pregnant women about new medical possibilities and creating more choices, seems to be in line with the feminist philosophy of self-empowerment. But the bump we see in the picture does not belong to the pregnant woman: It belongs to the fetus, who lives within it and whose shoes are ready for *stepping outside* (Figure 6.1). If medical check-ups can be carried out without any risk, would it be irresponsible not to perform them? The headless depersonalised woman's body in the figure demonstrates that the topic here is not female empowerment. However, because Down syndrome is

Figure 6.1 Image of a headless pregnant body (*Bild*, 2015c)

presented as a pathological fact, this public provocation constitutes a narration of the neoliberal social order, in which the empowerment of women – in the name of choice – is actively reversed (McRobbie & Villa, 2010). McRobbie understands this undoing of feminism as women being pushed into new post-feminist dependence – not only by the beauty and health industries but also by declaring pregnancy a pathological state. These kinds of popular representations are part of a social contract in times of post-welfare states. Not only is reproduction now a private responsibility, but ideally working women should also support themselves and find their own work-life balance. McRobbie calls these women of the post-feminist era 'Top Girls' (ibid.).

Women as monsters

In articles that focus on different aspects of the fetus, a certain image, related to the post-feminist Top Girl, emerges: its negative counterpart. Several articles report on stories about *the fetus and the woman as a monster*, describing women who carried a dead fetus for years. All these reports have a common structure. They describe a woman who is middle aged or older and has some sort of physical disorder. Experts test her and discover one or more dead fetuses and finally free her from the pain (e.g. *Bild*, 2015a). The aging female body appears as a sick and disgusting body, while the male expert appears as a saviour. He is able to control nature's proliferation, its rampant play, and the following deformities – all linked to female reproduction. This drawing of misogynist gender relations is similar to another type of repulsive woman appearing when *Bild* reports on *violence and the fetus*. On the one hand, they concentrate on violence against pregnant women. The offenders in these reportings are not usually men, but mostly jealous women who try to cut a fetus out of another woman's body. Then, on the other hand, *Bild* also focusses on murdering and criminal mothers: hysterical women who behave with cruelty and violence towards their newborn baby. Such stories are well known – not just from popular media: mothers who kill their babies or let them die by neglecting them, then hide them and bury them until they are found by accident (e.g. Wegener, 2014). These mother-figures seem to correlate with what media sociology characterises as monsters – not just grotesque figures, but characters that mark the edge of normality. Two main types of monsters can be identified. First, the corporeal-monster I just described, whose monstrosity is the counterpart of an ideal body; it refers to everything a female body should not be. Second, we find moral monsters (Hoffarth, 2015). Nevertheless, no matter whether the monstrosity is bodily or moral, the narrative character of the female monster targets the normalisation of womanhood in a heteronormative pattern (ibid.).

The old sick women with their unproductive and un-re-productive bodies as well as the irresponsible, libidinous, immoral baby murderer function as a negative pole in contrast to the positive image of the post-feminist Top Girl.

Images of female fertility and pregnancy

The image of the Top Girl dominates the discourse of the fetus and appears in a wide range of articles that focus on the main topic as well: *how to be a good mother* or, more precisely, *how to be a good pregnant woman*.

In popular reporting, female fertility is a main issue; being a good mother starts with taking care of her own egg cells. As in biological textbooks, it is imagined in contrast to male fertility:

> Men are fertile throughout a big part of life, being able to produce fertile sperm. Women on the other hand start having their periodic cycle WITHOUT ovulation from age 30 and over. By the time they are 50, fertility has faded. [...] During the embryonic phase, a high number of female egg cells are already formed. A 20 week-old female fetus has developed around 6 to 7 million egg cells that die bit by bit. By the time a girl reaches puberty, the number is already reduced to around 400 000. In contrast to the male sperm cells, egg cells are NOT constantly reproduced. The female body has to manage with that amount throughout her life.
>
> (Raupach, 2013, emphasis in original)

Emily Martin has analysed how social gender identity is produced and reproduced by heteronormative metaphors, structuring the language of biological concepts of fertilisation. The egg is described as passive and difficult to conquer, while the sperm is active and aggressive. Representations of the female's menstrual cycle picture the unfertilised egg as monthly waste and the limited supply of egg cells reduces month by month. Conversely, the male body constantly produces new sperm cells – about 100 million a day (Martin, 1991). Considering this, Martin asks: 'The real mystery is why the male's vast production is not seen as wasteful' (Martin, 1991: 488). Why are trillions of sperm cells, which a male body might produce during 60 reproductive years of living, not described as wasteful, if only the average of two or three lead to an offspring? In contrast, a woman might release from her ovaries perhaps 500 egg cells during a reproductive life of 40 years (Martin, 1991).

Using this and many more examples which Martin selected from medical textbooks used in classes for medical students, it becomes clear that scientific knowledge is indeed loaded with cultural and social meaning. In this manner, it produces social order by accessing ideas of heteronormative gender roles.

The quoted *Bild* article continues: 'The egg cells must survive all sorts of stress, for instance pollutants, alcohol consumption, extreme physical stress triggered by being heavily underweight, or overweight' (Raupach, 2013). Consequently, women not only carry responsibility for a fetus but also put their egg cells at risk through their habits, long before fertilisation takes place. A lot of articles argue in a similar way, mainly focusing on risks of alcohol and nicotine consumption

Figure 6.2 Image of a sporty, young pregnant woman (*Bild*, 2014b)

during pregnancy. The term 'risk' is strongly connected to the fetus and ideas of pregnancy: 'A lot of scientists believe that the basis of our health is already being formed in our mother's womb [...] People having a lower weight at the moment of their birth bear a higher risk of heart diseases!' (*Bild*, n.d.b). From the known nutritional taboos concerning pregnant women to harmful sunscreen, and the ideal weight during pregnancy; the articles give a lot of advice on how to lower the risk, which the fetus is exposed to, in the uterus. Fetal risks create maternal responsibility: 'Soft sports like yoga enhance the mental development of the fetus' declares the commentary to Figure 6.2.

In order to be a good citizen or woman, taking preventive self-care of one's health and one's body is obligatory, while the idea of actively inducing a healthy pregnancy marks a significant turn in conceptualising pregnancy. Being aware of risks has not always been a part of medicine. By the middle of the twentieth century, medicine began to concentrate on avoiding health hazards and the prevention of chronic diseases, instead of treating acute conditions. The concept of risk arises and evolves into a guiding principle (Lemke, 2004: 19). Barbara Duden and Silja Samerski state that pregnancy, in times of genome analyses, transformed from being a *Zustand der guten Hoffnung*[9] into dealing with risks (Duden, 2002; Samerski, 2013).

The conceptualisation of the fetus does not allow having a discourse about it, without talking about motherhood and womanhood. At the same time, the fetus and its needs are discussed; questions about the social role of the mother arise, whose answers consist of her being obliged to regulate and optimise herself in the interest of the fetus. This idea of motherhood includes a traditional care-taking aspect. As far as this aspect was concerned, motherhood acquired new responsibilities imposed by the idea of preventive health which women are expected to handle privately. Referring to McRobbie's post-feminist Top Girls, Lisa Malich calls this concept of motherhood, which began in the 1990s, the concept of the 'Top Mom' (Malich, 2014: 156). Until the eighteenth and nineteenth centuries, motherhood was strongly characterised by religious aspects, but has become more and more naturalised and linked to the biological body since then (Malich, 2014). The Top Mom is no longer desexualised but, rather, is a slim, white, sporty, attractive, young woman, wearing a coral coloured bikini. Regarding the figure of the MILF ('mother I like to fuck'), mothers have to be both sexy and carers at the same time. They embody – as I implied above – a neoliberal idea of being a woman under the social order of late capitalism (ibid.).

Concluding remarks

Finally, through these discourses the fetus is designed as a specific individual biological and social entity, engaged in actions, and having a concrete impact on how images of being pregnant and being a woman are structured. Popular reportings about reproductive technologies and the fetus are understood as technologies of governance that serve economic logics, such as productivity, efficiency, and cost-reduction programmers (McRobbie & Villa, 2010). Haraway puts it this way:

> Communication technologies and biotechnologies are the crucial tools recrafting our bodies. These tools embody and enforce new social relations for women world-wide. Technologies and scientific discourses can be partially understood as formalizations, i.e. as frozen moments, of the fluid social interaction constituting them, but they should also be viewed as instruments for enforcing meanings.
>
> (Haraway, 1991: 164)

Through popular discourses on new diagnostic options, such as NIPT, the fetus is increasingly understood as an independent individual. It is not described as a tool that enables screenings of the mother and her future child as a union but of the mother alone. Finally, the effect is the equalisation of the fetus' status with the mother's.

Unfortunately, the conflict that could arise between the pregnant woman and the fetus is rarely explicitly discussed. The main part of the reportings we have analysed is seen to focus on the health of the fetus and thereby ignores what consequences might develop for the mother. Referring to the slogan of choice, responsibilities, and decisions regarding the fetus are described as the mother's private affair, that does not involve any physician or expert. She becomes the sole bearer of duties. In the name of the fetus and its health, the maternal body suffers the loss of its autonomy.

References

Altmann, B. (November 30, 2007) Forscher können Hautverjüngen. *Bild*. Available from: www.bild.de/tipps-trends/gesund-fit/genetische-manipulation-3117658.bild.html [Accessed February 25, 2015]

Bild (May 26, 2009) Neue Herzinfarkt-Gene entdeckt. *Bild*. Available from: www.bild.de/ratgeber/gesundheit/entdeckt-neue-therapieformen-bessere-vorbeugung-7375202.bild.html [Accessed February 25, 2015]

Bild (November 25, 2011) Arzt erwischt das falsche Baby – Beide Kinder tot. *Bild*. Available from. www.bild.de/news/ausland/behandlungsfehler/arzt-erwischt-das-falsche-baby-beide-kinder-tot-21215754.bild.html [Accessed Februauy 25, 2017]

Bild (January 26, 2014a) Schwangere Koma-Patientin gestorben. *Bild*. Available from: www.bild.de/news/ausland/tod/hirntote-schwangere-klinik-koennnte-in-revision-gehen-34402146.bild.html [Accessed February 25, 2015]

Bild (2014b) Schwangeren-Sport fördert Fötus-Hirn. *Bild*. Available from: www.bild.de/ratgeber/gesundheit/medizin/medizin-ticker-schwangeren-sport-foerdert-die-geistige-entwicklung-von-ungeborenen-34380000.bild.html [Accessed February, 25th 2015]

Bild (June 25, 2015a) Frau trug mumifizierten Fötus im Bauch. *Bild*. Available from: www.bild.de/news/ausland/embryo/frau-trug-mumifizierten-foetus-im-bauch-41482048.bild.html [Accessed February 25, 2015]

Bild (January 18, 2015b). Gendercide – Der Krieg gegen Mädchen in Asien. *Bild.* Available from: www.bild.de/news/ausland/haeusliche-gewalt/maedchenmorde-asien-indien-china-39387124.bild.html [Accessed February 25, 2017]

Bild (2015c) Von der Befruchtung bis zur Geburt. *Bild.* Available from: www.bild.de/themen/specials/schwanger/ratgeber-schwangerschaft-02-42332664.bild.html [Accessed February, 25 2015]

Bild (n.d.a) Stammzellen sollen biologische Uhr aufhalten. *Bild.* Available from: www.bild.de/ratgeber/gesundheit/stammzellen-sollen-biologische-uhr-aufhalten-13969258.bild.html [Accessed February 25, 2015]

Bild (n.d.a) Wie die Zeit im Mutterleib unsere Gesundheit prägt. *Bild.* Available from www.bild.de/ratgeber/gesundheit/gesundheit-neun-monate-praegen-14157820.bild.html [Accessed February 22, 2017]

Bockholt, J. (August 18, 2008) Migräne. Was gegen das Gewitter im Kopf wirklich hilft. *Bild.* Available from: www.bild.de/news/2008/was-gegen-das-gewitter-im-kopf-wirklich-hilft-5507594.bild.html [Accessed February 25, 2015]

Blumenberg, H. (2002). *Die Lesbarkeit der Welt.* Frankfurt/Main, Suhrkamp.

Dawkins, R. (2006). *The Selfish Gene.* Oxford, Oxford University Press.

Derrida, J. (1996). *Grammatologie.* Frankfurt/Main, Suhrkamp.

Duden, B. (1991) *Der Frauenleib als öffentlicher Ort: vom Missbrauch des Begriffs Leben.* Hamburg, Luchterhand-Literaturverlag.

Duden, B. *et al.* (ed.) (2002). *Geschichte des Ungeborenen.* Göttingen, Vandenhoek & Ruprecht.

Foucault, M. (1983). *Der Wille zum Wissen. Sexualität und Wahrheit.* Frankfurt/Main, Suhrkamp.

Foucault, M. (1991). *Die Ordnung des Diskurses.* Frankfurt/Main, Fischer.

Foucault, M. (1997). *Archäologie des Wissens.* Frankfurt/Main, Suhrkamp.

Haraway, D. (1991) *Simians, Cyborgs and Women. The Reinvention of Nature.* New York, Routledge.

Hauser-Schäublin, B. (1995) *Das Ende der Verwandtschaft? Zeugung und Fortpflanzung zwischen Produktion und Reproduktion.* In: Wolfgang Kaschuba (ed.). Kulturen – Identitäten – Diskurse. Berlin, Akademie Verlag, pp. 163–185

Hoffarth, B. (2015) *Ungeheure Weiber. Monster, Bildung, Disposition.* In: Orthner, J. (ed.), *Medien – Bildung – Dispositive. Beiträge zu einer interdisziplinären Medienbildungsforschung.* Wiesbaden, Springer, pp. 203–220.

Jäger, S. (1997) *Spiel mir das Lied vom Tod. Biopolitik in Bild.* In: Jäger, M., Jäger, S.,Ruth, I., Schulte Holtey, E., & Wichert, F. (eds.), *Biomacht und Medien. Wege in die Biogesellschaft.* Duisburg, DISS, pp. 62–99.

Jost, S. (December 22, 2012) Ungeborenes Baby sucht seinen Papa. *Bild.* Available from: www.bild.de/regional/berlin/baby/ungeborenes-baby-sucht-seinen-papa-22761996.bild.html [Accessed February 25, 2017]

Koschorke, A., Lüdemann, S., Frank, T., Matala de Mazza, E. (2007) *Der fiktive Staat. Konstruktionen des politischen Körpers in der Geschichte Europas.* Frankfurt/Main, Fischer.

Latour, B. (2002). *Wir sind nie modern gewesen. Versuch einer symmetrischen Anthropologie.* Frankfurt/Main/Fischer.

Lemke, T. (2004). *Veranlagung und Verantwortung.* Bielefeld, transcript.

Lemke, T. (2006). *Die Polizei der Gene.* Frankfurt/Main, Campus.

Malich, L. (2014). *Verunsicherungsmaschinen – Anmerkungen zu feministischer Mutterschaft*. In: Franke, Y. (ed.), *Feminismen heute. Positionen in Theorie und Praxis*. Bielefeld, transcript, pp. 155–168.

Martin, E. (1991). The Egg and the Sperm. How Sciene Has Constructed a Romance Based on Male-Female Roles. *Signs*,3, (6), 485–501.

McRobbie, A., Villa, P., Hark, S. (2010) *Top Girls. Feminismus und der Aufstieg des neoliberalen Geschlechterregimes*. Wiesbaden, VS Verl. für Sozialwiss.

Rabinbach, A. (1998). *Ermüdung, Energie und der menschliche Motor*. In: Sarasin, P. and Tanner, J. (eds.), *Physiologie und industrielle Gesellschaft*. Frankfurt/Main, Suhrkamp, pp. 286–312.

Raupach, A. (September 24, 2013) Wie viel Zeit bleibt mir noch für ein Kind? *Bild*. Available from:

www.bild.de/ratgeber/kind-familie/kinderwunsch/fruchtbarkeitscheck-wie-viel-zeit-bleibt-mir-noch-fuer-ein-kind-32496478.bild.html [Accessed February 22, 2017]

Samerski, S. (2013). *Entmündigende Selbstbestimmung. Wie die genetische Beratung schwangere Frauen zu einer unmöglichen Entscheidung befähigt*. In Graumann, S. & Schneider, I. (eds), *Verkörperte Technik – Entkörperte Frau*. Frankfurt/Main, Campus, pp. 213–232.

Sarasin, P. (2003). *Geschichtswissenschaft und Diskursanalyse*. Frankfurt/Main, Suhrkamp.

Sell, A. (September 9, 2014) Warum ist Inzest ein Risiko für die Nachkommen? *Bild*. Available from: www.bild.de/ratgeber/gesundheit/inzest/inzest-geschwister-gefahr-37909074.bild.html [Accessed February 25, 2015]

Strathern, M. (1992). *After Nature. English Kinship in the Late Twentieth Century*. Cambridge, Cambridge University Press.

Tanner, J. (2009). Populäre Wissenschaft: Metamorphosen des Wissens im Medium des Films. *Gesnerus*, 66), 15–39.

Voss, C. (1999). *Textgestaltung und Verfahren der Emotionalisierung in der Bild-Zeitung*. Frankfurt/Main, Peter Lang.

Wegener, A. (October 28, 2014) Totes Baby im Keller war ein Mädchen. *Bild*. Available from: www.bild.de/regional/ruhrgebiet/kindstoetung/totes-baby-gefunden-38325952.bild.html [Accessed February 25, 2015]

Notes

1 For instance, the character of the fetus (presumed nature) illustrates this thesis because through technologies of visualisation (presumed culture) its basic qualities were shaped. Donna Haraway states, human beings are already cyborgs – bodies that consist of both, nature and culture.

2 Author's own translation.

3 From a historical perspective, metaphors of the body have been used to organise society like Hobbes's body politic regards a state as a corporal entity for example (Koschorke *et al.*, 2007).

4 Author's own translation.

5 All *Bild* quotes are based on the author's own translation.

6 Author's own translation.

7 Galileo Galilei already considered that nature is 'written in mathematical language'; Descartes talked about 'reading the big book of life' as well (Derrida, 1996: 32). It can be traced back to the Christian idea of life and nature as a book

that was written by God. This idea implies that there was a deeper sense of being. The world and human beings were construed as secret divine documents. And this is what the text-metaphor in genetics refers to: the idea of the genetic code as a text written by God (Blumenberg, 2002). Therefore, only under these discursive circumstances is the geneticist able to become the person to decode this text.

8 During the fifteenth week of pregnancy an 18-year-old woman died in a car accident. Still she was treated in intensive care unit at the University Hospital of Erlangen to continue the pregnancy. A few weeks later she deteriorated until she had a spontaneous abortion during the nineteenth week of pregnancy. This case led to uproar and concern among the German press in 1992.

9 A German expression that can be literally translated as *state of good hope.* It describes the stage of expecting a child before clinical vocabulary found its way into pregnancy.

7 The fetus as a patient: professional and patient discourse

Heather Strange

This chapter explores how the figure of 'the fetus' appears and is discussed in association with patient and professional experiences of NIPT (non-invasive prenatal testing) and NIPD (non-invasive prenatal diagnosis). Building on the findings of a small-scale qualitative PhD study which examined early user experiences of NIPT and NIPD in the UK and tracked the development of this emergent prenatal testing technology (Strange, 2015), this work draws directly from in-depth participant accounts of pregnancy, prenatal testing and patienthood.

Prenatal testing in the UK

Appealing to a common and long-standing desire to predict and influence human reproduction (Gammeltoft and Wahlberg, 2014), and mirroring developments in many other countries and health-systems worldwide (Ginsburg and Rapp, 1995), prenatal testing – as conducted for the purposes of both screening and diagnosis – has become a well-established and thoroughly routine form of public health practice and prenatal care within the UK. The 'combined test' is routinely offered to all women whose antenatal care is provided through the UK's National Health Service (NHS), and the Fetal Anomaly Screening Programme (FASP) – which was introduced formally in 2004 to 'address gaps and deficiencies' in regional NHS prenatal testing services (Kirwan, 2010) – currently ensures that screening tests for three types of autosomal trisomy (Down's, Edward's and Patau's syndromes) is offered to all women receiving prenatal care through the NHS during pregnancy. Programmes such as FASP allow for the systematic and population-wide identification of pregnancies which are 'at increased risk' of trisomies, particularly Down's syndrome. Women whose pregnancies are more likely to have one of the trisomies tested for are then offered the targeted use of invasive tests (amniocentesis and Chorionic Villus Sampling/CVS) which definitively diagnose the presence or absence of a condition following receipt of a 'screen positive' result.

The routinisation and normalisation of prenatal testing technologies – as well as the ongoing consolidation of screening practices via public health programmes such as FASP – has attracted significant bioethical and social-scientific discussion. Research on some of the first populations exposed to routine prenatal diagnosis

(PND), highlighted the significant levels of anxiety women experienced in connection with PND (Rapp, 1999) and demonstrated how they responded by adopting a 'tentative' approach towards pregnancy (Rothman, 1994), delaying maternal-fetal 'bonding' until after receipt of (negative) test results. Scholars have shown how the population-wide (and global) extension of PND technology raises significant moral, social and political concerns (Ginsburg and Rapp, 1991; Lippman, 1991; Marteau *et al.*, 1992; Rapp, 1999), and they have demonstrated also how technologies such as ultrasound – though introduced as clinical/diagnostic tools – have both evolved into and have been promoted as *social* tools; visualisation technologies which provide opportunities to *'make real'* the fetus, and purposively *'enhance maternal-fetal bonding'* (Mitchell, 200; Roberts, 2012; Thomas, 2015).

The successful routinisation of prenatal testing has depended on – and has been driven in large part by – the ongoing development, deployment, and gradual normalisation of specific technologies. Technologies that have come to be very widely and routinely used include ultrasound anomaly scanning, nuchal translucency scanning, amniocentesis, CVS, and maternal serum screening (MSS). The particular type of screening and/or diagnostic technologies which are made available within the NHS vary according to a number of factors; primarily whether local services are practically and financially able to offer a particular form of testing, and whether a pregnancy is categorised as being sufficiently 'high risk' for techniques such as amniocentesis – which carry a risk to the pregnancy but provide definitive, diagnostic results – to be deemed appropriate. Less routine testing technologies (such as CVS, or NIPD) are offered in a more limited range of circumstances, typically to women who are receiving specialist care (from within fetal medicine or clinical genetics for instance) during their pregnancy. Where particular tests are not available as part of NHS care, they may be available to purchase via private prenatal clinics. Currently, this is the case with NIPT: though implementation within routine NHS screening programmes is planned for 2018 (Montgomery, 2017; UK National Screening Committee, 2016) to date women have been able to access NIPT testing only through the many private practices that have come to offer testing since NIPT's initial introduction into the UK market in 2012 (Genomeweb, 2012).

NIPT and diagnosis

Both NIPT and NIPD stand apart from preceding technologies in that they are the only forms of prenatal testing which promise to simultaneously provide diagnostic/highly accurate results, which can be made available at an early stage of pregnancy (within the first trimester, typically at around 8–10 weeks of gestation), and which do not confer any direct risk of harm to the fetus. NIPD and NIPT tests are similar in that both techniques function by exploiting the presence of cell-free fetal DNA (cffDNA) within the maternal blood stream. They operate differently at the molecular level however, and with regards to test accuracy, they differ significantly. NIPD is used within the fields of clinical genetics, fetal medicine and obstetrics, for the targeted diagnosis of disease/disorder in pregnancies which are known to be 'at risk'. Current NIPD tests are able to provide results for a growing number of conditions/diseases/disorders including fetal sex, certain forms of skeletal dysplasia, cystic fibrosis, spinal muscular atrophy and Duchenne muscular dystrophy, and the results produced are of sufficient accuracy to allow them to be treated as clinically *diagnostic* (and as such, patients may choose to undergo termination of pregnancy/TOP on the basis of a 'positive' NIPD test result).

By contrast, results provided by the various forms (or brands) of NIPT currently offered each carry some degree of risk that they will provide either false negative or false positive results. NIPT is therefore typically categorised as a tool for prenatal *screening* only, and is not used for providing independently-definitive diagnostic results. This entails that when a 'screen positive' result is provided, patients are required to undergo follow-up diagnostic testing before undergoing TOP. The boundary between what is categorised and understood as being diagnostic/certain and what is understood as being uncertain/appropriate for screening only, is however, somewhat troubled by the introduction of NIPT. The significant difference in accuracy between those screening tests which are currently routine (ultrasound and the combined nuchal translucency scan/serum screen), which for Down's syndrome have a maximum detection rate of between 82–87 per cent during the first trimester (Malone *et al.*, 2005) and a positive-predictive value of 3.4 per cent (Norton *et al.*, 2015) and NIPT, which for Down's syndrome has a sensitivity and specificity of over 99 per cent and a positive-predictive value of between 76 per cent and 80.9 per cent (Norton *et al.*, 2015), entails that NIPT is positioned somewhat differently to other prenatal screening tests. As such, the introduction of NIPT has attracted much discussion and debate.

NIPT also stands apart from NIPD in that it has been the subject of significant global commercial investment. Established companies (such as Roche/Hoffman-La-Roche Ltd. and Illumina Inc.) have invested heavily in NIPT development, and for many smaller-scale companies (such as the UK-based Premaitha Health Plc.) NIPT remains their main area of focus for ongoing research and development. The 'global market' for NIPT testing has been predicted to reach '2.38 billion dollars by 2022' (Transparency Market Research, 2015) and the commercial significance of NIPT was greatly enhanced by the fact that the development of testing for conditions such as Down's syndrome – already routinely tested for within whole pregnant populations – was a key area of focus from the outset. The publication of proof-of-principle research on NIPT testing for Down's syndrome (Lo *et al.*, 2007; Fan *et al.*, 2008) – which was quickly followed by research on an expanded range of trisomies (Fan *et al.*, 2009; Tsui *et al.*, 2009) – was hailed as a 'watershed moment' during which both the commercial and clinical potential of NIPT was made abundantly clear. Another 'watershed moment' in the development of NIPT arrived in 2010, when researchers demonstrated the 'whole fetal genome' was represented in the maternal blood (Lo *et al.*, 2010; Thung *et al.*, 2015). This opened up the further possibility that NIPT would come to exploit the 'full potential' of next generation genetic sequencing technologies (Hall *et al.*, 2014). With increased market activity came a corresponding increase in the range and volume of web-based information on NIPT that was made publicly available. Companies such as Sequenom, Ariosa and BGI developed NIPT-specific websites, enabling them to disseminate information on various branded NIPT test options to both clinicians and consumers. These websites typically stress the high sensitivity and specificity rates that are achieved by NIPT: BGI for instance currently describe their test, (within their parent FAQ section), as being 'accurate to 99.5 per cent for detection of Downs Syndrome Edwards Syndrome and Patau Syndrome (BGI Diagnostics Co., 2017).

The 'therapeutic gap'

Within any critical discussion of prenatal testing – but particularly within those that seek to examine questions around fetal patienthood – it is important to recognise the significance of what has been termed the 'therapeutic gap' (Holtzman and Shapiro, 1998; Kelly, 2009). Prenatal testing – whether screening or diagnosis – aims to provide women/parents with some type of health-related information on the status of their fetus, and within a limited range of circumstances the information gained through testing may be used to direct the clinical management of pregnancy, fetal healthcare or birth. NIPD, for instance is currently used to 'diagnose' sex in pregnancies which are at known risk of sex-linked diseases such as haemophilia, as this information may be used to inform the clinical management of pregnancy and birth. Additionally, a restricted range of surgical procedures or invasive therapeutic interventions – such as fetal blood transfusions, cardiac procedures, and laser treatment of twin-twin transfusion syndrome – have been performed directly on the fetus or the pregnant patient. Such pioneering therapies, however, are currently appropriate for use only within a small number of 'at risk' pregnancies, and access to fetal therapeutic intervention remains severely limited (Van Mieghem *et al.*, 2014). Hence, though opportunities to test the fetus are widespread and growing in number and scale, concurrent opportunities to provide therapeutic intervention after a diagnosis is made, are rare. The existence of this 'therapeutic gap' entails that, in the vast majority of circumstances, after any kind of diagnosis is made prenatally (typically via use of amniocentesis or CVS), the only form of treatment that is available is 'therapeutic' termination of pregnancy/abortion. This practice has variously been termed 'genetic termination' (Thachuk, 2007), 'selective termination' (Press and Browner, 1997; Shakespeare, 1998) and therapeutic termination/abortion (Clarke, 1997; Priaulx, 2008).

As the vast majority of women, post-diagnosis, are offered only the binary choice to either continue with a pregnancy, or end the pregnancy via 'therapeutic termination' (which takes materially/physically very different forms depending on the gestation at which a diagnosis is made, or the point at which TOP becomes available), the practice of PND – and by extension the practice of prenatal screening (PNS) – sits directly alongside the practice of TOP/abortion. Abortion remains a matter of significant and ongoing political and philosophical debate (Theodosiou and Mitchell, 2015). The legal frameworks that govern abortion provision differ significantly state-to-state, and within the UK – though abortion has been legal under a range of closely-defined circumstances since the late 1960s (UK Parliament, 1967) – the matter nevertheless attracts ongoing media attention, and remains the subject of ongoing parliamentary debate and discussion (Bruce, 2013; UK Parliament, 2017). Numerous empirical studies have reported that women who experience abortion – whether for 'social' or 'medical' purposes, post-diagnosis – frequently experience stigma, guilt and shame, and feel compelled to keep their abortion experiences 'secret' (Thachuk, 2007; Ludlow, 2008; Sanger, 2012; Cowan, 2014; Hanschmidt *et al.*, 2016). The wider implication of the 'therapeutic gap' then is that – through direct entanglement with abortion/TOP – both PNS and PND raise significant social, moral and political concerns. Prenatal testing – as conducted within the wider context of this therapeutic gap – has important implications for any discussion of the 'fetal patient'; the very act of testing of this type of 'patient' may entail that its continued existence comes into question. With many debates around the political, social and moral dimensions of abortion/TOP focussing on issues such as the moral status of the fetus (Jensen, 2014; Kluge, 2015) and a clinician's right to exercise conscientious objection (Gerrard, 2009; Faundes *et al.*, 2013; Nordberg *et al.*, 2014), the 'therapeutic gap' has acute implications for the concept, and discussion of the 'fetal patient'.

Research methodology

The data presented here were collected as part of a PhD research project examining the development and use of emergent NIPD/T tests in the UK. The original research was conducted between 2011 and 2015, a time during which a number of significant developments in the technological, clinical and policy-related aspects of NIPD and NIPT occurred. As such, the field of enquiry was open and dynamic, and the range of participants that came to be included in the study was accordingly broad. NIPD/T 'experts' (defined within the study as those with direct professional experience of using, encountering or developing relevant technologies) were exceptionally open and willing to participate. Additionally, being recruited through both clinical spaces and parent-and-baby social groups, women who had both used and refused prenatal testing came to be included. The study was also expanded in response to the 2012 introduction of NIPT into private UK clinics, allowing women who were some of the earliest users of NIPT to also be included. Participants took part in narrative, semi-structured interviews with the researcher, the form of which was designed to prioritise participants' own perspectives and concerns, and to encourage in-depth discussion and reflection of significant themes. Data from both professional and patient accounts are presented here. The analysis that is presented both supplements and stands alongside a larger body of work, as published in the form of a PhD thesis (Strange, 2015).

Talk of 'the fetus': multiple framings, maternal patienthood and relationality

Where direct talk of the 'fetus' appeared within the data, it occurred largely within accounts provided by clinicians, scientists and policy makers; nineteen of the twenty-two expert participants spoke of the fetus at some point during their interview. Typically entering the frame as they discussed the clinical use and ongoing development of NIPD/T, direct references to the 'fetus' appeared as these participants discussed the technical and practical aspects of NIPD and NIPD, and reflected on the differences between current (routine) screening tests and emerging non-invasive tests. Chloe (an NIPD/T researcher) for instance, emphasised the significance of the fetus as she recounted how she felt this form of testing stood apart from other screening technologies. Describing how NIPT functioned by 'directly testing' the fetus via analysis of cffDNA,[1] Chloe explained how she viewed the fetus as being both the recipient of, and location for NIPT testing:

> I think it's significant that you are directly, you are testing the fetus, I know it's a screening test but it's much more accurate than the serum screening or something like that, and it, it for us in genetics, it's a huge step.
>
> (Chloe, NIPD/T research)

Cerys – a clinician who had encountered NIPD as a tool for the targeted diagnosis of fetal sex in an 'at risk' population of women – also spoke of the 'fetus' as she explored some of the fears and anxieties she experienced in relation to the possibility that early NIPD results may, under certain circumstances, be used (illegitimately) to directly inform decisions around TOP/abortion:

> And I don't think we have had any terminations of male fetus, I don't think so. Unless, maybe one or two, one perhaps, that I- you hear a whisper that it is happening but I don't think so. We did have a mum who did, didn't want another boy with [rare disease], but she had the NIPD and it didn't show male, and she did have a girl.
>
> (Cerys, nurse/midwife at rare disease clinic)

And elsewhere, Beth, an NIPD/T researcher, described how array testing[2] had come to be used within the fields of genetic counselling and fetal medicine, and she compared this existing practice with newly-emergent possibilities for the use and extension of NIPD/T. Reflecting particularly on some of the challenges that are raised when comparing postnatal and prenatal diagnoses, she speaks directly of 'the fetus', and refers to its 'very limited phenotype':

> So it's easier in postnatal cos you kind of know what you're trying to diagnose, whereas with the fetus you might pick up something, but it doesn't fit with the very limited phenotype that you've got, and then you don't know

> whether to report it or not, because you think, well I've found something but is it actually relevant to why the fetus was referred?
>
> (Beth, NIPD/T research)

As Beth stresses how fetal/prenatal testing provides only a 'very limited phenotype' she explains that by generating results of uncertain interpretation, testing presents the dilemma of 'whether to report [findings] or not'. With the complex work of providing a PND – which is dependent on the testing and imaging of the fetus – being held here in direct contrast with the '*easier*' work of providing a diagnosis postnatally (which may be accomplished by using a wider range of testing techniques, and by engaging in a more direct examination of the baby/child), the fetus appears as a somewhat vague and elusive figure. Cerys' account also touches on this – the fetus is mentioned only because she hears only '*a* whisper' about possible TOP.

Though no single expert participant directly presented the fetus as 'a patient', and though the the fetus is typically characterised as something both abstract and intangible, it is during these expert accounts that the fetus comes close to appearing as some kind of patient. Beth refers not to the mother/pregnant woman but to the fetus *itself* as that which has been 'referred' for diagnostic testing. Subtle and indirect descriptions of what could be considered fetal patients are scattered throughout the expert accounts gathered here – references are made for example to clinical interactions with (or on) the 'fetus' – talk of collecting 'fetal material' and 'fetal samples', performing 'fetal sexing', encountering 'abnormal' or affected' fetuses and dealing with 'fetal loss' – appears within many expert interviews. The somewhat contradictory positioning of the fetus within Beth's account – as a subject of medical intervention and interaction that is at once definite, and identifiable, and yet whose exact form remains profoundly difficult to grasp – points towards an ambiguity and tension underlying the way in which 'the fetus' is being described and understood. Though the concept of the 'fetal patient' certainly seems to appear within the expert accounts gathered here, it does so only faintly, and is in no way foregrounded or made central.

Whilst talk of the fetus appeared regularly within expert accounts, by clear contrast, it appeared infrequently within patient and parent accounts (just four of the seventeen women interviewed spoke directly of the 'fetus'). Where this group of participants used the term fetus, it did not appear as a 'natural' or everyday use of language, being spoken about only in connection with some of the more clearly medicalized experiences of pregnancy that were reported within the dataset. Interviewees typically only referred to the 'fetus' when describing the way in which their healthcare providers, and not themselves or their partners, had approached the subject of prenatal testing. Joan, for instance, an NHS patient who had used NIPD testing for fetal sex during a 'high risk' pregnancy, spoke of how 'they' (her healthcare providers) had 'called it a fetus' during a phone-call which was made in order to communicate her NIPD test results:

And you said around the NIPD, the communication of results was a bit mixed ...

Yeah absolutely, yeah. Well, because the time I miscarried, um. You know it was his secretary ringing me, and just. Ok I know it's not a baby at that point, they call it, it's a fetus. And just being told 'it's male' over the phone, when you are looking at knowing that that male is ... I hadn't miscarried at that point, is going to be a baby with severe [rare disease] and how is that going to affect us? Um, I was really upset.

(Joan, NHS patient who had used NIPD)

Joan describes experiencing health care professionals' reference to her 'fetus' as upsetting and impersonal, an approach which lay in stark contrast to her own perceptions of, and approach towards, pregnancy and her much-wanted 'baby'. Elsewhere, Yasmin – a mum who received additional care in the form of early ultrasound scans, in response to a history of repeated miscarriage – spoke of the seeing 'a little fetus' during her second early scan:

I was wondering ... you had a scan at five weeks. How was that?

Well, I did see it ... I think I've got a picture upstairs. I mean, she scanned me, you could just see the yolk sac really, and then, um she said I'll scan you again in ten days' time. And it's amazing then, how much it changes ... you've got a little fetus there then. And that was a bit ... particularly the first early one, it was really surreal. It was ... oh my god, is that really me, sort of thing. It was really odd.

(Yasmin, parent recruited though mother and baby group)

Yasmin uses 'fetus' here to describe what she saw of her early pregnancy, as visualised through ultrasound scanning. She uses the term to differentiate between the very early 'yolk sac' she viewed during her first scan, and the many images of her 'baby' that she describes viewing during subsequent scans at several other points in the interview. Though talk of the 'fetus' is not experienced as distressing here – as it was for Joan – it is similarly distant from Yasmin's everyday and embodied experience of pregnancy; she describes the experience of seeing the very early fetus – 'it' – as being both 'surreal' and 'really odd' and she questions her bodily connection to the early fetus; 'is that really me?'

Within the remainder of the patient and parent accounts gathered here the fetus is mentioned directly just two more times, again in connection only with the way in which others – clinicians or the imagined 'public' at large – spoke of pregnancy and prenatal testing. Responding perhaps to the ambiguity and lack of definition that so clearly surrounded talk of the fetus within the expert accounts gathered here, and to the sense of distance and detachment present within patient and parent accounts, participants from across the dataset drew upon a range of alternative descriptions of the fetus as they discussed their thoughts on and experiences of prenatal testing (and – as performed within the context of the therapeutic gap – TOP): they spoke variously of the fetus in terms of being 'a bunch of cells', 'a wanted pregnancy', and 'a source of hope and expectation'. Such findings parallel the work of scholars elsewhere, who have explored how prenatal testing constructs a particularly fragmented understanding of the 'fetus': we have 'shifting meanings and understandings of "the fetus" as waste, corpse, research tool, baby, body part of the woman' (Kent, 2012). Though talk of the fetus appears frequently (within expert accounts at least), corresponding talk of the fetal patient appears only faintly, and no single, unified picture of either the fetus, or the fetal patient, emerges out of the data gathered here.

Standing in clear contrast with this however, patients, parents and experts spoke very commonly – and with reference to a wide variety of pregnancy and parenting experiences – of the 'child' or the 'baby'. The term 'baby' was in fact mentioned within every one of the seventeen patient or parent interviews conducted, and frequent reference to the 'baby' or the 'child', the 'boy' or the 'girl' characterised the vast majority of these accounts. Talk of the 'baby' appeared to be equally relevant to experiences of both the early and later stages of pregnancy. Alana, for instance, who had purchased NIPT testing 'for peace of mind' through a private prenatal clinic, speaks only of 'the baby' as she describes and recounts both the pre-testing stage of her pregnancy, as well as the time during which she received her NIPT test results:

> I had read up about it before, to see exactly what happens. Because it's quite confusing to think that they can tell by taking my blood, if there is anything wrong with the baby, so I had already looked it up ... I was just surprised they could do it really. Because I knew that when you are pregnant you had more blood in your system, but I didn't realise that the baby's blood was within your blood.
>
> the lady from the clinic phoned us on Sunday evening to give us the results. I can't remember exactly what they were now. Genetic tests all came back as low risk, which was fine, and um they told us the sex of the baby was a girl.
>
> (Alana, private NIPT screening patient)

Though NIPT testing had taken place at an early stage in her pregnancy (around 12 weeks) – before the point at which a pregnancy would typically have been visible to others, and before fetal movement would typically have been experienced – Alana describes how, even at this early stage of pregnancy, she viewed the subject of testing as being her 'baby'. The (presumed) boundary between the maternal body and that of the fetus (here, 'the baby') also begins to come under question within Alana's account. Though she describes being confused by the fact that testing would require a sample of *her* blood, after gaining greater understanding of how NIPT functions, she came to recognise that material from the fetus would be present within her own body: 'the baby's blood was within your blood'.

Jamie, an 'older mum' who had sought NIPT for 'reassurance' during her pregnancy (and who was interviewed during the second trimester of her pregnancy), also spoke of her 'baby' throughout, referring to both her pregnancy and to the imagined future baby/child she would have as a result. She also stood apart from many interviewees in that she was able to speak very openly about abortion/TOP, an issue she felt was bound closely to the aims and purposes of NIPT testing:

> For me, because as I say, I mean my son is ten, um and I am forty-two, one of the other reasons was because, um, if I knew that there was an issue, i.e. that the baby had Down's syndrome for example, I can be straight with you and say, I may strongly, would have considered having um, an abortion. Because I think at my time of life, genuinely I don't think I could have coped with that. So I think that was another thing- so there were lots and lots of reasons, really why I thought it was the right thing to do.... the issue for me was Down's, Down's Syndrome... because you know the older you get the more sort of high risk you become if you like, from having a Down's baby, so I was a little bit concerned about that
>
> (Jamie, private NIPT screening patient)

As one of the few participants who had experienced both fetal loss and motherhood, Jamie appeared able to speak of abortion/TOP with little hesitation. She openly considers the possibility that her NIPT results, were they to have indicated she was at 'high risk... of having a Down's baby', could have resulted in her taking the decision to end her much-wanted pregnancy: 'I may strongly, would have considered having um, an abortion'. The reasoning process that Jamie explains guided her thinking on this focused in on both self-directed concerns – relating to her pregnancy/fetus, her age, and her previous experiences of miscarriage – as well as a range of concerns which were directed outwardly, towards her family members. Jamie refers directly to her existing son's age, and later in the interview (as she elaborates on her position regarding TOP for Down's syndrome) she highlights how the needs and perspectives of her whole family were crucial to her thinking; 'I just think, if we are all honest with each other that would have been a massive, massive problem for us, it would have been a big issue.'

The complexity and depth of consideration that is evident here suggests that within such circumstances it is the pregnant woman/mother – rather than the fetus – who most clearly takes on the patient role. Jamie's body is quite clearly the focus of and location for clinical intervention – she explains how the abortion would have been something *she* would have – and elsewhere she also speaks of how she needed and valued the 'support' that was given directly to *her* by a range of healthcare providers ('I've got everything that I need because the support is in place for me'). Similar accounts – of their bodies/pregnancies being the location for clinical investigation and care, of spending time discussing and deliberating complex medical decisions and visiting a range of clinical spaces – are provided by women across the dataset. Though the experience of *maternal* patienthood very clearly appears as central here, it also emerges as something that – by simultaneously taking into account concerns relating to the self, the pregnancy at hand, to loved ones and the whole family unit (in Jamie's words, 'us') – is characterised by an explicitly *relational* approach. This framing of maternal patienthood – as something that extends out to encompass the needs of an entire familial network – is strongly evident elsewhere in the data:

> I just think, you probably, if you had a high chance of Down's syndrome you probably wouldn't abort the pregnancy. But at least you would have time to prepare for it and you know what's to come. I think that's more the case, especially now with the second one. Where, you bend your life around your first child, but when you have a second one you still have got the first one to bear in mind as well, so. I think it's forewarned I think is, forearmed. Yeah and both of us work fulltime and the baby is going to nursery. And if you know you are not going to be able to carry on with that any more you are going to be able to make decisions a lot earlier
>
> (Alana, private NIPT screening patient)

Though Alana's perspective on TOP and Down's syndrome clearly differs to Jamie's, her approach to decision making appears to be even more clearly embedded in a relational approach towards maternal patienthood. The key factors that shape Alana's approach towards testing, relate not simply to her own experiences of pregnancy and motherhood, but extend out to encompass a broad network of concerns such as the needs of her existing child, and the practical constraints of her (and her partner's) career. Elsewhere, Louise speaks of holding similar concerns, as she explains that TOP for Down's syndrome would have been a likely course of action were her NIPT results to come back 'screen positive':

> Probably selfish reasons really, I just thought the age that we are- and I didn't really want burden [daughter] with a child who would be, potentially quite dependent. So that was in my mind really. Well, obviously it would have been heart breaking to make a decision, and I'm not sure I would have made that decision if I'd had that kind of a result. I don't know what I would have done. But I think, going into it I thought that might be what might have to be done.
>
> (Louise, private NIPT screening patient)

Though she describes her reasoning as 'selfish', Louise clearly prioritises the needs of her family and her existing child as she thinks through her decision to use NIPT. As such, the boundary between the maternal self and the lives of others is again called into question, and a relational approach towards pregnancy, motherhood and parenting is foregrounded. The significance of this relational approach towards patienthood was also made clear within certain expert accounts, particularly those provided by genetic counsellors, who – because genetic diagnoses frequently entail strong familial implications – often treat and encounter multiple family members (Knoppers, 1998; Rantanen *et al.*, 2008). Naomi provides a particularly powerful account of how the interests of individual patients are inevitably interleaved with those of their partners, offspring, siblings and other family members:

And when you say four patients?

Well that's four slots so that might be, that might be a couple, that might be siblings, um it's a whole variety of things really, you never know quite who is going to come to clinic. Yeah so we, there is a big kind of debate about your numbers in genetics, you know who do you count as your patients? Because it's, I think it is very different to other areas of medicine. So we try and separate out who is a significant attendee, so it might be that you see the parents of a child with a problem, and actually the child is the significant person. But if you see a woman with a family history of breast cancer and she brings her sister and you end up having a conversation with both of them about their risk, and referring them both for screening you are essentially seeing two patients at once.

(Naomi, genetic counsellor)

If patienthood in general – and particularly maternal patienthood – may be understood *relationally* (as the accounts gathered here would suggest) then the fact that the 'fetal patient' only faintly appears does not entail that the possible interests of such a figure are displaced entirely. Rather, as a picture emerges of maternal patienthood as an expansive and inclusive experience, any interests that may be ascribed to the 'fetal patient' can be positioned alongside the many other interests this understanding of maternal patienthood provides space for. It is only through the very real and tangible *maternal* patient that the (potential) interests of the frequently mentioned 'baby', or 'future child', and the more vague and elusive 'fetal patient' are given weight and significance; as is evident within the accounts gathered here, the interests of the fetus are in no way foregrounded when examined alongside the multitude of interests which are generated through the lived and social experience of the maternal patient. Such findings sit alongside and contribute to existing discussions of how contemporary, technologically-mediated experiences of parenting and kinship may be best understood in multiple and explicitly *relational* (rather than individual and rational), terms (Latimer, 2008; Strathern, 1988, 1991).

Concluding comments

The data drawn upon here were gathered during a very particular moment, as NIPT testing first began to reach out to patient populations within the UK, and they were generated by a broad range of voices. As such, though the results presented here provide some insight into how fetal patienthood may be approached by those engaging with contemporary prenatal testing practices and debates, additional research, for example with a larger number of patients from a variety of socio-economic backgrounds, will be required for a full picture to emerge of how the discussion and concept of 'fetal patienthood' is affected by experiences of pregnancy and prenatal testing.

As explained above, participants' experiences with NIPT and NIPD (and all other forms of prenatal testing) are profoundly shaped by the broader context of the 'therapeutic gap'. Recent developments including 'gene editing' technologies – such as CRISPR/cas-9 and the more recently-reported 'base editor system' (Liang *et al.*, 2017), coupled with the potential growth of 'fetal personalized medicine' (Bianchi, 2012), present the real possibility however that this 'therapeutic gap' may begin to close. If, in line with developments discussed elsewhere in this book (see chapters by Verweij, Clarke, De Wert and Dondorp), the range of fetal therapies made available were to increase, what might this mean for our understanding of 'fetal patienthood'? Would it begin to appear as something more tangible, and if so, how might this alter the way in which we approach and discuss maternal patienthood? Is there a risk that women's right to exercise reproductive choice would be under further strain?[3]

Acknowledgements

This work was funded by the National Institute for Social Care and Health Research (NISCHR) in Wales, and was undertaken with the support of Cardiff University's School of Social Sciences and the School of Medicine's Centre for Trials Research (CTR).

References

Bgi Diagnostics Co., L. 2017. *How accurate is the NIFTY test?* [Online]. Available: www.niftytest.com/expecting-parents/faq/ [Accessed 15 October 2017].

Bianchi, D. W. 2012. From prenatal genomic diagnosis to fetal personalized medicine: progress and challenges. *Nature Medicine*, 18, 1041.

Bruce, F. 2013. Parliamentary Inquiry into Abortion on the Grounds of Disability. London: UK Parliament.

Clarke, A. 1997. Prenatal genetic screening: paradigms and perspectives. *Genetics society and clinical practice*. Oxford: BIOS Scientific.

Cowan, S. 2014. Secrets and misperceptions: the creation of self-fulfilling illusions. *Sociological Science*, 1, 466–492.

Fan, H. C., Blumenfeld, Y. J., Chitkara, U., Hudgins, L. and Quake, S. R. 2008. Noninvasive diagnosis of fetal aneuploidy by shotgun sequencing DNA from maternal blood. *Proc Natl Acad Sci U S A*, 105, 16266–71.

Fan, H. C., Blumenfeld, Y. J., El-Sayed, Y. Y., Chueh, J. and Quake, S. R. 2009. Microfluidic digital PCR enables rapid prenatal diagnosis of fetal aneuploidy. *Am J Obstet Gynecol*, 200, 543 e1–7.

Faundes, A., Duarte, G. A. & OSIS, M. J. 2013. Conscientious objection or fear of social stigma and unawareness of ethical obligations. *Int J Gynaecol Obstet*, 123 Suppl 3, S57–9.

Gammeltoft, T. M. and Wahlberg, A. 2014. Selective reproductive technologies. *Annual Review of Anthropology*, 43, 201–216.

Genomeweb. 2012. *Q&A: Prenatal screening pioneer Kypros Nicolaides on introducing non-invasive testing in the UK* [Online]. [Accessed 18/01/14 2014].

Gerrard, J. W. 2009. Is it ethical for a general practitioner to claim a conscientious objection when asked to refer for abortion? *J Med Ethics*, 35, 599–602.

Ginsburg, F. D. and Rapp, R. 1991. The politics of reproduction. *Annual Review of Anthropology*, 20, 311–43.

Ginsburg, F. D. and Rapp, R. 1995. *Conceiving the new world order: the global politics of reproduction*, Berkeley and Los Angeles: University of California Press.

Hall, A., Finnegan, T. and Alberg, C. 2014. *Realising genomics in clinical practice*, Cambridge: PHG Foundation.

Hanschmidt, F., Linde, K., Hilbert, A., Riedel-Heller, S. G. and Kersting, A. 2016. Abortion stigma: a systematic review. *Perspectives on Sexual and Reproductive Health*, 48, 169–177.

Holtzman, N. A. and Shapiro, D. 1998. Genetic testing and public policy. *BMJ*, 316, 852–6.

Jensen, D. 2014. Birth, meaningful viability and abortion. *J Med Ethics*.

Kelly, S. E. 2009. Choosing not to choose: reproductive responses of parents of children with genetic conditions or impairments. *Sociol Health Illn*, 31, 81–97.

Kent, J. 2012. *Regenerating bodies: tissue and cell therapies in the twenty-first century*, London and New York: Routledge.

Kirwan, D. 2010. NHS Fetal Anomaly Screening Programme. *18+ 0 to 20+ 6 Weeks Fetal Anomaly Scan National Standards and Guidance for England.*

Kluge, E. H. 2015. Ethical considerations on methods used in abortions. *Health Care Anal*, 23, 1–18.

Knoppers, B. M. 1998. Towards a reconstruction of the "genetic family": new principles? *Int Dig Health Legis*, 49, 241–53.

Latimer, J. 2008. Working paper 112: Unsettling Bodies: Frida Khalo's portraits and in/dividuality. Cardiff, Cardiff School of Social Sciences.

Liang, P., Ding, C., Sun, H., XIE, X., XU, Y., Zhang, X., Sun, Y., Xiong, Y., Ma, W., Liu, Y., Wang, Y., Fang, J., Liu, D., Songyang, Z., Zhou, C. and Huang, J. 2017. Correction of beta-thalassemia mutant by base editor in human embryos. *Protein & Cell*, 8, 811–822.

Lippman, A. 1991. Prenatal genetic testing and screening: constructing needs and reinforcing inequities. *Am J Law Med*, 17, 15–50.

Lo, Y. M., Tsui, N. B., Chiu, R. W., Lau, T. K., Leung, T. N., Heung, M. M., Gerovassili, A., Jin, Y., Nicolaides, K. H., Cantor, C. R. and Ding, C. 2007. Plasma placental RNA allelic ratio permits noninvasive prenatal chromosomal aneuploidy detection. *Nat Med*, 13, 218–23.

Lo, Y. M. D., Chan, K. C. A., Sun, H., Chen, E. Z., Jiang, P., Lun, F. M. F., Zheng, Y. W., Leung, T. Y., Lau, T. K., Cantor, C. R. and Chiu, R. W. K. 2010. Maternal plasma DNA sequencing reveals the genome-wide genetic and mutational profile of the fetus. *Science Translational Medicine*, 2, 61ra91.

Ludlow, J. 2008. The things we cannot say: witnessing the trauma-tization of abortion in the United States. *Wsq: Women's Studies Quarterly*, 36, 28–41.

Malone, F. D., Canick, J. A., Ball, R. H., Nyberg, D. A., Comstock, C. H., Bukowski, R., Berkowitz, R. L., Gross, S. J., Dugoff, L., Craigo, S. D., Timor-Tritsch, I. E., Carr, S. R., Wolfe, H. M., Dukes, K., Bianchi, D. W., Rudnicka, A. R., Hackshaw, A. K., Lambert-Messerlian, G., Wald, N. J., D'Alton, M. E., First and Second-Trimester Evaluation of Risk Research, C. 2005. First-trimester or second-trimester screening, or both, for Down's syndrome. *N Engl J Med*, 353, 2001–11.

Marteau, T. M., Slack, J., Kidd, J. and Shaw, R. W. 1992. Presenting a routine screening test in antenatal care: practice observed. *Public Health*, 106, 131–41.

Mitchell, L. M. 2001. *Baby's first picture: ultrasound and the politics of fetal subjects*, Toronto ; London: University of Toronto Press.

Montgomery, J. 2017. Non-invasive prenatal testing: ethical issues. *Nuffield Council on Bioethics*. London: Nuffield Council on Bioethics.

Nordberg, E. M., Skirbekk, H. and Magelssen, M. 2014. Conscientious objection to referrals for abortion: pragmatic solution or threat to women's rights? *BMC Med Ethics*, 15, 15.

Norton, M. E., Jacobsson, B., Swamy, G. K., Laurent, L. C., Ranzini, A. C., Brar, H., Tomlinson, M. W., Pereira, L., Spitz, J. L., Hollemon, D., Cuckle, H., Musci, T. J. and Wapner, R. J. 2015. Cell-free DNA analysis for noninvasive examination of trisomy. *N Engl J Med*, 372, 1589–97.

Press, N. and Browner, C. H. 1997. Why women say yes to prenatal diagnosis. *Soc Sci Med*, 45, 979–89.

Priaulx, N. 2008. Testing the margin of appreciation: therapeutic abortion, reproductive "rights" and the intriguing case of Tysiąc v. Poland. *European Journal of Health Law*, 15, 361–39.

Rantanen, E., Hietala, M., Kristoffersson, U., Nippert, I., Schmidtke, J., Sequeiros, J. and Kaariainen, H. 2008. What is ideal genetic counselling? A survey of current international guidelines. *Eur J Hum Genet*, 16, 445–52.

Rapp, R. 1999. *Testing women, testing the fetus: the social impact of amniocentesis in America*, New York: London, Routledge.

Roberts, J. 2012. "Wakey wakey baby": narrating four-dimensional (4D) bonding scans. *Sociol Health Illn*, 34, 299–314.

Rothman, B. K. 1994. *The tentative pregnancy: amniocentesis and the sexual politics of motherhood*, London: Pandora.

Sanger, C. 2012. About abortion: the complications of the category. *Ariz. L. Rev.*, 54, 849.

Shakespeare, T. 1998. Choices and rights: eugenics, genetics and disability equality. *Disabil Soc*, 13, 665–81.

Strange, H. 2015. Non-invasive prenatal diagnosis: the emergence and translation of a new prenatal testing technology. Unpublished PhD Thesis, Cardiff University.

Strathern, M. 1988. *The gender of the gift: problems with women and problems with society in Melanesia*. Berkeley, University of California Press.

Strathern, M. (1991). *Partial connections*. Lanham, MD: Rowman and Littlefield.

Strathern, M. 1995. Displacing knowledge: technology and the consequences of iinship *In:* Ginsburg, F. D. and RAPP, R. (eds.) *Conceiving the new world order: the global politics of reproduction*. Berkeley and Los Angeles: Univ of California Press.

Thachuk, A. 2007. The space in between: narratives of silence and genetic terminations. *Bioethics*, 21, 511–4.

Theodosiou, A. A. and Mitchell, O. R. 2015. Abortion legislation: exploring perspectives of general practitioners and obstetrics and gynaecology clinicians. *Reprod Biomed Online*, 30, 197–202.

Thomas, G. M. 2015. Picture perfect: "4D" Ultrasound and the commoditisation of the private prenatal clinic. *Journal of Consumer Culture*, 17, 359–377.

Thung, D. T., Beulen, L., Hehir-Kwa, J. and FAAS, B. H. 2015. Implementation of whole genome massively parallel sequencing for noninvasive prenatal testing in laboratories. *Expert Review of Molecular Diagnostics*, 15, 111–124.

Transparency Market Research. 2015. *Accurate results and low risks to patients lead to increased demand for non-invasive prenatal tests: market to worth*

US$2.38 billion by 2022 [Online]. Transparency Market Research. Available: www.transparencymarketresearch.com/article/noninvasive-prenatal-diagnostics-market.htm [Accessed 27 September 2015].

Tsui, N. B., Wong, B. C., Leung, T. Y., Lau, T. K., Chiu, R. W. and Lo, Y. M. 2009. Non-invasive prenatal detection of fetal trisomy 18 by RNA-SNP allelic ratio analysis using maternal plasma SERPINB2 mRNA: a feasibility study. *Prenat Diagn*, 29, 1031–7.

UK National Screening Committee 2016. *Screening in the UK: making effective reccomendations*, Crown Copyright.

UK Parliament 1967. The Abortion Act 1967.

UK Parliament. 2017. *Reproductive Health (Access to Terminations) Bill 2016–17* [Online]. Available: https://services.parliament.uk/bills/2016-17/reproductivehealthaccesstoterminations.html [Accessed 01 October 2017].

Van Den Veyver, I. B., Patel, A., Shaw, C. A., Pursley, A. N., Kang, S. H. L., Simovich, M. J., Ward, P. A., Darilek, S., Johnson, A. and Neill, S. E. 2009. Clinical use of array comparative genomic hybridization (aCGH) for prenatal diagnosis in 300 cases. *Prenatal Diagnosis*, 29, 29–39.

Van Mieghem, T., Al-Ibrahim, A., Deprest, J., Lewi, L., Langer, J. C., Baud, D., O'Brien, K., Beecroft, R., Chaturvedi, R., Jaeggi, E., Fish, J. and Ryan, G. 2014. Minimally invasive therapy for fetal sacrococcygeal teratoma: case series and systematic review of the literature. *Ultrasound Obstet Gynecol*, 43, 611–9.

Notes

1 CffDNA in fact originates from the placenta rather than the fetus. NIPT does not therefore directly test fetal genetic material. The way in which cffDNA is discussed however – within the expert accounts gathered here and within much of the relevant literature – typically presents the fetus as being the direct recipient of testing.

2 Array-based comparative genomic hybridization (aCGH) is a genetic testing/analysis technique that 'allows for fast and accurate detection of unbalanced structural and numerical chromosomal abnormalities' (Van den Veyver *et al.*, 2009).

3 See Chapter 12 (Dondorp and De Wert) where the ethical implications of a possible narrowing of the therapeutic gap are further explored.

8 Means, ends, and the fetal patient

Anna Smajdor

Introduction

As medical knowledge increases, the possibility of diagnosing and treating fetuses *in utero* expands likewise. One example of this is fetal surgery, which has been practised in the US for some decades and has been gaining prominence in the UK and Europe more recently. In 2014, the Wellcome Trust funded a £10,000,000 research project on fetal interventions (University College, London, 2014). The most invasive form of fetal surgery involves hysterotomy: the uterus is lifted away from the woman's body and an incision is made to expose the fetus. The fetus remains attached to the placenta and umbilical cord while surgery is undertaken. Once the procedure on the fetus is completed, the fetus is replaced in the uterus, the uterine incision is sutured, the uterus is replaced in the abdominal cavity and finally the abdominal incision is sutured. This kind of intervention represents perhaps one of the starkest illustrations of how the treatment of the fetus of a patient can affect gestating women.

The prospect of treating a fetus as a patient has been regarded as risky, in that it carries an implicit suggestion about the moral status of the fetus. That is, patients are usually *persons*, and persons are commonly regarded as having full moral status. If we accept the term 'fetal patient' therefore, it may entail that the fetal patient's moral status is equal to that of the woman who is gestating it. In turn, this may lead to a conflict of interest between the two. In many jurisdictions where fetuses do not have *legal* personhood, pregnant women have a more or less absolute right to accept or reject medical treatment, irrespective of its effect on the fetus. It may be feared that this right would be diminished or negated by the association between patient-hood and moral status. Some of those who have written on this subject have attempted to show how these risks could be mitigated: that we do not have to ascribe *full* moral status alongside patient-hood (Dickens and Cook, 2003).

In this chapter, I will show that even where we do consider fetal patient-hood as implying full moral status, there are clear limits on what we are entitled to do to pregnant women on behalf of the fetus. I undertake this analysis from a Kantian perspective, asking whether treating the fetus as a patient justifies treating the gestating woman as a mere means to the fetus' ends. I will also ask whether fetal surgery is qualitatively different from other forms of prenatal intervention (such as inoculating pregnant women against whooping cough so that the baby is born ready-immunised) (Department of Health, 2014). I suggest that in fact any treatment of pregnant women aimed at benefiting the fetus is ethically problematic and that while some interventions are riskier than others, the deepest ethical question is not dependent on the degree of risk, but relates to the Kantian injunction that we should always treat humanity, whether in others or ourselves, as an end in itself, rather than as a mere means.

Kant and the Formula of Humanity

The German philosopher Immanuel Kant urged: 'Act in such a way that you always treat humanity, whether in your own person or in the person of any other, never simply as a means, but always at the same time as an end' (Kant, 1948). This injunction is known as the 'Formula of Humanity' (FH) and has a powerful intuitive appeal. As I have suggested, the treatment of the fetus as a patient seems to pose a problem for the FH, since – unlike other patients – when we intervene medically in the life of the fetus, we must treat the body in which it is gestated either as an impediment, or a means of accessing the fetus.

Part of the point of the FH is that human persons are not *things* and it is wrong to treat them as though they are: 'It is impossible to be a person and a thing, the proprietor and the property' (Kant, 1997). However, in pregnancy, this does not seem so obviously to be true. Women are routinely treated differently from other people solely because they are also things that contain fetuses. A pregnancy in itself involves the use of the mother's body by the fetus for its own ends/interests. A gestating woman can be viewed as a thing that contains another human organism, and at the same time, as a human organism that contains a thing. It is precisely this relationship of containment that is problematic here. But the fetus itself does not wrong her in this regard; it makes no conscious choice to occupy her body. However others, including doctors, the rest of society, and the pregnant woman herself, may be guilty of treating the pregnant woman as a mere means.

If a woman's containing function is *all* that dominates our understanding of her and our treatment of her, we treat her as though she were a mere container: a mere means, rather than an end in herself. Medical advances have made these questions much more than a speculative philosophical exercise. Women's bodies can be opened and operated on in order to access the fetus. The more we discover through medicine, the more pressing this question becomes.

When fetuses become patients

Pregnancy is regarded as a phenomenon that requires medical attention. One reason for this is that pregnancy and childbirth themselves involve significant medical risks for women. These risks can result in lifelong health problems or even death (Raymond and Grimes, 2012). Therefore, there seems to be a fairly straightforward justification for medical concern relating to the mitigation or avoidance of these risks where possible. To the extent that obstetric medicine attempts to achieve this, it does not raise very new ethical concerns. These interventions do not treat the fetus itself as a patient. However, many of the medical interventions that are undertaken in pregnancy do not focus primarily or even at all on the woman's medical welfare, but rather on the welfare of the fetus. As medical knowledge and expertise concerning fetal development advances, the scope for medical interventions during pregnancy increases, generating new questions about the medical and moral status of the fetus. Can it be treated as a patient? What does this imply for the relationship between the fetus and its gestator?

If fetuses are construed as patients, it makes sense to think about their welfare, and to undertake medical interventions when this is necessary to avoid risk or improve their health, just as we might do for any other patient. However, this may appear to place the fetal patient in conflict with the interests of the gestating woman. In granting fetuses patient status, do we risk systematising the treatment of gestating women as mere means to the ends of the fetus? I do not seek to answer the question of what moral status a fetus has in this chapter. However, my position is loosely based on that of Judith Jarvis Thomson (Thomson, 1976). In my usage of the term, 'fetal patient' implies that the fetus is – or could be – both a person and a patient: the subject of medical intervention designed to improve its health or to save its life. In this regard, its moral status is assumed to be no different from that of other patients. And with Jarvis Thomson, I will show that even where we do assume that the fetus has moral status equal to other patients, there remain questions about what can legitimately be done to other persons/ patients on its behalf.

Patients in patients

I start, therefore, from the position that the fetus could be treated as a patient like any other. However, the ethical difference here is that the fetal patient cannot be treated without thereby involving another person, who may or may not also be a patient. Any treatment of the fetus as a patient requires some interaction with the woman who is gestating it. Her body may be treated as a receptacle, a channel, an obstacle or impediment in the attempts by medical professionals to diagnose or treat the fetus. Ultrasound goes 'through' the body of the mother, as do nutritional supplements. Efforts to persuade or help women change their behaviour during pregnancy likewise treat her body as a means of benefiting or harming the fetal patient.

The risk of contravening the FH is especially high when interventions are aimed primarily or solely at benefiting the fetus. Interventions that are intended to benefit the mother herself and which indirectly benefit the fetus are less troubling in this regard. For example, pregnant women may receive treatment for diabetes or depression and this may also benefit the fetus indirectly. But what about whooping cough vaccine that is designed to benefit the fetus itself with no specific intention to protect the mother? Or fetal surgery that – from a purely medical perspective – only imposes harm on the pregnant woman with no benefit at all to her own health?

Interventions aimed solely at benefiting fetuses may entail that healthy pregnant women themselves are *rendered* patients by virtue of undergoing procedures that may not be beneficial, and indeed may be directly harmful to them. This is a case in which one person is put at risk for the benefit of another patient. And it seems an inescapable facet of most if not all interventions involving fetal patients. Yet, although this is challenging, it is not an entirely unprecedented situation in medicine. For example, in living kidney donation, an otherwise healthy person is rendered a *patient* in order to alleviate the medical problems suffered by another person. Not only this, but the previously healthy person undergoes serious surgical intervention that carries a risk of death (Tan *et al.*, 2015).

Arguably, the treatment of the fetus in utero can be regarded as a similar endeavour, conceptually. However, in both such scenarios, there is a kind of ethical unease that attaches to the medical practice in question. This unease arises, I suggest, from the sense that we may be *using* the person whose health is sacrificed as a mere means, rather than an end in herself. That is, that the procedure may contravene Kant's Formula of Humanity. In order to avoid this, a variety of ethical and legal constraints are imposed on people's freedom to benefit from the altruism of others, or indeed their freedom to *be* altruistic towards others.

A further point here is that one may be tempted to think that the fetus' patienthood is not qualitatively the same as that of other patients who may be benefited by the sacrifices of other people. This is because the fetus depends on the sacrifice *of the pregnant woman and no other person* for its very survival. It is this that makes the decision to regard the fetus as a patient such a weighty ethical choice. If we take the fetus to be a patient, it might be argued that this automatically means that its interest in survival might eclipse other interests that the pregnant woman may have. It is precisely in this context that the Kantian perspective, in conjunction with the kidney donor analogy, is helpful. Even where a prospective kidney recipient can only be saved through the donation of a specific person, and even when that person is the prospective recipient's mother, a coercive donation is not permitted. The maternal bond does not justify our concluding that a mother must donate her organs, even if the child will otherwise die. In this situation, the importance of ensuring that one patient is not used as a mere means prevails. I suggest that the same approach should be taken where the patient is *within* the person whose body is to secure the means of medical benefit.

But perhaps we should worry that if we grant the fetus the status of patient, we have to weigh the ethics of treating the *fetus itself* as a mere means, against treating its mother as a mere means. For example, if a pregnant woman refuses treatment that might save the fetus' life, does *she* then fall foul of the FH? The kidney analogy shows that this anxiety is misplaced. To fail to benefit a patient is not the same thing as to use him or her as a mere means. When a person refuses to donate their kidney, they may fail to embody the highest ideals of altruism, but a failure of altruism is not identical to the use of the prospective beneficiary as a mere means. These are separate moral categories. According to my argument, therefore, granting the fetus patient status need not imply that any specific medical measures are justifiable to secure its benefit if these benefits are dependent on treating another person as a mere means. This is so even though it may result in harm or death for the patient in question. And as this applies in other areas of medicine, it applies equally in questions of fetal treatment. (Nevertheless, I would say here that from a Kantian perspective, there are things that could be done to the fetal patient that would involve treating it as a mere means: to destroy it for use in research, for example, or to disaggregate it and use its component parts either for scientific work or in therapies for other patients.)

Consent

Stephen Wilkinson points out that people frequently fail to consider the scope of Kant's Formula of Humanity. It is only when we treat people as *mere* things that we go wrong. Otherwise, he says, we could do very little, since arguably getting into taxis or eating at restaurants might be construed as using people as a means (Wilkinson, 2003). To use people only *partly* as a means is not ethically problematic. But the distinction between treating people as mere means, partial means, or ends, is very complex. Wilkinson explores a number of possible approaches to the Formula of Humanity in this context. He suggests we consider the possible truth of the following statement: 'if A seeks and obtains from B valid consent to do x to B, that is sufficient to guarantee that B's status as an end in itself is respected by A' (Wilkinson, 2003: 42).

We can reformulate this for the fetal patient situation as follows:

> If a doctor seeks and obtains from a pregnant woman consent to perform an intervention designed to benefit a fetal patient, that is sufficient to guarantee that the woman's status as an end in herself is respected by the doctor.

Since of course most mothers want to secure the health of their offspring it may be that in many – and perhaps most – cases where medical intervention is proposed, pregnant women will eagerly consent. In such cases one could argue that the intervention no longer treats her as a mere means; rather, her ends are aligned with those of the fetus, and perhaps also with the medical professional. If we continue with the kidney donor analogy, it seems as though we *can* treat the fetus as a patient, even in ways that entail considerable medical risk on the part of the mother, without *necessarily* treating her as a mere means.

Using oneself as a mere means

However, Kant's moral requirements as expressed in the FH do not seem to be adequately accommodated by the bare consent requirement. On the formulation given above, for example, there would seem to be no intrinsic limit to what one could consent to. Thus consenting to be cannibalised would appear to be acceptable. Moreover, if we invest consent with too much importance we cannot make sense of Kant's application of the FH to oneself: if one's actions are always or nearly always taken to imply one's own consent to them, there could be no instances of an individual's transgressing his or her own humanity. Clearly with the exception of a few extraordinary psychiatric or neurological conditions, any use of oneself by oneself, comes with some sort of implied consent. But these exceptional cases are not obviously what Kant means when he says we should not use *ourselves* as mere means. Anyone who wants to sell their organs, commit suicide, or engage in prostitution on Kant's view, is using him or herself as a mere means.

On this basis, the bare fact of a mother's willingness to consent to medical interventions designed to benefit the fetus may not be sufficient to show that she is not using *herself* as a mere means. Matti Häyry points out that the moral restriction on what we can do *to ourselves* reveals a tension between the value of self-determination and the importance of inner worth in Kant's philosophy (Häyry, 2005). Counter to common assumptions, the intrinsic value of inner worth actually *restricts our liberty* to behave as we might wish with regard to our own bodies. Thus, in Kant's view, we use ourselves as mere means if we take our own lives, or sell integral parts of our body. This makes the problem of fetal patient-hood still more complex. A woman may eagerly consent to allow her body to be used as a means of benefiting the fetus. And if so, this may help us to believe that the medical professionals concerned are not using here as a mere means through which to benefit the fetus. But she may still be using *herself* as a mere means.

Risk

As I have suggested, consent is not an absolute guarantee that a person is not being treated as a mere means, where they are involved in medical procedures designed to benefit another patient. If consent is not sufficient, what other criteria might we take into account? One possibility is to think about the degree of risk involved. We do not usually accept consent as an absolute ethical justification for acts of extreme self-sacrifice. Thus, a person with only one kidney will not be allowed to donate it, whether or not he or she wishes to do so; and live heart donation is not permitted. Moreover, all live organ donors are rigorously scrutinised to ascertain *how much* harm will be caused by the removal of a kidney. It is precisely because of this that the lifespan of altruistic kidney donors was thought for some time to be higher than average (Fehrman-Ekholm *et al.*, 1997). Not because altruism makes you live longer, but because only the healthiest of people are 'allowed' to donate. (It is important to note here that harm is not itself a key part of the Kantian position, but is a more pragmatic concern for medicine, as we can see in the kidney donor analogy.).

Wilkinson suggests that if we cannot accept the purely consent-based approach outlined above, we might be satisfied with a more cautious harm avoiding formulation:

> If A seeks and obtains from B valid consent to do x to B and x is not substantially harmful to B, that is sufficient to guarantee that B's status as end in itself is respected by B.
>
> (Wilkinson, 2003: 42)

Since here we are interested in the question of whether the woman herself is using herself as a mere means, we could re-word this as follows:

> If A seeks and obtains from herself valid consent to do x to herself and x is not substantially harmful to her, she does not use herself as a mere means.

It certainly seems that the risks and harms involved in interventions such as fetal surgery could count as 'substantially harmful'. Indeed, pregnancy itself might fall foul of this harm-based interpretation, since as previously noted pregnancy involves a substantial risk to women, broadly comparable with the risks involved in live kidney donation. And of course pregnant women are not vetted for health in the way that live kidney donors are.

Nevertheless, if we accept the idea that pregnant women can only consent to fetal interventions within certain harm-limiting parameters, this would suggest that minimally invasive techniques such as the previously-mentioned whooping cough vaccine, might be more acceptable than the most invasive forms of fetal surgery. However, there may be some procedures that should not be available to anyone because they are so risky. And in all cases, while consent is not a sufficient justification for intervention, it is *necessary*. Only with consent are we justified in supposing that the pregnant woman's ends are indeed aligned with those of the fetus. This applies equally to the least invasive procedures, since breach of the FH is not directly correlated with the risks involved. Thus, although it may not harm a pregnant woman very much to undergo vaccination against whooping cough on behalf of the fetus, to do so without gaining her consent still involves using her as a mere means.

Social pressure in pregnancy

There are more or less coercive ways of gaining consent, and it is not clear that the circumstances surrounding women's involvement in fetal interventions are ideal in this respect. I have argued that the moral framework for accommodating living kidney donation offers a useful parallel for the treatment of the fetal patient. However, the social expectations surrounding kidney donation and gestation are very widely different. We live in societies that strongly reinforce expectations of maternal sacrifice. A woman has a lifetime risk of death from gestation and childbirth of 1 in 3700 in the developed world (World Health Organization, 2014). This is not so far off the risk of death in live kidney donation: approximately 1 in 3000 (Lentine and Segev, 2016). But despite this, while kidney donation is viewed as commendably and exceptionally altruistic, the sacrifices involved in gestation are often regarded as being morally *obligatory.* There is a powerful symbolism of maternal martyrdom, passivity and suffering in our societies (Smajdor, 2011). Because of the social expectations of pregnant women in our society, one might argue that to use oneself as a mere means during gestation is regarded almost as a badge of maternal honour rather than a source of moral concern.

While we might agree that consent is a necessary condition for fetal interventions, it may therefore not be sufficient to show us that the person is not being used as a mere means to benefit others, or that they are free from social coercion. In the context of kidney donation, potential donors and recipients are interviewed both separately and together (Reese *et al.*, 2015). Their motivations for the donation are carefully scrutinised, and they are required to state whether they have felt themselves to be under any duress, emotional or otherwise, and whether any reward, financial or otherwise, has been offered to them. Pregnant women, on the other hand, are *expected* to feel a degree of compulsion in their perceived obligations during pregnancy. We take far less care to guard against coercion in pregnancy and in maternal-fetal medicine.

When facing extreme social pressure, a person may consent against their better judgement, or because they are suffering from emotional anguish, or indeed because they have internalised the expectations they perceive are required of them (Lowe, 2016: 216). In such situations, the validity of their consent may be undermined. In fact, the more emotional pressure the person is under, the less confident we should be in the quality of their consent. In this context, the heavy social pressure and expectations of maternal altruism weigh *against* the plausibility that pregnant women's consent is sufficient to show that they are not being used as a means to benefit the fetal patient. Arguably in this case, the pregnant woman is regarded *by society* as a mere means, or is under social compulsion to regard herself in this way. Just as in the case of the altruistic kidney donor, if there is evidence of heavy pressure, this may be a reason to halt the process. However, in the fetal patient situation, the pressure comes from society itself, which makes it far more difficult to ensure that people are free from this form of coercion. This might be taken as a reason to exercise extreme caution in pursuing medical research into interventions that impose ever more burdensome duties on gestating women.

Conclusion

I have suggested that there may be good reasons to think that consent given by pregnant women for fetal interventions, is a necessary, but not always sufficient basis to ensure that she is not being treated as a mere means, either by herself or others. But what should we do in cases where it is not clear that women's choices are freely made? It is not clear that we can we make distinctions between women whose consent is valid, and those who are effectively 'coerced' by the expectations of doctors, society, or their own desire to be altruistic mothers. All women in our societies are confronted with weighty expectations concerning their duties and obligations.

To reduce the options of pregnant women with regard to their willingness to undergo altruistic medical interventions on behalf of the fetus also risks transgressing Kantian principles. Although we have moral reasons to avoid treating others as mere means, we cannot necessarily override their wishes in order to prevent them from treating themselves in this way. But this might seem to suggest we have to do everything that the mother asks in terms of her requests for fetal interventions. The place to emphasise the importance of women's worth as being more than a mere means to fetal ends is not at the point of medical intervention: not the point at which the fetus becomes a patient, but at a more general social level. If women's maternal altruism is excessive, it does not resolve the situation to compound the problem by restricting her autonomy in the clinic.

Given these challenges, perhaps we should not pursuing fetal medicine at all, in societies where the expectation of maternal sacrifice is valued so highly (Smajdor, 2011). While this may initially appear to be an unreasonably paternalistic response to the prospect of fetal medicine, it simply represents a suggestion as to the order of moral priorities. The continuing push towards greater knowledge of and power over the fetal patient does not happen in a vacuum. It is happening in societies where the known implications and burdens of such development are in conflict with the moral requirements of our treatment of others. *These* are the problems that should be occupying our moral attention.

My conclusion therefore is that to grant the fetus the status of patient does not in itself pose an insurmountable problem in maternal-fetal medicine, provided that we approach such interventions from a Kantian perspective in which neither the fetus nor the pregnant woman must be treated as a mere means. However, this is not the context in which fetal medicine is currently developed and practised. Therefore, if fetal interventions continue to be undertaken, we should approach them with extreme caution, remembering that the expectations we have of pregnant women do not always align with the moral principles that apply to other areas of medicine in which one patient becomes the means of treating another. This discrepancy lacks moral justification, and presents the biggest ethical problem relating to the treatment of the fetus as a patient.

References

Department of Health and Public Health England. (2014) Continuation of whooping cough vaccination programme in pregnancy advised. *Department of Health and Public Health England*. Available from: www.gov.uk/government/news/continuation-of-whooping-cough-vaccination-programme-in-pregnancy-advised [last accessed April 2017].

Dickens. B.M and Cook R.J. (2003) Ethical and legal approaches to 'the fetal patient'. *International Journal of Gynecology & Obstetrics*, 183 (1), 85–91.

Fehrman-Ekholm, I., Elinder, C.G., Stenbeck, M., Tydén, G., and Groth, C.G. (1997) Kidney donors live longer. *Transplantation*, 64 (7), 976–978.

Häyry, M. (2005) The tension between self-governance and absolute inner worth in Kant's moral philosophy. *Journal of Medical Ethics*, 31 (11), 645–647.

Kant, I. (1948) *Groundwork of the Metaphysic of Morals* (first published 1785), In: Paton, H. (ed.), *The Moral Law*. London: Hutchinson, p. 91.

Kant, I. (1997) *Lectures on Ethics*. Cambridge: Cambridge University Press, p. 157.

Lentine, K.L. and Segev, D.L. (2017) Understanding and communicating medical risks for living kidney donors: a matter of perspective. *Journal of the American Society of Nephrology*, 28 (1), 12–24.

Lowe P. (2016) *Reproductive Health and Maternal Sacrifice: Women, Choice and Responsibility*. New York: Springer, p. 216.

Raymond, E.G. and Grimes, D.A.. (2012) The comparative safety of legal induced abortion and childbirth in the United States. *Obstetrics & Gynecology*. 119 (2, Part 1), 215–219.

Reese, P.P., Boudville, N., and Garg, A.X. (2015). Living kidney donation: outcomes, ethics, and uncertainty. *The Lancet*. 385 (9981), 2003–2013.

Smajdor, A. (2011) Ethical challenges in fetal surgery. *Journal of Medical Ethics*. 37 (2), 88–91.

Tan, J.C., Gordon, E.J., Dew, M.A., Rudow, D.L., Steiner, R.W., Woodle, E.S., Hays, R., Rodrigue, J.R., and Segev, D.L. (2015) Living donor kidney transplantation: facilitating education about live kidney donation – recommendations from a consensus conference. *Clinical Journal of the American Society of Nephrology*, 10 (9), 1670–7.

Thomson, J.J. (1976) A defense of abortion. In: *Biomedical Ethics and the Law*. New York Springer, pp. 39–54.

University College London. (2014) £10m awarded for foetal surgery research. *University College London News*. Available from: www.ucl.ac.uk/news/news-articles/0614/020614-foetal-surgery [last accessed April 2017].

Wilkinson, S. (2003) *Bodies for Sale: Ethics and Exploitation in the Human Body Trade*. New York: Routledge.

World Health Organization and Unicef. (2014) *Trends in Maternal Mortality: 1990 to 2013: Estimates by WHO, UNICEF, UNFPA*. New York; The World Bank and the United Nations Population Division.

9 Caring for pregnant cancer patients

Alma Linkeviciute

Introduction

> Olga (35) is a mother of a beautiful girl called Eliza who just turned five. She is also 20 weeks pregnant with her second child and a recent scan revealed that she is expecting a boy. Delight, however, is overshadowed by Olga's recent diagnosis of breast cancer. For the best chances to combat Olga's cancer immediate treatment is recommended. Hence this can compromise the healthy development of the fetus. Olga's husband does not feel comfortable with the possibility of bringing a disabled child to life or his wife compromising her health by continuing the pregnancy. Therefore, his attitude is that it is better to have one child with a mother than raise two orphans on his own. Olga has been feeling the movements of the fetus for a few weeks now. She is certain she does not want to die but she does not want to sacrifice the life of her soon to be born child.

It is not very common that pregnancy and cancer occur simultaneously. Hence such occurrences are often surrounded by clinical and ethical uncertainties. Cancer being the second leading cause of death among reproductive-age women is estimated to complicate 1 out of 1000 pregnancies (Koren *et al.*, 2013; Peccatori *et al.*, 2013). Estimates vary depending on the type of cancer and the age of the pregnant patient. One of the most common cancers diagnosed during pregnancy is breast cancer, followed by thyroid, cervical, ovarian cancers and melanoma (Pentheroudakis *et al.*, 2010). Older maternal age is associated with an increased number of benign tumours (Stagnaro-Green *et al.*, 2011) and also malignancies (Schedin, 2006). Therefore, it is predicted that the number of malignancies diagnosed during pregnancy will rise due to a social trend to delay childbearing (Oduncu *et al.*, 2003).

In order to offer a successful treatment of the mother and favourable outcome for the fetus, knowledge about the likely effect of the cancer on the course of the pregnancy and of the pregnancy on the progression of the cancer is of crucial importance (Morice, Uzan and Uzan, 2012). However, most professional guidelines are based on case studies, case study reviews and various registries. This can offer only a limited level of evidence. Therefore, some treatment decisions in the care of pregnant cancer patients remain surrounded by varying levels of uncertainty.

Leading clinical authors recognize that discussion concerning maternal prognosis remains open (Peccatori *et al.*, 2013) and even though the evidence on fetal outcomes after exposure to chemotherapy is reassuring (Peccatori, Corrado and Fumagalli, 2015), this evidence is still being consolidated. Currently available data concerning fetal outcomes suggest a modest increase in complications such as intrauterine growth restriction (IUGR) and preterm birth (Peccatori *et al.*, 2013), and potentially impaired functional and cognitive development, myocardial toxicity, spontaneous abortion (Rizack *et al.*, 2009) and impaired future fertility of the developing child (Hahn *et al.*, 2006), which may be considered clinically acceptable risks. However, some patients might not consider these risks to be acceptable and would seek alternative solutions. Furthermore, the effect of new targeted therapies is often still unclear and should therefore not be advised in pregnancy (Boere *et al.*, 2017). However, those targeted therapies might be the most effective treatment for a pregnant woman and some experts suggest that not all of them should necessarily be avoided in the course of a pregnancy as the structures and mechanisms of action of the relevant agents are diverse (Lambertini, Peccatori and Azim, 2015).

Cancer during pregnancy

One of the most problematic aspects clinically and ethically in simultaneous cancer and pregnancy care is that it cannot always be predicted how beneficial cancer treatment will be to the pregnant woman and what risks it will pose to the developing fetus. Nevertheless, professional recommendations suggest that most treatment regimens can be given to pregnant patients in the second and third trimesters (Amant *et al.*, 2015) without severe adverse implications for fetal development and the future health of the child (Cardonick *et al.*, 2015). However, what clinicians see as acceptable risks to the fetus might be weighed and valued differently by the pregnant women. Therefore, despite reports suggesting that pregnancy termination does not have any survival benefit for a pregnant patient (Marsden *et al.*, 2010; Koren *et al.*, 2013) and pregnancy is safe for cancer survivors (Pagani *et al.*, 2011), it is important to consider how the pregnant patient herself views her situation, what awareness she has and what values and beliefs lie behind her preferences.

Clinical practice guidelines for cancer management during pregnancy suggest that maternal health benefit should prevail where a conflict occurs between maternal and fetal health-related wellbeing (Koren *et al.*, 2013; Amant *et al.*, 2014; Follows *et al.*, 2014) while only a few put a strong emphasis on fetal interests and advocate never terminating the pregnancy because of maternal cancer (Papini *et al.*, 2010).

It must be recognized, however, that a pregnant woman might not consider her own health as a priority and might see a meaning in sacrificing her own life for another life to be born. Therefore, a conflict might arise between a pregnant woman and her physicians, who might have their own moral views and perceive their obligations to promote the best interests of their patients differently. Meanwhile, a pregnant woman is under no obligation to give the same importance to her health-related treatment benefits as her physician might do (Fleischman, Chervenak and McCullough, 1998) but most people working in healthcare try to serve the best interests of their pregnant patient and her fetus based on their personal and professional perception of what will be good and beneficial for both parties. Patients, however, might have different preferences based on their personal values, cultural and/or religious background or just individual circumstances.

This is where maternal and fetal interests have a potential to clash as pregnant cancer patients might have to take into consideration other factors too, not only clinical factors. The basis for ethical disagreements might not be limited to the health-related benefits for a pregnant woman and her fetus but might also involve the physicians treating her (Oduncu *et al.*, 2003). Physicians might have their own biases, prejudices and experiences, which could influence their clinical decisions, treatment recommendations and their approach to patient support (Linkeviciute *et al.*, 2014). Therefore, a deliberative and mindful analysis including multiple perspectives is needed (Azim, Peccatori and Pavlidis, 2010) supporting the patients in their unique relational, socio-economic and other circumstances. Different tools exist for addressing a need for deliberation in the clinical setting (Linkeviciute and Sanchini, 2016) but – considering the complexity, emotional charge and diversity of personal values and beliefs – such support might have to be offered to patients and clinicians separately (Boniolo and Sanchini, 2016).

The fetus in maternal cancer treatment

Decisions surrounding cancer treatment during pregnancy are not easy due to the multiple actors involved, uncertainties about the effects of treatment on the fetus and the potential outcomes for the mother. In addition, pregnant women have a unique relationship with their developing fetuses, which can be pictured as either requiring *self-sacrifice* or as creating a case for *self-defence*.

The self-sacrifice model pictures a pregnant woman as agreeing to give up some of her interests for the benefit of her fetus, while the self-defence model asserts a pregnant woman's right to defend herself from a pregnancy that threatens her health and might result in significant injury or damage to her health or even her survival (McDonagh, 2002). Meanwhile, the parental relationship in itself can be perceived as entailing a special responsibility towards a child, in which the parents are required to make some sacrifices (Lee and George, 2005), thus limiting the extent to which the self-defence model can be seen as a valid alternative.

Cancer occurring during pregnancy has often been seen as creating a maternal-fetal conflict which occurs when a pregnant woman's interests *(as defined by her)*, conflict with the interests of her fetus and herself *(as defined by the physician)* (Fasouliotis and Schenker, 2000). However, it is also possible that a pregnant cancer patient, just as in the opening case, faces an internal conflict when making decisions about her cancer treatment and pregnancy. One of the most elaborated frameworks, referred to as a *professional responsibility model* (Chervenak, McCullough and Brent, 2011), suggests that for healthcare professionals it is the scientific evidence and compassionate care that are the most important aspects when attending to pregnant women with cancer. The same authors have also proposed an ethical framework in which the physician's obligations to the developing fetus seem to be determined by the fetus's viability and the mother's wishes (Chervenak *et al.*, 2004). This framework is based on the idea that the debate about fetal rights and fetal moral status does not lead us anywhere and should be replaced with the notion of *seeing the fetus as a patient* (Chervenak *et al.*, 2004; Chervenak, McCullough and Brent, 2011). It is explained that being a patient has two components: 1) a human being is presented to the physician; 2) clinical interventions exist that are reliably expected to clinically benefit that human being (Chervenak, McCullough and Brent, 2011). A fetus can only be presented to the physician by a pregnant woman and of course any intervention for fetal benefit which also affects the pregnant woman's body is still open to debate and contest. In general, cancer treatment is for the benefit of the pregnant woman's health and might not have any direct and active benefit to fetal health. Actually, direct benefit for the fetus might not even be sought, which complicates the notion that the fetus could be a patient in the context of cancer care during pregnancy.

However, in a pregnancy during which a cancer affects the pregnant woman, the fetus does not necessarily need an intervention for its health benefit but it is in the interest of the fetus to remain in the functioning maternal body as close to term as possible and for the pregnant woman to survive indefinitely so she can fulfil her role as the child's mother (Amant *et al.*, 2015). The fetus is presented to the physician as a part of the pregnant woman who needs treatment, but not as an entity requiring specific intervention for itself. This means that, if cancer is diagnosed during pregnancy, it is the pregnant woman who needs treatment and, therefore, is the patient. Meanwhile, the fetus has to bear the effects of cancer treatment in exchange for remaining in a functioning maternal body until the end of its gestation. The pregnant woman and her fetus are connected and cannot be treated separately without impacting on the other. Hence, while interventions for fetal benefit require a pregnant woman to make some sacrifices for the benefit of the fetus, e.g. undergoing maternal-fetal surgery, decisions surrounding cancer treatment during pregnancy are more complex. The pregnant woman is facing life-threatening disease, pregnancy and uncertainty about both. Cancer treatment might help her to survive but might not be a cure. The fetus will have to bear the potential adversities affecting the health of the future child it will become, or it might not survive the treatment, or it might die as a result of pregnancy termination.

The ethical framework offered by Chervenak and McCullough (Chervenak *et al.*, 2004) together with other attempts to contribute to this debate (Oduncu *et al.*, 2003) suggest that two ethical principles are of key importance when maternal and fetal conflicts occur: first, respect for the patient's autonomy and second, beneficence.

Respect for maternal autonomy is often presented as a key component of informed consent and is critical for informed decision-making. Moreover, autonomy is not limited solely to 'the patient's wishes' but is specified as an informed choice free from ignorance and false beliefs (Beauchamp and Childress, 2013) where the decision is not taken in isolation (Dickens and Cook, 2003), which means that the decision-making process can be influenced by other people, individual circumstances and personal beliefs. Therefore, it has been argued that, in order to enable the patient to exercise her autonomy, an adequate amount of information about her diagnosis and reasonable medical alternatives should be provided, including the information about the alternative of non-intervention (Fleischman, Chervenak and McCullough, 1998). In addition, it is important to ensure that clinical information is presented in a manner easy to comprehend, and that statistical risks are presented accurately (Boniolo and Teira Serrano, 2016). This implies that the clinical care team as well as support counsellors should have a thorough understanding of statistical data (Ferretti, Linkeviciute and Boniolo, 2017). Under some circumstances, it may be crucial to involve the partner and other family members in the decision-making but such practices might also lead to situations where the woman's wishes and preferences might be compromised by the undue influence of her partner, relatives or even the social/cultural/religious milieu.

Fetal interests could be considered from various perspectives. Building on the work of Thomas Murray (Murray, 1987), the Health Council of the Netherlands has pointed out that a distinction has to be made between speaking about the *fetus as a fetus* and referring to the *fetus as a future child* (Health Council of the Netherlands, 2009). This distinction is important because lasting health damage to the future child could occur well before the fetus reaches viability and/or fulfils the requirements for being seen as a patient, although not all fetuses, as *potential future children*, will become *actual future children* (Callhan and Knight, 1992). It can be said, however, that any future child has an interest in being born healthy and having access to a reasonable level of welfare, which includes the availability of food and clothing, a safe, caring and stimulating environment and – if at all possible – a healthy mother.

One of the major critiques of the concept of fetal patienthood is the separation of the fetus from its mother, the pregnant woman (Lyerly, Little and Faden, 2008), which physically is not possible because it would result in fetal death. Therefore, if pregnancy was framed within an *embodiment* model (Shanner, 1998), it could possibly address better the potential conflicts arising in cancer care during pregnancy. The embodiment model recognizes that mother and fetus are not identical entities but that they are inseparable. The pregnant woman with her fetus can be said to transcend herself, which means that she experiences a change during which she becomes something more than her previous self by crossing the usual boundaries of herself. According to this model, pregnancy is seen as a gradual process whereby a pregnant woman is both herself and another person at the same time but, at birth, the 'other' individual fully emerges and the woman returns to a non-transcendental, non-pregnant state where she returns to being herself alone again (Shanner, 1998). In this light, a pregnant woman and her fetus are viewed as a larger *relational unit* rather than as two distinct individuals, as in the notion of the fetus as a patient and related accounts of maternal-fetal conflict. Thinking in terms of this unit, a pregnant woman who has accepted to carry a pregnancy (granted there was no coercion to become and remain pregnant), can be expected to make sacrifices for the benefit of her transcended self as including the fetus (Torres and De Vries, 2009). Cancer diagnosis in the course of pregnancy affects this relational unit, as in some cases, a pregnant woman might not be in a position to continue to nurture and protect her developing fetus.

The relationship between a pregnant woman and her fetus is not built solely on the individual autonomy of the mother but requires the competence to create and sustain a relationship of mutual inter-dependence (Held, 1993). The fetus is physiologically dependent on a pregnant woman while the pregnant woman might be psychologically and spiritually dependent on her fetus. In addition, the pregnant woman and her fetus might be perceived as one relational unit by close relatives, friends, extended family and even strangers. Therefore, a strict emphasis on individual autonomy carries a risk of disrupting the interpersonal relationships through discarding the relational aspect of the woman's identity, which extends further than her relation with a developing fetus (DeGrazia, 2005). One can perceive her identity through connections and relationships with people around her (e.g. life partner, children, friends, neighbours, colleagues, community members, etc.). Even if they do not literally constitute a part of the pregnant woman, they might certainly be part of her identity and to some extent their interests are also her interests. Such overlapping interests indicate that the wellbeing of others may in part constitute the pregnant woman's wellbeing. For example, in the opening case, if Olga's husband and daughter flourish, she is also better off. Offering patient support services through counselling could help to identify these relationships, deliberate and reflect on them in order to determine their importance to individual patients and the role they would like these relations to play in view of the medical and ethical aspects of the decision-making process.

Importance of patient support services

Healthcare ethics consultation (Tarzian, 2013) and ethics support services (Larcher, Slowther and Watson, 2010) are mainly targeted at healthcare professionals. Methodologies focusing on patients and offering ethics support to patients are less frequently mentioned in clinical ethics literature. Offering ethics support services to patients would mean that they can be independent users of such services; healthcare professionals (e.g. obstetricians, midwives, etc.) could be involved to provide or clarify clinical information but need not be an active part of the service's reflection on ethical issues. This would provide pregnant cancer patients a space to reflect on their medical condition, on different cancer care options and their implications, and on the individual values and beliefs that the patient finds important. This could help pregnant cancer patients to reach better informed and considered decisions and avoid *decisional paralysis* or their submission to external decisions while wondering whether this was a decision they wanted to reach themselves (Boniolo and Sanchini, 2016).

Two examples of such patient directed ethics support methodologies are *philosophical counselling* (Matchett, 2015) and *decisional counselling* (Chiavari *et al.*, 2015). They are precisely focused on an individual facing troubling ethical issues rather than a team of healthcare professionals. They are used to support an individual patient (and in some cases her relatives) in a decision-making process by allowing patients to explore their *personal philosophy* in more detail, reflected upon and clarified if needed (Linkeviciute *et al.*, 2015; Boniolo and Sanchini, 2016). *Personal philosophy* is understood as an individual way of approaching one's life and the world based on one's personal beliefs, assumptions, principles, and values. In other words, it is considered as the 'conceptual and value laden window' from which any individual starts reflecting in order to make judgements, consider the choices and decide about the actions (Boniolo and Sanchini, 2016; Ferretti, Linkeviciute and Boniolo, 2017).

Ethical counselling is developed to fit under the umbrella of philosophical counselling and offers two distinct methodologies for addressing ethical issues in healthcare settings. One of them is aimed to serve the patients directly (Boniolo and Sanchini, 2016), meaning that patients can be independent users of ethics support service. Ethical counselling is conceived as a non-directive method, which serves as an orientating tool for patients and clinicians when thinking about the choices available that surround them with ethical questions and uncertainties. Its structure is meant to assist a guided reflection process where ethical arguments supporting and rejecting each available option can be clarified and evaluated. This method takes a patient's personal values and beliefs into particular consideration in order to explore and understand the reasons behind a patient's wishes but does not intend to offer justification for one choice over another (Linkeviciute *et al.*, 2015). It offers a structured methodology for creating a space for critical reflection, where the counselling service user can make her choice with more awareness of the situation, the available choices, their implications for her wellbeing and that of others, too, if she deems that important, and her beliefs and values. Such service would require counsellors with in depth training in psychology, communication, philosophy, ethics and statistics as well as clinical aspects of cancer and pregnancy co-existence.

Decisional counselling assists patients in thinking about the choices available for them by describing and explaining what choices exist, deliberating about implications attached to each choice and forecasting how they might feel about potential outcomes of each choice (Chiavari *et al.*, 2015). This type of patient support can be incorporated in already existing services, e.g. psychological counselling (Lawson *et al.*, 2015) in a collaboration with clinical teams where a counsellor might serve as a mediator between clinicians and the patient in regards to ethical issues.

Evaluation of patient support services remains complicated by the fact that there might not be a single 'best' choice even from the clinical point of view as evidence on cancer treatment during pregnancy remains scarce. However, the consistency and coherence of counselling methodologies used for patient support can be evaluated and such attempts have emphasized that the diversity of methods in use, the differences in regional approaches and expectations, and the lack of clarity on service providers' accountability remain key challenges for developing standardized evaluation (Linkeviciute *et al.*, 2016).

References

Amant, F., Halaska, M. J., Fumagalli, M., Dahl Steffensen, K., Lok, C., Van Calsteren, K., Han, S. N., Mir, O., Fruscio, R., Uzan, C., Maxwell, C., Dekrem, J., Strauven, G., Mhallem Gziri, M., Kesic, V., Berveiller, P., van den Heuvel, F., Ottevanger, P. B., Vergote, I., Lishner, M., Morice, P. and Nulman, I. (2014) Gynecologic Cancers in Pregnancy. *International Journal of Gynecological Cancer*, 24 (3), 394–403.

Amant, F., Vandenbroucke, T., Verheecke, M., Fumagalli, M., Halaska, M. J., Boere, I., Han, S., Gziri, M. M., Peccatori, F., Rob, L., Lok, C., Witteveen, P., Voigt, J.-U., Naulaers, G., Vallaeys, L., Van den Heuvel, F., Lagae, L., Mertens, L., Claes, L. and Van Calsteren, K. (2015) Pediatric Outcome after Maternal Cancer Diagnosed during Pregnancy. *New England Journal of Medicine*, 373 (19), 1824–34.

Azim, H. A., Peccatori, F. A. and Pavlidis, N. (2010) Lung Cancer in the Pregnant Woman: To Treat or Not to Treat, That is the Question. *Lung Cancer*, 67 (3), 251–6.

Beauchamp, T. L. and Childress, J. F. (2013) *Principles of Biomedical Ethics*. 7th ed. New York: Oxford University Press.

Boere, I., Lok, C., Vandenbroucke, T. and Amant, F. (2017) Cancer in Pregnancy. *Current Opinion in Oncology*, 29 (5), 328–334.

Boniolo, G. and Sanchini, V. (eds) (2016) *Counselling and Medical Decision-Making in the Era of Personalised Medicine*. Heidelberg: Springer International Publishing (SpringerBriefs in Applied Sciences and Technology).

Boniolo, G. and Teira Serrano, D. (2016) The Centrality of Probability, in Boniolo, G. and Sanchini, V. (eds) *Ethical Counselling and Medical Decision-Making in the Era of Personalised Medicine: A Practice-Oriented Guide*. Heidelberg: Springer, pp. 49–62.

Callhan, J. C. and Knight, J. W. (1992) Women, Fetuses, Medicine, and the Law, in Holmes, H. B. and Purdy, L. M. (eds) *Feminist Perspectives in Medical Ethics*. Bloomington, IN: Indiana University Press.

Cardonick, E. H., Gringlas, M. B., Hunter, K. and Greenspan, J. (2015) Development of Children Born to Mothers with Cancer During Pregnancy: Comparing in Utero Chemotherapy-Exposed Children with Nonexposed Controls, *American Journal of Obstetrics and Gynecology*, 212 (5), 658.e1–658.e8.

Chervenak, F. A., McCullough, L. B. and Brent, R. L. (2011) The Professional Responsibility Model of Obstetrical Ethics: Avoiding the Perils of Clashing Rights, *American Journal of Obstetrics and Gynecology*, 205 (4), 315.e1–315.e5.

Chervenak, F. A., McCullough, L. B., Knapp, R. C., Caputo, T. A. and Barber, H. R. K. (2004) A Clinically Comprehensive Ethical Framework for Offering and Recommending Cancer Treatment Before and During Pregnancy. *Cancer*, 100 (2), 215–22.

Chiavari, L., Gandini, S., Feroce, I., Guerrieri-Gonzaga, A., Russell-Edu, W., Bonanni, B. and Peccatori, F. A. (2015) Difficult Choices for Young Patients with Cancer: The Supportive Role of Decisional Counseling. *Supportive Care in Cancer*, 23 (12), 3555–62.

DeGrazia, D. (2005) *Human Identity and Bioethics*. Cambridge: Cambridge University Press.

Dickens, B. M. and Cook, R. J. (2003) Ethical and Legal Approaches to 'the fetal patient'. *International Journal of Gynecology and Obstetrics*, 83 (1), 85–91.

Fasouliotis, S. J. and Schenker, J. G. (2000) Maternal-fetal Conflict. *European Journal of Obstetrics Gynecology and Reproductive Biology*, 89 (1), 101–7.

Ferretti, G., Linkeviciute, A. and Boniolo, G. (2017) Comprehending and Communicating Statistics in Breast Cancer Screening. Ethical Implications and Potential Solutions, in *Prediction and Prognosis: Future Knowledge in Medicine*. European Association for Predictive, Preventive and Personalised Medicine, pp. 30–41.

Fleischman, A. R., Chervenak, F. B. and McCullough, L. B. (1998) The Physician's Moral Obligations to the Pregnant Woman, The Fetus, and the Child. *Seminars in Perinatology*, 22 (3), 184–8.

Follows, G. A., Ardeshna, K. M., Barrington, S. F., Culligan, D. J., Hoskin, P. J., Linch, D., Sadullah, S., Williams, M. V. and Wimperis, J. Z. (2014) Guidelines for the First Line Management of Classical Hodgkin Lymphoma. *British Journal of Haematology*. 166 (1), 34–49.

Hahn, K. M. E., Johnson, P. H., Gordon, N., Kuerer, H., Middleton, L., Ramirez, M., Yang, W., Perkins, G., Hortobagyi, G. N. and Theriault, R. L. (2006) Treatment of Pregnant Breast Cancer Patients and Outcomes of Children Exposed to Chemotherapy in Utero. *Cancer*, 107 (6), 1219–26.

Health Council of the Netherlands (2009) *Care for the Unborn Child*. 1st ed. The Hague.

Held, V. (1993) *Feminist Morality: Transforming Culture, Society and Politics*. Chicago: University of Chicago Press.

Koren, G., Carey, N., Gagnon, R., Maxwell, C., Nulman, I. and Senikas, V. (2013) Cancer Chemotherapy and Pregnancy. *Journal of Obstetrics and Gynaecology Canada*, 35 (3), 263–78.

Lambertini, M., Peccatori, F. a. and Azim, H. A. (2015) Targeted Agents for Cancer Treatment During Pregnancy. *Cancer Treatment Reviews*, 41 (4), 301–9.

Larcher, V., Slowther, A.-M. and Watson, A. R. (2010) Core Competencies for Clinical Ethics Committees. *Clinical Medicine (London, England)*, 10 (1), 30–3.

Lawson, A. K., Klock, S. C., Pavone, M. E., Hirshfeld-Cytron, J., Smith, K. N. and Kazer, R. R. (2015) Psychological Counseling of Female Fertility Preservation Patients. *Journal of Psychosocial Oncology*, 33 (4), 333–53.

Lee, P. and George, R. P. (2005) The Wrong of Abortion, in Cohen, A. I. and Wellman, C. H. (eds) *Contemporary Debates in Applied Ethics*. Oxford, Blackwell, pp. 13–26.

Linkeviciute, A., Boniolo, G., Chiavari, L. and Peccatori, F. A. (2014) Fertility Preservation in Cancer Patients: The Global Framework, *Cancer Treatment Reviews*, 40(8), 019–1027. doi: 10.1016/j.ctrv.2014.06.001.

Linkeviciute, A., Dierickx, K., Sanchini, V. and Boniolo, G. (2016) Potential Pitfalls in the Evaluation of Ethics Consultation: The Case of Ethical Counseling. *The American Journal of Bioethics*, 16 (3), 56–7.

Linkeviciute, A., Peccatori, F. A., Sanchini, V. and Boniolo, G. (2015) Oocyte Cryopreservation Beyond Cancer: Tools for Ethical Reflection. *Journal of Assisted Reproduction and Genetics*, 32 (8), 1211–20.

Linkeviciute, A. and Sanchini, V. (2016) Ethics Consultation Services: The Scenario, in Boniolo, G. and Sanchini, V. (eds) *Counselling and Medical Decision-Making in the Era of Personalised Medicine*. Heidelberg: Springer, pp. 3–12.

Lyerly, A. D., Little, M. O. and Faden, R. R. (2008) A Critique of the 'Fetus as Patient'. *The American Journal of Bioethics*, 8 (7), 42–6.

Marsden, J. R., Newton-Bishop, J. A., Burrows, L., Cook, M., Corrie, P. G., Cox, N. H., Gore, M. E., Lorigan, P., MacKie, R., Nathan, P., Peach, H., Powell, B. and Walker, C. (2010) Revised UK Guidelines for the Management of Cutaneous Melanoma 2010. *Journal of Plastic, Reconstructive and Aesthetic Surgery*, 63 (9), 1401–19.

Matchett, N. J. (2015) Philosophical Counseling as an Alternative Process to Bioethics Mediation. *The American Journal of Bioethics*, 15 (1), 56–8.

McDonagh, E. (2002) Models of Motherhood in the Abortion Debate: Aelf-sacrifice versus Self-defence, in Dickenson, D. L. (ed.) *Ethical Issues in Maternal-Fetal Medicine*. Cambridge: Cambridge University Press, pp. 213–31.

Morice, P., Uzan, C. and Uzan, S. (2012) Cancer in Pregnancy: A Challenging Conflict of Interest. *Lancet*, 379 (9815), 495–6.

Murray, T. (1987) Moral Obligations to the Not-yet Born: The Fetus as Patient. *Clinical Perinatology*, 14 (2), 329–43.

Oduncu, F. S., Kimmig, R., Hepp, H. and Emmerich, B. (2003) Cancer in Pregnancy: Maternal-fetal Conflict. *Journal of Cancer Research and Clinical Oncology*, 129 (3), 133–46.

Pagani, O., Partridge, A., Korde, L., Badve, S., Bartlett, J., Albain, K., Gelber, R. and Goldhirsch, A. (2011) Pregnancy after Breast Cancer: If You Wish, Ma'am. *Breast Cancer Research and Treatment*, 129 (2), 309–17.

Papini, E., Negro, R., Pinchera, A., Guglielmi, R., Baroli, A., Beck-Peccoz, P., Garofalo, P., Pisoni, M., Zini, M., Elisei, R. and Chiovato, L. (2010) Thyroid Nodule and Differentiated Thyroid Cancer Management in Pregnancy. An Italian Association of Clinical Endocrinologists (AME) and Italian Thyroid Association (AIT) Joint Statement for Clinical Practice. *Journal of Endocrinology Investigation*, 33, 579–86.

Peccatori, F. A., Azim, H. A., Orecchia, R., Hoekstra, H. J., Pavlidis, N., Kesic, V. and Pentheroudakis, G. (2013) Cancer, Pregnancy and Fertility: ESMO Clinical Practice Guidelines for Diagnosis, Treatment and Follow-up. *Annals of Oncology*. 24(suppl 6), vi160–vi170.

Peccatori, F. A., Corrado, G. and Fumagalli, M. (2015) Risk Factors: After Gestational Chemotherapy, The Kids Are All Right. *Nature Reviews Clinical Oncology*, 12 (5), 254–5.

Pentheroudakis, G., Orecchia, R., Hoekstra, H. J. and Pavlidis, N. (2010) Cancer, Fertility and Pregnancy: ESMO Clinical Practice Guidelines for Diagnosis, Treatment and Follow-up. *Annals of Oncology*, 21(suppl 5), 266–73.

Rizack, T., Mega, A., Legare, R. and Castillo, J. (2009) Management of Hematological Malignancies During Pregnancy. *American Journal of Hematology*, 84 (12), 830–1.

Schedin, P. (2006) Pregnancy-associated Breast Cancer and Metastasis. *Nature Reviews. Cancer*, 6 (4), 281–91.

Shanner, L. (1998) Pregnancy Interventions and Models of Maternal-Fetal Relationship: Philosophical Reflections on the Winnipeg C.F.S. Dissent. *Alberta Law Review*, 36 (3), 751–67.

Stagnaro-Green, A., Abalovich, M., Alexander, E., Azizi, F., Mestman, J., Negro, R., Nixon, A., Pearce, E. N., Soldin, O. P., Sullivan, S. and Wiersinga, W. (2011) Guidelines of the American Thyroid Association for the Diagnosis and

Management of Thyroid Disease During Pregnancy and Postpartum. *Thyroid*. 21 (10), 1081–25.

Tarzian, A. J. (2013) Health Care Ethics Consultation: An Update on Core Competencies and Emerging Standards from the American Society For Bioethics and Humanities: Core Competencies Update Task Force. *The American Journal of Bioethics*, 13 (2), 3–13.

Torres, J. M. and De Vries, R. G. (2009) Birthing Ethics: What Mothers, Families, Childbirth Educators, Nurses, and Physicians Should Know About the Ethics of Childbirth. *The Journal of Perinatal Education: An ASPO/Lamaze Publication*, 18 (1), 12–24.

Part IV

The fetus as a patient: challenges for clinical care pathways and interactions

10 Treatments and trials for the fetal patient: imposing the burdens of enthusiasm?

Angus Clarke

Establishing the diagnosis of a fetal disorder has often achieved little for the fetus. There have been few therapeutic efforts that provide the fetus with a direct benefit, as distinct from indirect benefits achieved through improvements to the mother's health. These direct benefits have included long-established interventions, such as intrauterine blood transfusion for Rhesus haemolytic disease, cardiac drugs for tachycardia, and the selection of an appropriate centre for delivery if the fetus might require surgery soon after birth for a cardiac, abdominal or spinal malformation. The benefits of a fetal diagnosis can, however, be broader than this account might suggest. While many parents choose to terminate a pregnancy affected by a malformation, or destined to be affected by a serious disease, others will decide to continue the pregnancy and to welcome their infant into the world. Being prepared in advance that their child will have a specific disorder may enable the parents to cope better with the period of adjustment following delivery. If a lethal malformation has been diagnosed *in utero*, the decision to continue the pregnancy will mean that the parents and professionals can ensure the comfort of the fetus as s/he becomes a newborn infant, for however long s/he has in which to live.

Developments in fetal (i.e. maternal-fetal) surgery have begun to improve the prognosis for some congenital malformations, as with the treatment of open spina bifida, although such procedures are far from being available universally.

This chapter turns to consider a different category of intervention: 'gene-based' developments, that are just on the cusp of becoming available. We consider new rational therapies for a fetus affected by rare, inherited disorders, as some of these treatments may be more effective when used *in utero*, when compared to treatments commencing after birth, and some may only be effective if used before birth. The circumstances in which it might be proper to use such therapies have not been defined and remain contentious, especially when there are other ways of avoiding the birth of an affected infant such as prenatal diagnosis (PND) and the selective termination of an affected pregnancy, or preimplantation genetic diagnosis (PGD) and, thereby, the 'evasion' of an affected pregnancy.

We explore what is meant by the term 'new, rational treatment' and what possibilities are open to a pregnant woman if her health professionals inform her and her family about a potential treatment of that sort. We consider the reasoning and motivation underlying these various approaches and whether and/or how society's interests may also need to be considered, alongside those of the parties more directly involved. We address some challenging questions around the approach to consent for experimental fetal treatments and the potential for conflicting interests of mother, fetus, and society.

Questions

What are the motivations in such endeavours, of both the parents and the investigators? The drive for clinical researchers to be innovators and develop new treatments is strong, with commercial motivations existing alongside pressure from academia. What are the pressures operating on a woman whose fetus is known to be 'affected', when she is asked to consider recruitment to an experimental clinical trial? How available is 'No, thank you' in her interactional repertoire at such a moment? How does the offer of experimental gene-based treatments differ from the giving of information about intrauterine surgery? What else needs to be considered in weighing up the decisions about whether to offer and whether to consent to these new treatments?

The balance between the interests of the mother, the fetus, the investigator, and society may alter if the fetus is likely to be affected by a serious, and expensive, medical condition or multiple physical, sensory and/or cognitive impairments. The family and investigator may perhaps wish to choose the treatment option, while 'society' may prefer to avoid the high cost and uncertain outcomes of an experimental treatment for yet another of the many thousands of rare diseases. Will the interests of society be conceived of in a narrowly economic frame, so that the humanity of the fetus and mother is forgotten?

New rational treatments

The last forty years have seen immense strides in the understanding of human genetics and the genetic contribution to disease. This began with the mapping (localization) and then the cloning (isolation) and sequencing of small numbers of disease genes. The Human Genome Project, that determined the DNA base sequence of all human chromosomes, then changed the pace of disease gene identification. Many disease-relevant genes have now been sequenced, or their previously known gene sequence has now been recognized as associated with disease, and our understanding of the mechanisms of disease has grown enormously. For example, the mapping and isolation of the gene for Duchenne muscular dystrophy (DMD) enabled the recognition of the dystrophin protein, which has led to massive progress in understanding muscle structure and function in both health and disease. However, while real progress has been made towards developing treatments for DMD, there have not yet been many comparable cases of therapeutic advance grounded in a knowledge of the genetic basis of the disease. There is a frustratingly long time lag between determining the sequence of a disease gene and intervening with an effective treatment designed on the basis of an improved understanding of the disease mechanism.

Promising treatments have emerged for at least some cases of DMD and cystic fibrosis, that depend upon a knowledge of the disease gene sequence and its expression. These treatments are potentially applicable to those with specific types of disease-causing mutation. In other diseases, treatments have been devised that may apply to all affected patients, as with inhibitors of the mTOR complex in patients with tuberous sclerosis. Gene therapy, inserting a functioning copy of the relevant disease gene into appropriate target cells, has given promising results in a few recessive diseases, such as spinal muscular atrophy, some immunodeficiencies, and some recessive disorders of retinal function. Further progress is being made towards therapeutic strategies that will reverse the effects of genetic diseases, or even 'correct' the mutations that cause them, such as gene editing technologies.

Whether a particular approach to designing a treatment is likely to be effective depends on multiple factors. These include whether the disease is inherited as a recessive or a dominant trait, the stage of development or stage of life when the disease process can first be demonstrated, and when the condition typically becomes apparent and presents as a disease. While many recessive disorders resulting from lack of gene product can be corrected by boosting levels of the gene product in one way or another, dominant disorders that result from a dominant negative process (that interferes with the function of the intact copy of the gene) will not be amenable to such an approach. A condition that results from a disorder of embryonic development is not likely to be amenable to interventions following birth. The feasibility of long-term treatment will also depend on how well the patient tolerates repeated therapies, the route of access needed to target the relevant tissue and other very practical matters. Thus, can the normal protein product of the gene be introduced so as to access the appropriate tissues and cells and function normally, without eliciting an obstructing immune response?

Some proposed therapeutic advances are tantalizingly close to becoming standard clinical treatments but many have not reached that point, and the process of evaluating new treatments for their efficacy and their safety remains as important as ever. Such powerful new therapeutic methods carry potential dangers, as with the off-target mutations that may result from gen(om)e editing technologies (Schaefer *et al.*, 2017).

When may it be appropriate to develop and introduce a 'new, rational treatment'?

There is a good case for developing a new treatment when existing approaches are unsatisfactory, when knowledge of the disease mechanism reveals a potential opportunity to reduce or abolish the risk of disease, and when this rationally-designed treatment appears likely to be safe, effective, and cost-effective. However, many such treatments are experimental, or will be experimental once they have been devised, and this situation will be slow to change for many reasons. One key reason is that it is very difficult to attract financial support for research into rare diseases. This is so because of the very large number of such conditions and the likely small size of any group of patients identified as the potential beneficiaries. These small numbers of patients inevitably mean that it will be difficult to recruit enough participants to any proposed clinical trials and the likely small size of any potential group of patients seeking treatment, even internationally, means that commercial enterprises seeking to invest in a health care venture will be discouraged by the likely difficulty of obtaining much return on their investment.

Furthermore, there are other ways to avoid having a child affected by many of the rare genetic disorders. Once a condition has been recognized within a family, whether through the birth of an affected child or through genetic screening of the prospective parents, it will often be possible to prevent the birth of future cases, using one of at least two different strategies: either PND and the selective termination of a wanted but affected pregnancy (i.e. a fetus that would have been wanted if unaffected); or the use of reproductive technologies such as PGD to achieve a pregnancy with a fetus already known to be unaffected. Neither of these approaches is 'easy' for anyone involved but they are known to be reasonably safe, fairly effective, and much simpler and cheaper than the cost of developing 'new rational treatments' for the 6,000+ rare genetic diseases. Population-based approaches, screening parents and/or screening pregnancies, hold out the potential of recognizing every couple at increased risk of a child affected by some categories of disorder, especially recessive disease, and every fetus affected by recessive disease or a chromosomal disorder. Until now, such testing to identify carriers and affected fetuses has – realistically – only been available in a family once an affected child has been born and the parents have decided to prevent a recurrence.

Once a condition has arisen in a family, society may assume that parents should not risk having further affected children if that could be avoided, with unaffected children being born instead. Treatments would then be of value for the first affected child in a family but thereafter the condition would more often be avoided than treated. However, the situation would in fact be much more complex, as parents may not wish to make such a detached and impersonal assessment of 'the sensible thing to do'. They may, for example, feel a full parental commitment to their child from early in the pregnancy (McDougall, 2007), even if they know there is a substantial chance that s/he may be affected, so that the selective termination of affected pregnancies would be unacceptable. They may understand that the success rate of PGD is only modest while its physical, emotional, and financial toll can be great. The condition in the family may cause very real problems but the parents may still feel that it is not sufficiently severe to warrant the selective termination of a wanted pregnancy. Any of several factors, such as a sense of loyalty to the affected individual in the family, or the sense of self-esteem in an affected parent, or a personal ethical or religious commitment, or personal experiences from earlier in their own lives, may rule out the use of abortion as a way of avoiding the condition. In any case, the condition may be one where most affected individuals are the only affected person in their family: it may usually arise by new mutation. For these reasons, and more, the avoidance of recurrence within the family may not be an adequate way to tackle the problem.

This leads us to consider the development of new, rational treatments. We turn to examine treatments that may need to be given *in utero* in order to be effective.

Possible fetal therapy for X-linked hypohidrotic ectodermal dysplasia (XHED)

XHED arises from the failure of development of a set of structures in the body's epithelia, especially the ectoderm but also the endoderm. The epithelial appendages include structures whose fate depends upon where in the body they develop. When formed by the ectoderm, and incorporating elements of the underlying mesoderm, they develop into hair, teeth, or sweat glands, or related structures such as the lacrimal and salivary glands and the breast. When formed by the endoderm, they become mucus-secreting glands in the airways or the bowel. The failure to form these structures correctly leads to serious health problems, such as overheating, failure to thrive in infancy and a susceptibility to chest infections, atopy, and immune dysfunction; these contribute to the significant mortality of XHED in early childhood (Clarke *et al.*, 1987). XHED can also lead to stigmatization, because of its impact on physical appearance, and problems of social adjustment (Clarke, 2013; 2016); the social effects of the condition can be experienced as at least as problematic as its physical consequences.

The *EDA* gene, in which mutations cause XHED, was isolated and sequenced in 1996. Ectodysplasin, the protein encoded by the gene, was found to be a developmental signalling molecule required for the induction of the relevant epithelial structures. An ingenious treatment strategy was developed, which entails substituting the ectodysplasin protein with a closely related, recombinant DNA-derived molecule (known as EDI200). This was shown to be a highly effective treatment when given on just a few occasions to affected fetal or newborn mice (Gaïde & Schneider, 2003). It was also highly effective when given to newborn dog pups (Casal *et al.*, 2010). Only a few doses are required in the mouse or dog if given at the point in development when the relevant structures are being formed.

After EDI200 was shown to be safe when given to adult males affected with XHED (clinicaltrials.gov NCT01564225), it was administered to a small number of newborn affected infants (clinicaltrials.gov NCT01775462) as a 'Phase 2 Study to Evaluate Safety, Pharmacokinetics, Immunogenicity and Pharmacodynamics/Efficacy of EDI200 in Male Infants With X-Linked Hypohidrotic Ectodermal Dysplasia'. This study also showed EDI200 to be safe but, as one would anticipate, it was not effective when given to newborn human infants as most of the relevant structures form so long before birth, in contrast to the XHED animal models. The next step in developing rational treatments for this condition, therefore, will be to give treatment *in utero*, either by intra-amniotic fluid injection or by injection into the mother's circulation (as the EDI200 molecule will be actively transported across the placenta into the fetus). This would be timed to match when the human fetus would usually be developing some of the key ectodermal structures. The human fetus would then have the prospect of benefiting from the striking clinical improvement seen in affected animal models.

Experience with recruitment to the trial of neonatal treatment (to be reported elsewhere) has shown the enormous commitment of participating families despite the very substantial barriers and deterrents. The barriers include the need to move the family to another city for ~3–4 weeks shortly after delivering an affected infant, the need for the newborn infant to be monitored intensively, especially during and after each of five intravenous infusions, and numerous associated venepunctures. Furthermore, while it appeared likely that the therapeutic molecule would be safe, it is clearly a very powerful biological agent and its safety could not be guaranteed in advance. Thus, there was some potential for discomfort, pain and hazard to the infant, as well as disruption to family life far beyond that of most normal births. In addition, signing up to the trial entailed commitment to a schedule of follow-up visits over the first few months and then the first year, and was expected to lead into a programme of annual review.

The motivators that drove participation included considerations such as attachment to affected family members, living or deceased, a general wish to advance treatment for those affected by the condition, and more specific hopes that the infant in question – or perhaps other family members – might benefit directly from the trial treatment. Another potential benefit reported by practitioners related to various types of shame: the parents of some participating children wanted to be able to say to their affected child(ren) that they (the parents) had 'done all they could' to advance research into their family's – and their child's – condition and to work towards treatments. They wanted to be able 'to look into the eyes of their child' and account for the decisions they made now, without regrets (in the future) when they would be explaining what they had done when the child was newborn.

Tuberous sclerosis (TS)

There are both parallels with and differences between managing a fetus at risk of XHED and managing a fetus likely to be affected by TS. One difference is that treatment for XHED is probably only needed in a few doses at critical stages of development while treatment for anyone affected by TS will probably be required life-long; another difference is that a fetus affected by XHED is unlikely to be recognized unless it arises in a known family and is actively looked for, while a new mutation case of TS will often be recognized in a fetus because a high proportion will develop a cardiac tumour (a rhabdomyoma), which will be noted on fetal ultrasound scan and will often be recognized as indicating a likely diagnosis of TS. The diagnosis of TS can then be confirmed if NIPT identifies a mutation in one of the two TS genes (*TSC1* or *TSC2*).

The treatment of TS with sirolimus and everolimus, inhibitors of the mTOR complex, is effective in controlling the growth of renal tumours and cortical tubers in TS, and in managing angiomyolipomas, but has been less effective at controlling seizures and the neuropsychiatric manifestations of TS even when used in infancy (Gipson *et al.*, 2014). The use of intrauterine therapy with these drugs may, however, have much to offer in controlling the growth of cardiac rhabdomyomata and the 'micromalformations' of the cerebral cortex that occur in fetuses affected with TS. This could then, very plausibly, have major benefits for the long-term neurological outcomes of affected patients. Certainly, some very preliminary experience of everolimus in the mouse model of TS suggests it may have some beneficial effects (Anderl *et al.*, 2011), and preliminary experience in patients suggests it may at least be safe in pregnancy (Yamamura *et al.*, 2017). The advantages of intrauterine treatment with everolimus and similar drugs would of course be particularly apparent when the condition had been inherited from the mother as the same treatment might be of benefit to mother and fetus, while the scope for benefit would be somewhat less when it was transmitted from an affected father or had been inherited from neither parent as a mutation arising *de novo.*

Whether long-term benefits will accrue from treatment *in utero* is not known but there is a persuasive case for setting up clinical trials of treatment of the affected fetuses of parents affected by or carrying TS, or the fetuses identified by ultrasound scan as having cardiac rhabdomyomata and therefore likely to be affected by TS. Of course one should not prejudge the outcomes of such trials but it is entirely reasonable to argue in favour of setting them up.

Therapeutic interventions for the fetus as patient. something must be done: everything or anything?

As is made clear throughout this volume, the relationship between mother and fetus is complex. One can hardly talk of 'fetal surgery' when the mother is so inevitably and intimately involved in the surgery too: of course it has to be 'maternal-fetal surgery' (Lyerly & Mahowald, 2001). The approach of McCullough and Chervenak (2008) is to attempt to evade the debate about the moral status of the embryo by claiming that we can have obligations to be beneficent towards the fetus without any assumption that the fetus has rights. However, this position cannot be sustained if the two sets of interests conflict (Brown, 2008; Lyerly *et al.*, 2008). McCullough and Chervenak in fact ascribe greater weight to the interests of the mother than the fetus and only attend seriously to the interests of the fetus if the mother has already demonstrated her commitment to the fetus/pregnancy (Rodrigues *et al.*, 2013).

This impasse may be resolved by recognizing this as the actual situation: we argue that the fetus becomes a patient once the mother/parents accept the fetus and regard the pregnancy as no longer tentative (in the sense of Rothman, 1988) but see the fetus as her/their unborn child, to be fully accepted and welcomed into the world (McDougall, 2007). The recognition of the fetus as a patient is, in effect, in the gift of the mother.

The question then arises as to how professionals interact with the mother who has committed herself to her fetus in this way. There is the potential for the degree of commitment to the fetus to be ramped up into an absolute demand that 'everything' be done for the sake of a fetus at risk of serious or perhaps fatal disease, rather as we have recently seen in the highly publicized case of the infant Charlie Gard, who was affected by a severe form of mitochondrial disease. This chapter was written in July 2017, with continuing legal disputes over the rights of the parents to access experimental treatments for their child in the face of a minimal chance of benefit, while their severely damaged child continued to be exposed to invasive and most likely painful medical interventions. Is there a point beyond which such 'heroic' attempts at treatment become something else, much less 'heroic'?

It must be remembered that either the parents or the professionals – or even third parties, such as religious advisers – could activate the rhetorical call to do 'everything'. Such a rhetorical move is difficult to counter in the contemporary world, although there may be sound arguments against the move, including (i) the argument that nothing counts as something (to be done) unless there is good reason for thinking it will be effective, and (ii) the appeal to justice, in the form of the need for us to consider the claims that other patients and other members of society can make on us. We may have to restrict our support for one person so as to offer our support to others, who may be equally needy and more likely to benefit from our intervention. In the case of fetal interventions, there is also (iii) the question of whether any possible hazards to the fetus's mother have been taken adequately into account (Lyerly *et al.*, 2001).

In today's maternal-fetal medicine, intensive fetal therapies are not as developed as in neonatal care, although this may change. However, the development of rational fetal therapies has begun (and may even be seen as heroic in itself) but we wish to consider how the discussion of what it is reasonable to offer or to expect is negotiated between practitioner and parent. The backdrop to this is twofold: the rhetorical force of the demand that 'everything be done for my/your baby' (whoever utters this demand) and the emotional force of the urge 'to do something', 'that something must be done' or that 'everything possible must be done'. These are powerful but dangerous forces because they are difficult to resist even when reason might urge caution and restraint. They seem to 'trump' most counter-moves, given the public values of today.

It is indeed important not to undermine hope in parents that their baby, whether or not already born, has a chance of survival and a decent life. But it is all too easy to cross the line between maintaining an appropriate hope and colluding with futile interventions that simply prolong inevitable suffering and death, and risk causing further harm. There is a subtle balance to be struck between supporting hope on the one hand and active deception, or collusion with futility, on the other (Ruddick, 1999).

In a pregnancy, when the fetus is at risk of a serious genetic disorder but has been accepted by its mother as her (unborn) baby, so that termination of the pregnancy is not an option under consideration, what are the factors that might shape parental thoughts and decisions about participation in a clinical trial? Might society take a view, that it is irresponsible for parents knowingly to bring into the world a child whose care will be expensive and whose ability to contribute to society will be limited? If they choose to do this, perhaps they should pay the costs of treatment, or participate in research into treatments that might mitigate these additional costs being borne by society? I must make it very clear that this view is not my own but that it is one current manifestation of the long-standing eugenic tradition of concern for the 'health of the people' as shaped by neoliberal values.

Framings and expectations of outcomes

When parents have committed themselves to the wellbeing of their sick or endangered infant (or fetus), then the role of hope in framing their receipt of information about the likely outcome of events – including perhaps their participation in a clinical trial – is crucial. Hope could be exploited by the unscrupulous vendors of quack remedies or by physicians who may be sincere but are too enthusiastic about the treatment that they hope will prove to be a therapeutic breakthrough (Martin, 2008). This is why we need tight regulatory control of medicines and of clinical trials, to ensure that natural human failings among the professionals, including excessive optimism and enthusiasm as well as self-interest, do not distort the expectations and decisions of patients and parents.

There is a general expectation on the part of patients that overestimates the likely benefits of healthcare interventions and underestimates the likely harms (Hoffmann and Del Mar, 2015). This is perhaps most evident in the context of clinical trials, where Appelbaum *et al.* (1982) first noted the tendency for trial participants to anticipate benefit from participation. Extensive research on this phenomenon of the 'therapeutic misconception' has shown that it rests on multiple misunderstandings, including sometimes a failure to comprehend the basis of randomization in a trial or the belief that the physician recruiting them to the trial will actually have assigned them to the 'best treatment for them' (Featherstone and Donovan, 2002; Appelbaum *et al.* 2004; Lidz *et al.*, 2015). When patients do come to appreciate what a therapeutic trial is really about – providing information for 'the big picture' rather than providing care for them as individuals – the realization may come with a shock (Corrigan, 2003).

There may be some occasions, especially in a market-oriented private health care system, where participation in a trial may actually give access to superior care than a person of modest means could otherwise afford (Timmermans and McKay, 2009a). This, however, would not usually apply within most of Europe (including the UK), although there may be other advantages to participation in a trial that we should not ignore, if we are to understand patients' decisions about participation (Timmermans and McKay, 2009b). For parents, these advantages may include developing closer links with their child's health professionals, a feeling of having contributed to the future welfare of others, and perhaps more active monitoring of the child and more involvement of senior staff than would otherwise occur.

Even when parents have signed the consent form, this does not ensure that they have adequately understood the decision they made (Chappuy *et al.*, 2013). There is quite a typology of misunderstandings about the purpose and operation of trials, as developed by Horng and Grady (2003) and by McDougall *et al.* (2016), which now includes not merely therapeutic misconception but also therapeutic misestimation, excessive optimism, and therapeutic appropriation. That last term describes the situation reported above (in Timmermans and McKay, 2009a) where participation in a trial may be 'forced' in some measure, as without the trial they might have no access to even barely adequate healthcare.

The failures of patient understanding of trials in the context of oncology, where much of the literature on therapeutic misconception has focused its attention (Behrendt *et al.*, 2011), are less likely to be a problem in fetal therapeutic trials, especially for the treatment of rare inherited disorders. In these conditions, there may be more time to make a decision because the parents will often have been aware for months or years of the potential for their family's disease to be transmitted to their children. Indeed, families active in the relevant disease advocacy and support organizations are likely to know about the possibility of participation in a fetal trial in advance of becoming pregnant: knowledge of such a trial could even play a part in the decision to become pregnant. In some settings, of course, fetal treatments for genetic diseases may only be raised for discussion once a fetal scan anomaly has been recognized at 19–20 weeks' gestation. In that case, the time pressure may be as intense as it can be in oncology.

There has been some discussion of the incidence of the therapeutic misconception (ThM). In contrast to much previous research, Kim *et al.* (2016a) assert that the frequency of the ThM is low, in that statements made by research participants may be misconstrued as being based on ThM when the explanation lies more in the way that participants make personal sense of their involvement. Applebaum regards this as indicating something that really amounts to a very conventional ThM (Applebaum, 2016) while Kim *et al.* do not. It seems that people can express a correct understanding of the purpose of the trial in which they are participating when challenged by an interviewer, while making personal sense of their participation in an emotional frame that is less clear. They may have hopes that are not entirely reasonable, and make decisions on the basis of these hopes that indeed reflect an unreasonable but emotionally grounded ThM. It would take sustained effort to 'correct' such misunderstandings, if this was seriously thought to be desirable, as this would entail substituting a scientific frame of mind for their currently comforting and hopeful one (Lidz *et al.*, 2015), which may be serving them well. Participants in trials should not be encouraged to accept half-truths that make their participation more likely but nor should researchers set out to challenge their entire world view and 're-educate' them so that they fit some ideal rationalist stereotype.

Debates about such nuances of 'informed consent' are healthy and show how seriously researchers take their obligations. However, their principal effect is to reinforce the need for governance processes that oversee research projects, ensuring that their policies and procedures are assessed by outside agents before research on human patients is allowed to proceed.

Returning to the XHED project and future trials of fetal therapies

The recent project described above, about a trial of neonatal treatment for XHED, entailed recruiting female carriers of XHED who were pregnant with a male fetus who might be affected by this condition. What factors will have led a pregnant woman to participate, when so many practical factors weighed heavily against? Of the factors favouring recruitment to the trial, which may be thought of as 'appropriate' or at least 'permissible', and which would make us concerned that her participation had been coerced or might have rested on a misunderstanding in clear need of correction? The adjudication of such motives is difficult and perhaps impossible, with the tangled motivations being in part social and in part internal so that they cannot be categorized as either 'selfish' or 'altruistic' but are inevitably both (Hallowell *et al.*, 2010).

Woods *et al.* (2014) discuss the mood of unreasonable and excessive hope that can operate within some patient support and advocacy groups: a 'collective' ThM. Could this excessive hope undermine a parent's ability to make a decision on behalf of their infant or their fetus? Could engagement in a support group generate social pressures imposing an expectation that pregnant women should participate and should be willing for their infants to be recruited at birth (as required in the XHED study)? While over-enthusiastic professionals might give the impression that families have a duty to participate in rare disease clinical trials, some advocacy and support groups might argue that this is their right (Woods and McCormack, 2013), although a 'right' to participate in research is a potentially confused concept as it can only operate under very specific conditions. However, the moral ethos of such groups may also impose a sense of obligation on their members to participate in trials, a manifestation of the idea of biological citizenship developed by Rose and Novas (Rose and Novas, 2005). When disease groups engage heavily in the science of their disorder, and especially if multiple groups compete for the same disease 'territory', their different approaches to the 'political economy of hope' will impact on their success in attracting recruits, providing family support, funding basic science research, or promoting clinical trials (Novas, 2006).

Woods *et al.* (2014) recognize the importance of hope as a motivator in families and distinguish carefully between an appropriate hope that energizes and sustains, contrasting this with an inappropriate hope that is unrealistic and may block an adequate understanding of the purpose of a trial, occasionally making it impossible to accept a patient as a recruit if they (or their parents) are unable to recognize that participation may not achieve the cure they hope for and might bring some potential hazards. The processes of research governance should block the setting up of any trial that would be likely to cause harm to the child, so that participation would be against their best interests. However, once a trial has been funded and approved, and has commenced, when might parental motivation be inappropriate because it in effect undermines the proper basis of consent? Making such decisions about the quality of a parent's consent runs the risk of a heavy-handed paternalism and comes down either to a decision about the child's 'best interests' or about the competence of the parent.

I hope that we did not recruit any infant to the trial of EDI200 whose parent believed that the child would definitely benefit from participation. They might have hoped that their son would benefit but that is different from believing that he would do so. In this trial, I am confident that no-one in the UK felt pressured by the medical team or the support group involved. However, the potential for pressure in such settings is real and, in larger and more powerful support groups, it would be possible for an atmosphere to develop akin to an emotional coercion. Protecting parents from having to make such decisions, controlling the way in which trials of treatments for rare disorders are structured and how recruitment to them operates, may be represented as paternalistic, although I would support such measures. However, such steps may be ineffective in our global society: the fact that a trial or treatment is unavailable in one country does not mean that it is not available at all (as in the Charlie Gard case).

The next step in developing treatments for XHED will be to establish trials of fetal treatment, when the EDI200 molecule is highly likely to be effective. However, as Sheppard (2016) indicates, pregnant women whose fetus may be affected by a rare genetic disorder are highly vulnerable, perhaps especially if they feel guilt for their fetus/child being at risk of a serious disorder. The pressure to 'do something', or even to 'do everything you possibly can', may be near to irresistible, so they might agree to participate in a trial that had not been well designed and did not pay sufficient attention to safety. The only response to such complex and tangled motivations, vulnerabilities and misunderstandings is to have robust governance processes in place (Kenyon *et al.*, 2006). These will protect the pregnant woman against undue pressure and vulnerability in any trials of fetal therapies, so that her fetus is protected too. Participation in trials should not be offered to children or fetuses unless an independent science review process and an independent ethics review committee have both examined the reasoning on which the proposed therapy is based and assessed the plausible risks and likely benefits to the child or to the fetus and mother as being acceptable given the context of what is at stake.

Concluding (uncomfortable) reflections

The very active engagement of parents in genetic disease advocacy and support groups has several aspects to it. This is enormously productive and helpful in many ways and promotes a most valuable empowerment of patients and families. However, there may be aspects where we should watch for potential problems. These need not necessarily apply in the context of XHED or of TS, but they are likely to apply at some point in the context of some (other) conditions and groups.

One potential problem is that decisions about participation in trials will be made by parents on behalf of their children, whether born or not yet born. If parents draw a major element of their identities from the advocacy group, then this may colour their decisions. That may be a particular issue if their advocacy group has close links with commercial 'partners', whose return on capital investment depends on a ready supply of participants in research projects or clinical trials. Where there are several advocacy groups competing for a limited pool of patients and families, as happens in some disorders and disease categories, then this may impact on the family's or patient's sense of identity in an unpredictable dynamic, destabilized by competition among the groups.

Even without such tensions, the simple sense of commitment to research into one's own disease may lead a conscientious, indeed altruistic, parent to volunteer their child or fetus for a research project or as a trial participant. It is impossible to know what decision that infant or fetus 'would have made' if given the choice but governance procedures should generally prevent parents from being invited to expose their offspring to any more than minimal risk in case they might feel competing commitments, to a cause beyond the narrow focus of the best interests of their child.

Are there circumstances in which it would be fair for a fetus or infant to be entered into a clinical trial with some substantial element of doubt about the safety of the process? This happens in trials of cancer treatments. Might it be appropriate in the case of conditions that cause neurodevelopmental disorders of great severity or that are relentlessly progressive?

These concerns relate back to the question of demands or expectations 'that everything be done'. If parents insist on this, then the fetus or child may be entered into trials that are (too) preliminary and may be too risky. If it is the professionals who adopt that perspective, and impose an expectation of compliant consent on parents, the concerns are reversed. Now, it is the professional who attempts to focus on the obligations of the family to allow their infant or fetus to contribute to the collective, future-oriented good of 'the disease community'. In such circumstances, how much moral strength will it take for the mother or the parents to challenge this 'obligation'? In short, how available is 'No, thank you' in the mother's or parents' interactional repertoire at such a moment?

A final, somewhat unsettling question relates to the various genetic tests that can be performed on a newborn or, using NIPT, on a fetus (Nuffield Council, 2017). Such tests can generate progressively more genetic information, up to a whole exome or whole genome sequence. The immediate applicability of such information will often be unclear but one possible application is to help parents and professionals to make decisions about the management of a fetus or infant currently at hazard. However, even if it answers some specific questions, any genome test is highly likely to introduce a substantial dose of uncertainty about the future health of the individual (Newson *et al.*, 2016). How will both the clear answers and the uncertainties that are generated by the genomic tests be understood and used in practice? Will variants that suggest a risk of behavioural problems, for example, be used to make decisions that will influence the chance of survival of the fetus or infant? Might a modestly increased risk of the complications of adult-onset degenerative disease be seen as sufficient to alter decisions about the fetus's mode of delivery or the continuing provision of neonatal intensive care to a sick newborn? All in all, is the future outlook for the health and success of the fetus or child 'good enough' to warrant continued intensive management? Or must 'everything be done', however poor the grounds for thinking that the proposed intervention will be beneficial?

Comparable 'information' about future risk, in the form of brain imaging, has long been used in neonatal care. It reflects evidence of structural brain damage. Is it legitimate, or even morally acceptable, to use information whose status is much more uncertain and is likely to shift over time in a similar way, as if it were much more solid than is the case?

References

Anderl S, Freeland M, Kwiatkowski DJ, *et al.* (2011) Therapeutic value of prenatal rapamycin treatment in a mouse brain model of TS complex. *Hum Mol Genet*, 20, 4597–604.

Appelbaum PS, Roth LH, Lidz C. (1982) The therapeutic misconception: informed consent in psychiatric research. *Law Psychiatry*, 5, 319–29.

Appelbaum PS, Lidz CW, Grisso T. (2004) Therapeutic misconception in clinical research: frequency and risk factors. *IRB*, 26, 1–8 (and correction and clarification, 2004, 26(5),18).

Behrendt C, Gölz T, Roesler C, Bertz H, Wünsch A. (2011). What do our patients understand about their trial participation? Assessing patients' understanding of their informed consent consultation about randomised clinical trials *J Med Ethics*, 37(2), 74–80.

Brown SD. 2008. The 'fetus as patient': a critique. *American Journal of Bioethics*, 8(7), 47–50.

Casal ML, Lewis JR, Mauldin EA, Tardivel A, Ingold K, Favre M, Paradies F, Demotz S, Gaïde O, Schneider P. (2007). Significant correction of disease after postnatal administration of recombinant ectodysplasin A in canine X-linked ectodermal dysplasia. *Am J Hum Genet*, 81, 1050–6.

Chappuy H, Bouazza N, Minard-Colin V, *et al.* (2013) Parental comprehension of the benefits/risks of first-line randomised clinical trials in children with solid tumours: a two-stage cross-sectional interview study. *BMJ Open*, 3, e002733. doi:10.1136/bmjopen-2013-002733.

Clarke A. (2013). Stigma, self-esteem and reproduction: talking with men about life with hypohidrotic ectodermal dysplasia. *Sociology*, 47(5), 975–93.

Clarke A. (2016). Anticipated stigma and blameless guilt: mothers' evaluation of life with the sex-linked disorder, hypohidrotic ectodermal dysplasia (XHED). *Soc Sci & Med*, 158, 141–8. doi: 10.1016/j.socscimed.2016.04.027.

Clarke A, Phillips DIM, Brown R, Harper PS. (1987). Clinical aspects of X-linked hypohidrotic ectodermal dysplasia. *Arch Dis Child*, 62, 989–96.

Corrigan O. (2003). Empty ethics: the problem with informed consent. *Sociology of Health & Illness*, 25(3), 768–92.

Featherstone K, Donovan JL. (2002). 'Why don't they just tell me straight, why allocate it?' The struggle to make sense of participating in a randomised controlled trial. *Soc Sci & Med*, 55(5), 709–19.

Gaïde O, Schneider P. (2003). Permanent correction of an inherited ectodermal dysplasia with recombinant EDA. *Nature Medicine*, 9, 614–18.

Gipson TT, Gerner G, Srivastava S, Poretti A, Vaurio R, Hartman A, Johnston MV. (2014). Early neurodevelopmental screening in tuberous sclerosis complex: a potential window of opportunity. *Pediatr Neurol*, 51(3), 98–402.

Hallowell N, Cooke S, Crawford G, Lucassen A, Parker M, Snowdon C. (2010). An investigation of patients' motivations for their participation in genetics-related research. *J Med Ethics*, 36(1), 37–45.

Hoffmann TC, Del Mar C. (2015). Patients' expectations of the benefits and harms of treatments, screening, and tests: a systematic review. *JAMA Intern Med*, 175, 274–86.

Horng S, Grady C. (2003). Misunderstanding in clinical research: distinguishing therapeutic misconception, therapeutic misestimation, and therapeutic optimism, *IRB*, 25, 11–16.

Kenyon S, Dixon-Woods M, Jackson CJ, Windridge K, Pitchforth E. (2006). Participating in a trial in a critical situation: a qualitative study in pregnancy. *Qual Saf Health Care*, 15, 98–101.

Kim SY, Wilson R, De Vries R, *et al.* (2016a). Are amyotrophic lateral sclerosis patients at risk of a therapeutic misconception? *J Med Ethics*, 42, 516–20.

Kim SY, De Vries R, Holloway RG, Kieburtz K. (2016b). Understanding the 'therapeutic misconception' from the research participant's perspective. *J Med Ethics*, 42(8), 522–3.

Lidz CW, Albert K, Appelbaum P, Dunn LB, Overton E, Pivovarova E. (2015). Why is therapeutic misconception so prevalent? *Cambridge Quarterly of Healthcare Ethics*, 24, 231–41.

Lyerly AD, Little MO, Faden RR. (2008). A critique of the 'Fetus as patient,' *Am J Bioeth*, 8(7), 42–4.

Lyerly AD, Mahowald MB. (2001). Maternal-fetal surgery: the fallacy of abstraction and the problem of equipoise. *Health Care Analysis*, 9, 151–65.

Martin AM. (2008). Hope and exploitation. *Hastings Cent Rep*, 38, 49–55.

McCullough, LB, Chervenak, FA. (2008). A critical analysis of the concept and discourse of 'unborn child.' *American Journal of Bioethics*, 8(7), 34–9.

McDougall R. (2007). Parental virtue: a new way of thinking about the morality of reproductive actions. *Bioethics*, 21, 181–9.

McDougall R, Martin D, Gillam L, Hallowell N, Brookes A, Guillemin M. (2016). Therapeutic appropriation: a new concept in the ethics of clinical research. *J Med Ethics*, 42, 805–8.

Newson AJ, Leonard SJ, Hall A, Gaff CL. (2016). Known unknowns: building an ethics of uncertainty into genomic medicine. *BMC Medical Genomics*, 9(57), 1–8.

Novas C. (2006). The political economy of hope: patients' organizations, science and biovalue. *Biosocieties*, 1, 289–305 doi:10.1017/S1745855206003024.

Nuffield Council (2017). *Non-Invasive Prenatal Diagnosis. Report of a Working Party.* London: Nuffield Council on Bioethics, pp. 106–7.

Rodrigues HCML, van den Berg PP, Düwell M. (2013). Dotting the I's and crossing the T's: autonomy and/or beneficence? The 'fetus as a patient' in maternal–fetal surgery. *J Med Ethics*, 39, 219–23.

Rose, N, Novas, C. (2005). Biological citizenship. In A. Ong and S. Collier (eds.), *Global Assemblages: Technology, Politics, and Ethics as Anthropological Problems.* Malden, MA: Blackwell, pp. 439–59.

Rothman BK. (1988). *The Tentative Pregnancy: Prenatal Diagnosis and the Future of Motherhood.* London: Pandora.

Ruddick W. (1999). Hope and deception. *Bioethics*, 13, 343–57.

Schaefer KA, Wu W-H, Colgan DF, Tsang SH, Bassuk AG, Mahajan VB. (2017) Unexpected mutations after CRISPR–Cas9 editing in vivo. *Nature Methods*, 14, 547–8.

Sheppard MK. (2016). Vulnerability, therapeutic misconception and informed consent: is there a need for special treatment of pregnant women in fetus-regarding clinical trials? *J Med Ethics*, 42: 127–31.

Timmermans S, McKay T. (2009a). Bioethics and health care disparities in substance dependency. *Soc Sci & Med* 69: 1784–90.

Timmermans S, McKay T (2009b). The bioethical misconception: a response to Lidz. *Soc Sci & Med*, 69, 1793–6.

Woods S, McCormack P. (2013). Disputing the ethics of research: the challenge from bioethics and patient activism to the interpretation of the Declaration of Helsinki in clinical trials. *Bioethics*, 27(5), 243–50.

Woods S, Hagger LE, McCormack P. (2014). Therapeutic misconception: hope, trust and misconception in paediatric research. *Health Care Anal*, 22, 3–21.

Yamamura M, Kojima T, Koyama M, Sazawa A, Yamada T, Minakami H. (2017). Everolimus in pregnancy: case report and literature review. *J Obstet Gynaecol Res*, May 29. doi: 10.1111/jog.13369

11 Ethics of involving pregnant women in fetal therapy trials

E.J. (Joanne) Verweij

Introduction

With the increasing routinization of fetal ultrasound screening and developments in fetal therapy, new ethical dilemmas occur. Severe conditions of the fetus are detected with a poor prognosis. As a consequence, in the last few decades intra-uterine therapeutic options have been developed for otherwise fatal diseases. Nowadays opportunities for fetal therapy are on the increase, especially those for reducing morbidity. Counselling regarding these conditions is difficult.

As Casper has stated: 'Biomedical research has resulted in significant and amazing contributions to human life. But medicine and science, for all their promise, also raise pressing moral and political questions' (Casper, 1998: 138).

In this chapter, the current state of fetal therapy is discussed facing the transition from treatments developed with the aim of reducing mortality to newer treatments developed with the aim of reducing morbidity. The importance of trials will be discussed. Within trials in this field there are several challenges, like deciding on the inclusion criteria and reducing the risk of the therapeutic misconception. Probably the most important, but also the most difficult issue in fetal therapy is the unique fetal-maternal relationship. The mother gives informed consent, not only for herself, but also for her future child.

Current state: from saving lives to improving health

The history of fetal therapy is strongly related to developments in the techniques for visualizing the fetus (Health Council of the Netherlands, 2008). The first attempts at fetal therapy were mostly by open surgery. The results were disappointing because of the complications for mother and fetus. For this reason, minimally invasive techniques were developed with instruments of just a few millimetres.

An example of this development is the laser therapy for twin-to-twin transfusion syndrome (TTTS) in mono-chorionic twins. Problems arise in these pregnancies because of the shared circulation via vascular anastomoses. There is an unbalanced exchange of blood creating a transfusion from one twin to the other twin. TTTS results in a high risk of adverse perinatal outcome. The preferred treatment option for TTTS is fetoscopic laser coagulation of the vascular anastomoses. If not treated, the mortality rate in TTTS may be as high as 73–100 per cent (Berghella and Kaufmann, 2001). De Lia conducted intensive studies of treatment for TTTS, first in Rhesus monkeys. In 1990 he published the results of the first human cases treated, still exhibiting poor survival (De Lia *et al.*, 1990). De Lia and other fetal therapists worldwide refined the laser technique. Today, laser therapy is regarded as standard therapy for TTTS with good survival rates (Middeldorp *et al.*, 2007).

Until recently, the aim of fetal therapy was mortality reduction, but some new techniques are primarily developed to reduce morbidity. An example is the prenatal treatment of spina bifida. Spina bifida is the most common birth defect of the nervous system compatible with life. A myelomeningocele results in a lifelong disability, often including paralysis of bowel and bladder dysfunction. Despite the failure of neural-tube formation, the hypothesis is that there is also spinal cord injury because of the prolonged exposure of neural elements to the intra-uterine environment (Adzick *et al.*, 2011). Even with early postnatal surgery, the damage is irreversible. For this reason, a prenatal treatment was developed to decrease the duration of exposure of the neural tissue to the intra-uterine environment, by covering the defect to prevent further damage. The MOMS trial was performed to compare the outcome of prenatal and postnatal operations. In the prenatal intervention group, the researchers found a reduction of the need for shunting (ventriculoperitoneal shunts because of hydrocephalus) and improved motor outcomes at 30 months, but were associated with maternal risks (Adzick *et al.*, 2011). This operation is currently the only 'open surgery' done in fetal therapy. Fetal surgeons perform a laparotomy, the uterus is opened and a paediatric neurosurgeon closes the defect. Maternal risks of this operation should not be underestimated. In the MOMS trial, prenatal surgery was associated with higher rates of preterm birth, intraoperative complications, and uterine scar defects apparent at delivery, along with a higher rate of maternal transfusion at delivery. A uterine dehiscence has consequences for all subsequent pregnancies since it can result in a uterine rupture with severe maternal and fetal consequences (Adzick *et al.*, 2011).

Besides surgical interventions described above, fetal therapy could also be performed in a less invasive way by administering medication to the mother. An example is the use of steroids to accelerate fetal lung maturity in case of premature labour. This intervention is standard therapy as the benefits for the fetus are proven to be significant, with very little maternal risk.

One of the newest innovations in fetal therapy is the use of fetal mesenchymal stem cells for osteogenesis imperfect (OI) tested in the BOOSTB4-study. The goal of the 'Boost Brittle Bones Before Birth' (BOOSTB4) study is to develop a new treatment for osteogenesis imperfecta, resulting in a healthier start to life for children with osteogenesis imperfecta. The most important reason to treat OI prenatally is that OI causes damage early in fetal life. An additional reason includes higher engraftment rates after prenatal fetal stem cell transplantation in the pre-immune fetus than after postnatal stem cell treatment (Westgren and

Gotherstrom, 2015). The 'first in man' clinical trial transplants fetal mesenchymal stem cells before and/or after birth which aims to improve severe osteogenesis imperfecta. The BOOSTB4 study is planned to start at the end of 2017 (www.boostb4.eu).

Consensus on the importance of trials

Fetal therapy has been developed mostly by pioneers and in experimental settings. The distinction was made between lethal and non-lethal diseases. In case of lethal disease, fetal therapy was justified as an 'ultimo remedium': the untreated fetus would die anyway. The fetal therapist tried to save the fetus by surgery or by administering a drug. For some therapies, after an experimental period, studies have been conducted to prove the effectiveness of the therapy or to refine the therapy. An example of the refinement of an established therapy is the Solomon trial for TTTS (Slaghekke *et al.*, 2014). Although most innovations start with an experimental phase, innovations should be tested in a research setting to protect pregnant women and their fetus and future children from severe risks. The American College of Obstetricians and Gynecologists and the American Academy of Pediatrics jointly recommend: 'Although the first few uses of a new intervention may be motivated by a desire to help particular fetuses, once feasibility and potential benefit have been identified, innovations should be subjected to systematic formal research as soon as feasible' (Committee opinion ACOG, 2011). The first phases aim to test the safety and efficacy of the innovation. If these phases are completed successfully, the next phase is to determine the efficacy of the innovation comparing the innovation with standard interventions. Ideally, innovations are tested in large groups; however, this is not always possible.

It is important to note is that it is essential for innovations in fetal therapy to balance the benefit of treating the condition in utero versus ex utero. A clear benefit of fetal therapy should be apparent. If postnatal therapy has equal results, it will always be first choice, as it has less risk of premature labour and no maternal risks (Health Council of the Netherlands, 2008).

Currently, more and more fetal interventions are developed to improve the health and quality-of-life outcomes for the future child. Without any fetal therapy, the child is usually born, depending on the disease, with a normal life expectancy but severe morbidity. The intra-uterine treatment might improve the outcome. However, as the therapies are still very new, short and long-term outcome are uncertain. As a consequence it could also be that a child is born with a worse outcome because of the therapy.

One of the most important challenges of conducting and finishing a trial in fetal therapy with rare conditions is reducing the risk of patients receiving the treatment elsewhere, without participating in a trial. Fetal therapists should work in an international collaboration and under an agreement not to offer experimental treatments without inclusion in a trial if the treatment has not yet been proven to be beneficial. Especially if the tested innovation aims to reduce morbidity, time could be a problem as these trials will take many years. In some cases this could be difficult, for instance if the fetal therapist has an optimism bias or the patient 'forces' treatment.

Inclusion design

In most Western countries, a prenatal screening program is offered to provide opportunities for reproductive choice to decide whether or not to have a child with a (severe) congenital abnormality. After diagnosing a severe condition of the fetus, either by ultrasound or after genetic testing, the pregnant woman (and partner) will be counselled about the prognosis, but also about the option of continuation or termination of the pregnancy. For some conditions, fetal therapy has been developed and introduced as standard care. If fetal therapy is standard care, the pregnant woman is informed about this option too. However, for some conditions innovations in fetal therapy have been developed, and should be tested in a study. But how do we define the inclusion design?

First of all we should acknowledge that the pregnant woman and partner are confronted with a lot of information in a very emotional situation. Most pregnant women are already halfway through pregnancy and have been looking forward to the birth of the child. Suddenly they have to choose between life and death. In this situation, the patient is counselled with regard to the condition, therapeutic options and possible studies. Right from the start, when conducting a trial in fetal therapy, it is important to acknowledge the vulnerable position of a pregnant woman carrying a fetus with a severe condition.

Fetal therapy studies are conducted to first, refine an evidence based safe and effective fetal therapy with an innovation (for instance the Solomon trial mentioned before), and second, for a condition without previous fetal therapy possibilities (for instance the BOOSTB4 study mentioned before).

If a standard fetal therapy is refined with an innovation, the impact of a trial between the standard therapy and a possible refinement will not influence the decision-making essentially. The patient will choose between continuation or termination of pregnancy, fetal therapy or participation in a trial with fetal therapy. However, in the case of studies for a condition without previous fetal therapy possibilities, the parental decision-making might change radically when a study option is discussed. Especially for this group it is important to consider when to provide information about a fetal therapy study. The innovation has not been studied widely, so real data on outcome is not yet available. Counselling on the basis of multiple uncertainties is very difficult and it could induce therapeutic misconception. Therapeutic misconception will be discussed in depth in the next section of the chapter.

For most 'type 2' trials there are two options for the inclusion design. The first option (A) is to include patients who still have to decide whether the pregnancy is continued or terminated. The second option (B) is to only offer the possibility of participating in a fetal therapy trial to patients who have decided to continue the pregnancy. Choosing between options A and B could be seen as striving for a balance between the autonomy of the patient and beneficence.

If inclusion design A is chosen, the patient receives the information about continuation or terminating the pregnancy because of the severe condition together with the information about the study. After receiving all information, the patient is guided in a decision-making process. How the study is described is crucial for the decision-making, regarding participation. This information should include the knowledge gaps but also the uncertainties, and the (possible) risks and benefits for both mother and fetus. It should be made clear that the study is an experimental (often phase I/II) trial aiming to collect scientific information for the future. Inclusion design A enforces reproductive autonomy, as all choices are open. For the physician this might be a comfortable option as all information is given to the patient and the patient can never blame the physician for withholding information. If a patient opts for termination of pregnancy without receiving the information about the experimental fetal therapy, she might feel uninformed or that she has not been treated 'equally'. However, all patients are different, and not all patients are able to handle the complexity of the information. A difficulty could be the information overload. All information could distract attention from the (possibly) real decision, whether the patient wishes to proceed with the pregnancy. The central ethical issue here is the risk of uninformed reproductive choice. Couples who become confused, distressed, or overwhelmed by the complexity of information provided, might be unable to make choices that are consistent with their own values (Stapleton, 2017).

Patient regret

The prevention of future patient regret should be an important aim of clinical care pathways in this field. The burden of choice should not be underestimated. Regrets could flip both ways. The patient could regret her choice to terminate the pregnancy when the results of the innovation at a later stage are very positive. However, she may also come to regret her choice to continue the pregnancy and to participate in the study. The patient might have chosen for the innovation in fetal therapy as it gave her hope for a better outcome; however, the outcome is unknown and may be unfavourable. Nevertheless, might it not be very hard to choose against hope? Patients might be guided by the illusion of hope, i.e. the therapeutic misconception. The occurrence of the therapeutic misconception is a possibility in every study. However, in this case it has serious consequences, as the patient will proceed with the pregnancy because of the misconception. If the patient later regrets her choice, because of the poor outcome in that particular pregnancy, and perhaps the poor effectiveness of the innovation found in the trial overall, all involved will suffer enormously.

The risk of patient regret about continuation of the pregnancy and having a child with a severe disorder could be lowered if the second design (B) is undertaken. In study design B, participation is only offered after patients have decided to continue the pregnancy, and so with the knowledge of having a child with a severe condition. If a patient opts for continuing the pregnancy, they are considered to be informed and to have already accepted the severe prognosis.

Experimental studies are at first having the goal to assess the safety and efficacy of the intervention (phase I/II trial), and it will take some time to determine the treatment's real effect. An argument for this inclusion design is that it prevents decisions about pregnancy continuation being made on the basis of the therapeutic misconception; the illusion of hope can be very powerful (Ruddick, 1999; Woods *et al.*, 2014). It might be defensible to choose this inclusion design to avoid the interference of information about the trial of a still experimental treatment with the difficult choice of continuing or terminating the pregnancy. For the BOOSTB4 study this inclusion design is chosen (Westgren and Gotherstrom, 2015).

If avoiding interference with decision-making about a possible termination is the main reason for choosing option B for trial design, it should be noted that this intention may be undermined with the current access to information via the internet, as some women may find out about the option of participating in the fetal therapy trial prior to having decided whether or not to continue the pregnancy. Chervenak *et al.* state another argument for option B: 'from the perspective of investigators, to get the cleanest results about outcomes for fetuses and future children one would not want any pregnancies in which fetal surgery occurred to result in elective abortions' (Chervenak *et al.*, 2004: 227). Although this of course does not mean that patients should be expected or asked to refrain from the termination of pregnancy for the sake of the study.

The challenge of therapeutic misconception

Therapeutic misconception is described as research participants' assumptions that decisions relating to research interventions are made on the basis of their individual therapeutic needs but is used more broadly to refer to misunderstandings that trial participants might have (Lidz *et al.*, 2015; McDougall *et al.*, 2016). However, there is no widely accepted definition of the term (Lidz *et al.*, 2015; Kim *et al.*, 2016). The patients misunderstand the purpose of the trial. They do not understand that the goal of research is to generate knowledge for future patients and is not primarily aimed at treating the patient being recruited now into the trial, or the patient has unrealistic expectations of personal benefit (Lidz *et al.*, 2015). Unlike clinical care provided in routine settings, treatment provided in a clinical trial cannot follow the ethical precept of personal care described by Fried (Fried, 1974; Appelbaum *et al.*, 2004: Lidz *et al.*, 2015,). Research and medical practice are often narrowly intertwined. It is often difficult to draw the line between research and medical practice without risking therapeutic misconception. Or it can be stated the other way around; because research and medical practice are often narrowly intertwined, the line between research and medical practice is important to mark clearly to prevent therapeutic misconception. As Appelbaum has reported, the frequency of therapeutic misconception is related to several study characteristics (Appelbaum *et al.*, 2004). The risk of therapeutic misconception always exists, however, and both the doctor and the patient (i.e. parent) might be especially vulnerable to this in fetal therapy trials, although this has not yet been investigated. Possibly the most important consequence of therapeutic misconception in fetal therapy would be any impact of the offer of trial participation on decisions about continuing the pregnancy in the belief that this would benefit the fetus and result in a healthier child.

The patient is confronted with a poor prognosis for her child, a very difficult and emotional message to receive. A mother (to be) will often break her deepest principles and conventions for her (future) child. The patient may be faced with the prospect of doing nothing and possibly losing her unborn child. While the trial has potential benefits for the fetus, however minor, the woman may ignore any possible risks to herself (Sheppard, 2016). Williams describes that in her study practitioners recognized that women themselves might find it difficult to decide against treatment (Williams *et al.*, 2002). Sheppard describes how medical vulnerability due to restricted treatment choices can give rise to therapeutic misconception (Sheppard, 2016). Of course it should be very clear that the pregnant woman is under no obligation to participate for her own sake or for her fetus, because no benefit from the procedure has been established and it might prove, on balance, to be harmful (Chervenak *et al.*, 2004). Although the article of Woods *et al.* refers to parents of children (and not of a fetus) she mentions that parents are particularly vulnerable if the request to consent involves a serious condition or where the condition is acute and potentially life-threatening. 'Parents of acutely ill children recognized that their decision-making ability was impaired, sometimes regretted their decision and sometimes failed to recognize the voluntary nature of research' (Woods *et al.*, 2014: 14). As an example she mentioned that parents and children of very sick neonates, and children with cancer express a greater acceptance of risk in the hope of cure and felt a feeling of pressure to participate in phase I studies as a way of not 'giving up' on their child (Woods *et al.*, 2014).

Not only is the patient in a vulnerable position that might lead her to such a therapeutic misconception but also the physician may in fact easily *cause* this to happen. The physician's responsibility to 'do everything possible' are embodied in the physician's own attitude. Factors of impossibility and uncertainty in situations where there is a strong emotional interest in success are common. The physician is trained to act, not merely to be a passive observer. The patient is also under strong emotional pressures to 'get something done'. But in this particular case it is not only about the patient herself, it is also about the fetus, a potential future child. Until recently, fetal therapy could often have been seen as a remedy of last resort but now that the treatments are intended to improve morbidity this is no longer the case. The children will survive anyway, possibly in an improved situation, but also possibly in a worse situation because of the experimental therapy. In contrast, in the past the fetus often died if the treatment was not successful. The potential benefits for the child should be acknowledged too.

In this context it is important to mention equipoise, that state of genuine uncertainty about the risks and benefits of alternative interventions or non-interventions 'The ethics of clinical research requires equipoise, a state of genuine uncertainty on the part of the clinical investigator regarding the comparative therapeutic merits of each arm in a trial' (Freedman, 1987). The procedure should not be offered outside the context of a clinical trial, even if a patient urgently requests this. This is often very difficult, and a powerful antithesis to the problem of the 'technological imperative – the idea that if something can be done it should be done' (Chervenak *et al.*, 2004). Especially with the easy access to information on the internet, patients are often very well informed. It can be very difficult to resist the wish of the patient/parent to perform a certain intervention. For this reason, it is important to conduct a randomized controlled trial as soon as possible before the therapy has too many 'true believers' (both fetal therapists and patients/parents) resulting in a situation in which a study to gather evidence is no longer feasible. As a consequence, the treatment may be integrated into care without adequate scientific evidence (Lyerly and Mahowald, 2001).

A physician who is both physician and researcher is in a difficult position. In studies of fetal therapy this might often be the case. The differences between those roles are not always clearly understood by patients (Woods *et al.*, 2014), but are also difficult for the physician (de Vries *et al.*, 2011). There are just a few fetal therapists in every country. Research is often conducted in international collaborations because of the small numbers of patients involved. Often the patient is referred to the fetal therapist who is involved in the research, not only because the fetal therapist is the best informed but also because he or she is able to perform the fetal therapy. Clinical care and research are easily tangled. 'The informed consent process should be rigorously non-directive, which will be challenging for physicians who have participated in the innovation phase and have championed the procedure' (Chervenak *et al.*, 2004: 228). Often there is a real belief that by running clinical trials perfect harmony exists between the aims of patient care on the one hand and research progress on the other (de Vries and van Leeuwen, 2008). 'Physicians are more likely to prefer the perspective of a therapist over that of a researcher, and consequently they may truly come to believe that in the research setting they promote the child's best interests' De Vries et al argue, and 'with this position physicians potentially promote the existence of a therapeutic misconception between them and the parents' (de Vries *et al.*, 2011: 7). Another point to note is the fact that doctors are not well trained in obtaining informed consent. All doctors are expected to be able to counsel, but until recently extra training has often not been given with regard to ethics in the specific context of research. The situation is improving with the international requirement for clinical researchers to have training in Good Clinical Practice.

The key in reducing the risk of therapeutic misconception is awareness. In each study protocol the risk of a therapeutic misconception should be assessed, case by case. As a consequence, measures should be taken to reduce these risks, and this might entail preferring one set of inclusion criteria to another.

Conclusion

Innovation in medicine is the only way to improve treatments in health care. Nevertheless, any particular case of innovation might be harmful; until it has been trialled, there will be uncertainty as to whether it achieves a benefit. Regulations therefore demand evaluation of these innovations in clinical studies for which informed consent is a prerequisite. While experimental studies are not rare in health care, the situation is different in fetal therapy due to the fetal-maternal relationship. Patients are confronted with very difficult decisions in a very emotional situation. In this context, reducing the risk of therapeutic misconception is a challenge. To reduce (the effect of) therapeutic misconception, the inclusion design should be considered carefully. Especially in the early studies assessing the safety and efficacy of an innovation in fetal therapy, the study design should provide minimal risk for the patient and fetus. Risk to the patient could easily be defined as merely the risk attributed to the treatment itself, but should in fact be defined in a broader way. Researchers should be aware of the consequences of therapeutic misconception and false hope, so that they minimize the risk of regret. The risk of information overload should be reduced, so as not to interfere with the initial difficult choice of having a child with a severe disorder or terminating the pregnancy. Considering all these recommendations, a policy of informing and counselling patients about phase I/II studies only once they have decided not to terminate but to continue the pregnancy could be defended. A counterargument is that the patient should be able to have the maximum range of choice, following a simple application of the principle of autonomy. However, a wider range of choice does not always enhance autonomy. As a physician or a researcher, it is important to balance the important principles.

Notwithstanding, a large amount of research on therapeutic misconception exists, however no studies were found about therapeutic misconception in the specific case of fetal therapy. Although this is of course a small group, therapeutic misconception might have serious consequences. It might be interesting to investigate the occurrence of therapeutic misconception and counselling strategies in this group.

References

Adzick, N. S., Thom, E. A., Spong, C. Y., Brock, J. W., III, Burrows, P. K., Johnson, M. P., Howell, L. J., Farrell, J. A., Dabrowiak, M. E., Sutton, L. N., Gupta, N., Tulipan, N. B., D'Alton, M. E., Farmer, D. L. and Moms Investigators. 2011. A randomized trial of prenatal versus postnatal repair of myelomeningocele. *N Engl J Med*, 364, 993–1004.

American College of Obstetricians and Gynecologists Committee on Ethics (ACOG). 2011. *Committee opinion: Maternal-Fetal Intervention and Fetal Care Centers.* Available from: www.acog.org/Resources-And-Publications/Committee-Opinions/Committee-on-Ethics/Maternal-Fetal-Intervention-and-Fetal-Care-Centers [Accessed: June 1, 2017].

Appelbaum, P. S., Lidz, C. W. and Grisso, T. 2004. Therapeutic misconception in clinical research: frequency and risk factors. *IRB*, 26, 1–8.

Berghella, V. and Kaufmann, M. 2001. Natural history of twin-twin transfusion syndrome. *J Reprod Med*, 46, 480–4.

Casper, M. J. 1998. *The making of the unborn patient: a social anatomy of fetal surgery*, New Brunswick, NJ: Rutgers University Press.

Chervenak, F. A., Mccullough, L. B. and Birnbach, D. J. 2004. Ethical issues in fetal surgery research. *Best Pract Res Clin Anaesthesiol*, 18, 221–30.

De Lia, J. E., Cruikshank, D. P. and Keye, W. R., Jr. 1990. Fetoscopic neodymium:YAG laser occlusion of placental vessels in severe twin-twin transfusion syndrome. *Obstet Gynecol*, 75, 1046–53.

De Vries, M. C., Houtlosser, M., Wit, J. M., Engberts, D. P., Bresters, D., Kaspers, G. J. and Van Leeuwen, E. 2011. Ethical issues at the interface of clinical care and research practice in pediatric oncology: a narrative review of parents' and physicians' experiences. *BMC Med Ethics*, 12, 18.

De Vries, M. C. and Van Leeuwen, E. 2008. Ethics of medical scientific research: informed consent and the therapeutic misconception. *Ned Tijdschr Geneeskd*, 152, 679–83.

Freedman, B. 1987. Equipoise and the ethics of clinical research. *N Engl J Med*, 317, 141–5.

Fried, C. 1974. *Medical experimentation: personal integrity and social policy.* New York : American Elsevier.

Health Council of the Netherlands. 2008. *Fetal therapy. Update on the current level of knowledge. The Hague: Health Council of the Netherlands; publication no. 2008/10E.* Available from: www.gezondheidsraad.nl/nl/taak-werkwijze/werkterrein/preventie/foetale-therapie-update-van-de-stand-van-de-wetenschap [Accessed: June 1, 2017].

Kim, S. Y., Wilson, R., De Vries, R., Ryan, K. A., Holloway, R. G. and Kieburtz, K. 2016. Are patients with amyotrophic lateral sclerosis at risk of a therapeutic misconception? *J Med Ethics*, 42, 514–8.

Lidz, C. W., Albert, K., Appelbaum, P., Dunn, L. B., Overton, E. and Pivovarova, E. 2015. Why is therapeutic misconception so prevalent? *Camb Q Healthc Ethics*, 24, 231–41.

Lyerly, A. D. and Mahowald, M. B. 2001. Maternal-fetal surgery: the fallacy of abstraction and the problem of equipoise. *Health Care Anal*, 9, 151–65.

Mcdougall, R., Martin, D., Gillam, L., Hallowell, N., Brookes, A. and Guillemin, M. 2016. Therapeutic appropriation: a new concept in the ethics of clinical research. *J Med Ethics*, 42, 805–8.

Middeldorp, J. M., Sueters, M., Lopriore, E., Klumper, F. J., Oepkes, D., Devlieger, R., Kanhai, H. H. and Vandenbussche, F. P. 2007. Fetoscopic laser surgery in 100 pregnancies with severe twin-to-twin transfusion syndrome in the Netherlands. *Fetal Diagn Ther*, 22, 190–4.

Ruddick, W. 1999. Hope and deception. *Bioethics*, 13, 343–57.

Sheppard, M. K. 2016. Vulnerability, therapeutic misconception and informed consent: is there a need for special treatment of pregnant women in fetus-regarding clinical trials? *J Med Ethics*, 42, 127–31.

Slaghekke, F., Lopriore, E., Lewi, L., Middeldorp, J. M., Van Zwet, E. W., Weingertner, A. S., Klumper, F. J., Dekoninck, P., Devlieger, R., Kilby, M. D., Rustico, M. A., Deprest, J., Favre, R. and Oepkes, D. 2014. Fetoscopic laser coagulation of the vascular equator versus selective coagulation for twin-to-twin transfusion syndrome: an open-label randomised controlled trial. *Lancet*, 383, 2144–51.

Stapleton, G. 2017. Qualifying choice: ethical reflection on the scope of prenatal screening. *Med Health Care Philos*, 20, 195–205.
Westgren, M. and Gotherstrom, C. 2015. Stem cell transplantation before birth – a realistic option for treatment of osteogenesis imperfecta? *Prenat Diagn*, 35, 827–32.
Williams, C., Alderson, P. and Farsides, B. 2002. Is nondirectiveness possible within the context of antenatal screening and testing? *Soc Sci Med*, 54, 339–47.
Woods, S., Hagger, L. E. and Mccormack, P. 2014. Therapeutic misconception: hope, trust and misconception in paediatric research. *Health Care Anal*, 22, 3–21.

12 The 'normalization' of prenatal screening: prevention as prenatal beneficence

Wybo Dondorp and Guido de Wert

Introduction

From an ethical point of view, a distinction can be made between two types of prenatal screening that in this chapter we will call PS1 and PS2. Both are offered either in the form of a public health screening programme or on the initiative of individual practitioners in accordance with professional guidelines, depending on how health care is organized in different countries.

PS1 is directed at maternal or fetal conditions the timely detection of which allows taking preventive measures so as to improve pregnancy outcomes. For instance under the PSIE screening programme in the Netherlands ('Prenatal Screening for Infectious diseases and erythrocyte immunization'), all pregnant women are offered screening for hepatitis B, syphilis and HIV, as well as for rhesus factor (RhD and Rhc) and irregular erythrocyte antibodies. As a recent addition to this programme, rhesus D-negative women are offered NIPT (non-invasive prenatal test on cell-free fetal DNA in maternal blood) in week 27 in order to determine the rhesus status of the fetus. If the fetus is found to be D-negative, medication to protect it against rhesus disease can be avoided.

PS2 is directed at the early detection of serious fetal abnormalities. For instance, the British National Health Service provides a Fetal Anomaly Screening Programme under which all pregnant women are offered first-trimester screening for Down's syndrome (trisomy 21), and a mid-trimester ultrasound scan for structural abnormalities. Also in the UK, screening for carrier status of sickle cell and thalassemia disorders is routinely offered to pregnant women. Many countries, including the UK and the Netherlands, provide both PS1 and PS2 as forms of population screening in a public health setting.

As we will explain in the next section what distinguishes these types of prenatal screening in ethical terms, is their different aims, prevention for PS1, autonomy for PS2. This is important, because those aims are essential determinants of the moral framework governing prenatal screening. However, as will become clear in section 3, new forms of 'double-purpose screening' will challenge this distinction. Section 4 will discuss routine prenatal ultrasound as a precedent for this development. Interestingly, the precedent shows that combining PS1 and 2 may actually take away part of the concerns that have fuelled so much of the ethical debate about prenatal screening. As we will suggest in section 5, this provides ethical space for thinking about an adapted framework for a future scenario of integrated prenatal screening and care, with 'prevention as beneficence' as its primary aim.

Aims of prenatal screening

The aim of PS1 (improving pregnancy related health outcomes for the woman and her child) makes a perfect fit with the classical aim of most public health screening programmes. In line with the well-known criteria of Wilson and Jungner, these programmes (think of neonatal screening, screening for breast cancer or bowel cancer, etc.) are all aimed at reducing the burden of disease in the population by facilitating timely treatment or prevention (Juth & Munthe, 2012). But what is the aim of PS2, given that a prenatal diagnosis of most of the conditions tested for does not allow for treatment options that would significantly change the burden of disease?

Prevention through abortion?

Some have suggested that there is not really a difference here, given that for these disorders termination of pregnancy can serve as a form of prevention. For instance, in the early days of setting up prenatal screening programmes, Stein and colleagues (1973) argued that it was desirable from a public health perspective to aim for an 'almost total prevention of Down's syndrome (...) by screening all pregnant women' (p. 305).

However, ethically speaking, there are two problems with bringing PS2 under the prevention paradigm (Dondorp *et al.*, 2015). First, it turns termination of pregnancy into a public health instrument. One need not adhere to a 'pro-life' position to see why that is problematic. As views about the moral status of the fetus are inevitably world-view dependent (whether religious or secular), the choice to terminate a pregnancy should be respected as a personal decision of the woman and her partner. Making that choice should not in any way be presented as the obvious or socially desirable thing to do. It is difficult to see how that can be avoided if reducing the birth prevalence of children with DS, etc. is the very aim of PS2.

A second problem with bringing PS2 under a prevention paradigm is that it makes the screening offer vulnerable to what is known as the 'disability rights critique' (Parens & Asch, 1999: S1). From this perspective, the problem is not so much with abortion, or abortion decisions *per se*, but with *selective* abortion of fetuses with abnormalities. A programme inviting such choices would imply the discriminatory message that it is better for society if people with those conditions were never born. To answer this charge, it is not enough to stress that women who choose to terminate a pregnancy because of a fetal abnormality may have all kinds of personal motives that need not entail a discriminatory view of the worth of the lives of people living with those conditions. They may for instance reason that having a child with special needs is beyond their parenting abilities, or difficult to fit in with their life plans, or not in the interest of their other children. On the level of those personal choices the notion of 'prevention through abortion' is not necessarily discriminatory or otherwise problematic. But the disability rights critique seems less easily dismissed when the *screening offer* is motivated by a public policy aim of reducing the number of children born with Down syndrome or other conditions.

The autonomy paradigm

To avoid these moral pitfalls, a broad international consensus has emerged in the past decades that the aim of PS2 must not be understood in terms of prevention or health gain but as providing meaningful options for reproductive choice. It is important to note that this makes PS2 an atypical form of screening. Whereas all other public health screening programmes (including PS1) are aimed at furthering prevention, PS2 is aimed at facilitating well-informed reproductive decision-making. Although not all commentators do think that this really removes the sting of the disability rights critique, this account of the aim of PS2 is widely endorsed among policymakers and authorities in the field, and reflected in guidelines and position statements from professional societies (Dondorp *et al.*, 2015).

Historically, the ethos of respect for reproductive autonomy is rooted in the tradition of individual genetic counselling that itself arose in answer to the eugenic ideas and practices of the earlier twentieth century. Here, that same ethos is connected to PS2 as a routinely offered public health service. Clearly, this comes with a substantial challenge. If enabling autonomous decision-making is the very aim of the screening programme, then this should be reflected in every aspect of how the screening is presented, offered, carried out, and evaluated. The many reports suggesting that this is often not the case in practice have sparked much of the ethical debate on prenatal screening in the past decades. In this connection, Angus Clarke (1997) has spoken of 'the implicit goals' of prenatal screening (p. 121). If PS2 is offered in a way that ignores rather than furthers reproductive autonomy, and if such programmes are evaluated by their effect on the societal burden of disease rather than in terms of successfully providing women with meaningful reproductive choices, the official endorsement of the autonomy paradigm can be criticized as mere window dressing.

It is only with the recent prospect of whole genome sequencing (WGS) based prenatal testing, that the interpretation of the autonomy paradigm as meaning 'the more choice the better' has entered the inevitable debate about the scope of the screening offer. This interpretation is problematic, not just because of the limits of a publicly funded screening service, but also because the appeal to 'pure autonomy' as an end in itself will give free rein to the joint imperatives of commerce and technology, while in fact undermining meaningful reproductive decision-making through information overload (Donley, Hull & Berkman, 2012, Dondorp *et al.*, 2015). Moreover, if understood as giving parents-to-be the right to know everything that WGS can reveal about the health prospects of their offspring, reproductive autonomy seems at odds with respecting the autonomy rights of the future child (Deans, Clarke & Newson, 2015; de Jong & de Wert, 2015).

Avoiding mixed messages

If not clearly communicated, the different aims of PS1 and 2 may lead to misunderstandings among professionals and pregnant women. Given that PS1 serves the health interest of the woman and the future child, it is uncontentious to present this screening as a normal part of good quality prenatal care. However, with respect to PS2, the message should be that having this screening is not a normal part of prenatal care. As these messages are different, in fact opposed, it is important to avoid their becoming mixed up or confused. Mixed messages might lead to women thinking that having PS1 is not really recommended, or that having PS2 is simply a matter of course. To avoid misunderstandings, it has been recommended to keep the two types of screening apart (Dondorp *et al.*, 2015: 1446).

Double-purpose screening

But new developments lead to blurring this distinction with emergent forms of double-purpose screening. This includes the possible use of PAPP-A, and other first-trimester biochemical markers for detecting pregnancies at a high risk of developing pre-eclampsia and other placental complications. As some of the same markers are or may also be used in the combined first-trimester screening test for DS and other aneuploidies, it is not strange that proposals have been made for combining aneuploidy and placental complications screening (Zhong, Tuuli & Odibo, 2010).

Similar possibilities may arise with the new NIPT. Already, NIPT is used both as a PS2-type screening test for fetal aneuploidy and as a PS1 test for determining the rhesus status of fetuses of RhD negative women (Van der Schoot, Hahn & Chitty, 2008). These were developed as separate tests conducted in different stages of pregnancy, but in principle, they can be combined into one test in early pregnancy. There are conflicting reports in the literature about the possibility of using altered levels of cell-free DNA as a marker for placental complications such as pre-eclampsia, growth retardation, and preterm birth. That would be a further way of combining NIPT for PS1 and 2 purposes.

Looking further into the future, it has been suggested that NIPT might be used to pick up gene-expression patterns that would predict pregnancy complications and other problems with fetal development that would require adapted care or allow for tailored interventions. More insight into the epigenetics of in utero development may lead to personalized life-style recommendations for pregnant women aimed at improving long-term postnatal health outcomes (Hens, 2017). In addition to this, improvements in the field of prenatal therapy will more often allow in utero therapeutic intervention in the interest of the future child, giving women with affected pregnancies a further option in addition to a possible termination. An interesting instance of this is the development of prenatal pharmacotherapy aiming at better cognitive functioning in children with Down syndrome, for which the first clinical trial has just started (De Wert, Dondorp & Bianchi, 2017) (see also the next chapter in this volume). Referring to this future landscape of integrated prenatal screening and care, Diana Bianchi (2012) speaks of 'fetal personalized medicine' (p. 1041).

How can one respond to this trend towards double-purpose screening from an ethical point of view? Should the response be a call to hold and reverse this trend, or at least to keep PS1 and 2 aspects of double-purpose screening separate (Jorgensen *et al.*, 2014)? Is it realistic to think that the relevant tests can be kept separate in all practical respects? Or can the tests be combined in the laboratory but should the pre- and post-test information and counselling be done at different moments? Although such a conceptual (rather than material) separation may perhaps work for certain forms of double-purpose screening, it will not be feasible with more integrated forms of double-purpose screening.

Why routine prenatal ultrasound has not led to much debate

To see this, one need not look at scenarios beyond present prenatal screening practice. For with routine second trimester ultrasound, there is already a clear precedent for the future scenario that Bianchi envisages. As a fetal anomaly scan, routine ultrasound is a clear instance of PS2. The scan looks for abnormalities (structural defects, syndromes) that for the woman and her partner can be a reason for a termination. At the same time, the scan may also reveal maternal and fetal conditions that require adapted care or an adapted delivery setting, or that allow for a form of prenatal therapy. As a screening test for those conditions, the ultrasound scan aims at improving healthy pregnancy outcomes for mother and child and is as such a form of PS1. There is no way in which those aspects of ultrasound can be separated: the same test may lead to outcomes that can be relevant both in view of a possible abortion decision and in view of adapted care.

It is remarkable that there has been far less ethical debate about the fetal anomaly scan than about prenatal screening for DS and other chromosomal abnormalities (Dondorp & van Lith, 2015). It would seem that there was ample reason for such debate, given the obvious tension between the non-specific character of the scan and the autonomy paradigm. The clear impossibility to provide pretest information detailing all possible defects that the scan might bring to light, would seem to undermine the ideal of enabling well-informed decision-making with regard to the screening offer.

Part of the explanation for the relative lack of debate may be that precisely the non-specific character of routine ultrasound avoids much of the concerns about PS2 as inviting selective abortion. The charge of prenatal screening being a 'search and destroy mission' seems less convincing when no specific disorders are being targeted. Indeed, this is why some have argued that in a future scenario of non-invasive whole genome screening the scope of the screening offer should not be restricted, thus turning genomic screening into a counterpart of the fetal anomaly scan.

Interestingly, a further possible reason for the observed lack of debate may be that routine ultrasound is regarded as more than a PS2 screening test. Whereas typical PS2 screening invokes the notion of a tentative pregnancy, routine ultrasound serves as a bonding tool: pregnant women and their partners value the scan as the first opportunity to actually 'see the baby' (Health Council of the Netherlands, 2013: 40). Moreover, both professionals and pregnant women think of it as a pregnancy monitoring instrument necessary for providing good quality prenatal care and contributing to a healthy outcome for mother and child. The fact that this latter use introduces PS1 aspects in what is also an instance of PS2 screening seems to mitigate rather than to raise ethical concerns about routine prenatal ultrasound. After all, a better outcome for mother and child is a form of prevention that, unlike PS2, does not raise the red flags of (selective) abortion. That this is more than just a test for conditions that may lead to a request for termination in a way 'normalizes' prenatal ultrasound screening. It does so by connecting the screening with the classical aim of preventive medicine in a morally unproblematic way that as such is unavailable for typical PS2 screening.

This is not to say that the concerns raised about double-purpose screening, especially with regard to counselling challenges, do not apply. In addition to the non-specific nature of the scan, its double-purpose character is a further reason why counselling for routine ultrasound is complex (Edvardsson *et al.*, 2016). Given that the scan may give information relevant for optimizing pregnancy management, professionals who have no problem with being non-directive with regard to screening for DS, may find it difficult to accept that a woman would decide to refrain from ultrasound screening. Should they try to convince her to have the scan in her own interest and that of her future child? Conversely, for a woman who would reject all forms of PS2 because she finds that any child should be welcome in her life, PS1 may still be a reason to have the scan. Of course, she will have to be aware that this may then also lead to the PS2 type information about the fetus that she would rather not be confronted with.

Ethics of prenatal personalized medicine

If we accept Bianchi's prediction about the integrated future landscape of prenatal screening and care, routine ultrasound should no longer be regarded as an exception to the rule, but as providing a taste of that future. In the scenario of what – with a slight variation on Bianchi – we call 'prenatal personalized medicine' (PPM), PS1 and PS2 are not available or conceivable as distinct screening offers. As separation is not possible, a new ethical framework will be needed that accepts rather than rejects this reality. In the next sections, we will tentatively draw some of the contours of this framework.

Prevention as prenatal beneficence

How should the aim of prenatal screening in this future scenario be understood? Bianchi (2012) says that 'Historically, the goal of prenatal diagnosis has been to provide an informed choice to prospective parents. We are now at a point where that goal can and should be expanded to incorporate genetic, genomic, and transcriptomic data to develop new approaches to fetal treatment' (p. 1041). This seems to suggest that the autonomy paradigm would still be leading, with the only difference that women or couples are given a broader range of choices than in typical PS2 screening. However, this is not obvious for two reasons.

First, as the PS1-aspect of PPM will be even stronger than is already the case with present routine ultrasound, the same goes for the ensuing normalization (one might also say 'medicalization' (De Wert, 2013: 78)) of prenatal screening as a matter of what Conley and colleagues (2017) have referred to as 'beneficence in utero' (p. 28). Clearly, prenatal screening in the PPM scenario will still lead to findings that pregnant women may regard as a reason to ask for a termination. Providing them with relevant information to make such choices will remain important as an aim of prenatal screening. But to the extent that future prenatal screening will more often lead to findings relevant for improving pregnancy outcomes in the interest of mother and child, this screening can be regarded as primarily aimed at prevention as prenatal beneficence. This has the benefit of sidelining the mistaken idea of prenatal screening as concerned with the promotion of 'pure reproductive autonomy' (see above). Second, PPM requires an ethical framework that accounts for parental and professional responsibility for the interests of the child-to-be. Whereas the autonomy paradigm falls short of this, understanding PPM as aimed at prevention will provide the scope for the wider ethical framework that seems necessary here.

The future child, not the fetus

The ethical framework for PPM will have to be able to account for both the interests of the pregnant woman and those of the child-to-be. In most cases, these interests will coincide, but the framework must also be able to deal with possible tensions. In order to avoid limiting women's right to choose abortion, or to refrain from life-saving fetal therapy, it is important to stress that in prenatal care, there is only one patient, namely the woman. As we have argued elsewhere, talk about 'the fetus as a patient', if meant as a normative statement rather than an observation of empirical fact, is problematic (Dondorp & de Wert, 2018). As it rests on an inevitably contestable position in the world-view dependent debate about the status of the fetus, the notion of the fetus as a patient should not be used for defining parental and professional obligations.

However, regardless of whether the fetus is thought as having a high or low moral status, if the pregnancy leads to a child, this will be a person whose interests can be undermined or promoted by what happens to the fetus during pregnancy. As has been argued by several philosophers including Joel Feinberg and Thomas Murray, the fact that future persons are not-yet born is irrelevant: the point is that *if* they come to be born, they will *then* have interests that should already count during pregnancy (Feinberg, 1984, Murray, 1987).

Our use of 'prenatal' rather than 'fetal personalized medicine' (as in the quoted original phrasing from Bianchi) is meant to flag the ethical importance of this distinction between the undeniable interests of the future child and the presumed interests of the fetus. The framework for PPM should account for the former, not the latter.

Counselling challenges

Given that PPM will present pregnant women with a complex array of choices, counselling will remain a challenge, both with regard to decision-making about options arising with a diagnosis and with regard to the screening offer.

Concerning post-test choices, a distinction should be made between two types of situation: where termination is considered as one of the options, and where the woman has the intention of giving birth to the child. As the interests of the future child are not at stake in termination decisions, non-directive counselling remains essential with regards to termination as a possible reproductive choice. From the fact that established and safe prenatal treatment provides women with a further option next to the choice between termination and preparation, it does not follow that this new option should be presented as morally superior. However, when women decide not to have a termination, the moral landscape changes because the interests of the child-to-be need to be taken into account. If the woman intends to bring the child into the world, then if there is an established and safe life-style choice or intervention that would significantly further its interests, she has a moral responsibility as a parent to adopt that life style or to have that intervention. Most women do not need to be reminded of this but some do. According to a recent statement from the American College of Obstetrics and Gynecology (2016) on how to deal with refusals of medically recommended treatment during pregnancy, directive counselling may well be appropriate in such cases, as non-coercive recommendations 'do not violate but rather enhance the requirements of informed-consent' (p. 3). We agree with this: in the context of a pregnancy that is intended to be carried to term, addressing women in their parental role need not be at odds with respecting them as autonomous persons.

Does this also apply to the screening offer? Given that prevention would be the (primary) aim of screening for PPM, it is at least not obvious that pre-test counselling should be absolutely non-directive. Of course, the justification for any directiveness in this context will be stronger to the extent that PPM becomes more successful in improving health outcomes through established non-invasive and safe interventions, such as life-style modification or drug treatment. But even with successful PPM, there will continue to be findings that allow for no other choice than that between termination and preparation, with which some women may wish not to be confronted. And even though more and more prenatal treatment options may become established, many will also be new and experimental and come with possible risks both for the woman and the child. Do women act irresponsibly if, in order to avoid having to face such options, they reject the screening offer? These are issues for further ethical debate and analysis.

Conclusion

The distinction between prevention- and autonomy-aimed prenatal screening is not sustainable in view of new developments in the field. We have argued that from an ethical point of view, this is less problematic than it may seem, given that these same developments will lead to 'normalizing' prenatal screening as a beneficence-driven, and to that extent morally non-problematic, form of preventive medicine. Although helping women to make autonomous reproductive choices will remain an important aim for the future integrated landscape of prenatal screening and care, the new ethical framework needed for this scenario will also have to account for the interests of the future child and how these shape parental and professional responsibilities. This means there will still be tensions between autonomy and prevention, though from a different from than those that led to separating PS1 and 2.

References

American College of Obstetricians and Gynecologists – Committee on Ethics. (2016) Committee Opinion No. 664: Refusal of Medically Recommended Treatment During Pregnancy. *Obstetrics and Gynecology*, 127 (6), e175–82.

Bianchi, D.W. (2012) From prenatal genomic diagnosis to fetal personalized medicine: progress and challenges. *Nature Medicine*, 18 (7), 1041–51.

Clarke, A.J. (1997) Prenatal screening. Paradigms and perspectives. In: Harper, D.S. & Clarke, A.J. (eds.) *Genetics, Society and Clinical Practice*. Oxford: Bios Scientific Publishers, pp. 119–40.

Conley, W.K., McAdams, D.C., Donovan, G.K. & FitzGerald, K.T. (2017) Beneficence in utero: a framework for restricted prenatal whole-genome sequencing to respect and enhance the well-being of children. *American Journal of Bioethics*, 17 (1), 28–9.

de Jong, A. & De Wert, G.M. (2015) Prenatal screening: an ethical agenda for the near future. *Bioethics*. 29 (1), 46–55.

de Wert, G. (2013) 'Medicalisering' van de voortplanting: een ethische verkenning van prenatale screening. *Tijdschrift voor Gezondheidszorg en Ethiek*, 23 (3), 78–83.

de Wert, G., Dondorp, W. & Bianchi, D.W. (2018) Fetal therapy for Down syndrome: an ethical exploration. *Prenatal Diagnosis*, 37 (3), 222–8.

Deans, Z., Clarke, A.J. & Newson, A.J. (2015) For your interest? The ethical acceptability of using non-invasive prenatal testing to test 'purely for information'. *Bioethics*, 29 (1), 19–25.

Dondorp, W., de Wert G., Bombard Y., Bianchi, D.W., Bergmann, C., Borry, P., Chitty, L.S., Fellmann, F., Forzano, F., Hall, A., Henneman, L., Howard, H.C, Lucassen, A., Ormond, K., Peterlin, B., Radojkovic, D., Rogowski. W., Soller, M., Tibben. A., Tranebjærg, L., van El, C.G. & Cornel, M.C. (2015) Non-invasive prenatal testing for aneuploidy and beyond: challenges of responsible innovation in prenatal screening. *European Journal of Human Genetics*, 23 (11), 1438–50.

Dondorp, W. & de Wert, G. (2018) Ethical issues in maternal-fetal medicine. In: Rodeck, C.H. & Whittle, M.J. (eds). *Fetal Medicine: Basic Science and Clinical Practice*. London: Elsevier, Chapter 15.

Dondorp, W. & van Lith, J. (2015) Dynamics of prenatal screening: new developments challenging the ethical framework. *Bioethics*, 29 (1), ii–iv.

Donley, G., Hull, S.C. & Berkman, B.E. (2012) Prenatal whole genome sequencing: just because we can, should we? *Hastings Center Report*, 42 (4), 28–40.

Edvardsson, K., Lalos, A., Ahman, A., Small, R., Graner. S. & Mogren, I. (2016) Increasing possibilities – increasing dilemmas: a qualitative study of Swedish midwives' experiences of ultrasound use in pregnancy. *Midwifery*, 42, 46–53.

Feinberg, J. (1984) *Harm to Others. The Moral Limits of the Criminal Law*. New York and Oxford, Oxford University Press.

Health Council of the Netherlands. (2013) *NIPT: dynamiek en ethiek van prenatale screening*. The Hague: Gezondheidsraad.

Hens, K. (2017) Neurological diversity and epigenetic influences in utero. An ethical investigation of maternal responsibility towards the future child. In: Hens K., Cutas, D. & Horstkoetter, D. (eds.) *Parental Responsibility in the Context of Neuroscience and Genetics*. International Library of Ethics, Law, and the New Medicine. New York Springer, pp. 105–19.

Jorgensen, J.M., Hedley, P.L., Gjerris, M. & Christiansen, M. (2014) Including ethical considerations in models for first-trimester screening for pre-eclampsia. *Reproductive Biomedicine Online*, 28 (5), 638–43.

Juth, N. & Munthe, C. (2012) *The Ethics of Screening in Health Care and Medicine: Serving Society or Serving the Patient?* Dordrecht, Heidelberg, London, New York: Springer.

Murray, T.H. (1987) Moral obligations to the not-yet born: the fetus as patient. *Clinical Perinatology*, 14 (2), 329–43.

Parens, E. & Asch, A. (1999) The disability rights critique of prenatal genetic testing. Reflections and Recommendations. *Hastings Center Report*. 29 (5), S1–22.

Stein, Z., Susser, M. & Guterman, A.V. (1973) Screening programme for prevention of Down's syndrome. *The Lancet*. 1 (7798), 305–10.

van der Schoot, C.E., Hahn, S. & Chitty, L.S. (2008) Non-invasive prenatal diagnosis and determination of fetal Rh status. *Seminars Fetal and Neonatal Medicine*, 13 (2), 63–8.

Zhong, Y., Tuuli, M. & Odibo A.O. (2010) First-trimester assessment of placenta function and the prediction of preeclampsia and intrauterine growth restriction. *Prenatal Diagosis*, 30 (4), 293–308.

13 Beyond the fetal patient: the ethics of fetal treatment for Down syndrome

Guido de Wert and Wybo Dondorp

Introduction

The field of fetal therapy has seen important changes in the past decades (Deprest *et al.*, 2011). With improving technology, there has been a shift away from high risk 'open fetal surgery' (which involves opening the uterus in order to operate on the fetus) to minimally-invasive endoscopic procedures and pharmacotherapeutic approaches. As these may still come with significant risks both for the pregnant woman and the developing fetus, a second important development is the move beyond 'heroic' attempts at saving fetuses against all odds towards evidence-based treatments. There is now a shared understanding that new fetal treatments ought to be introduced in a clinical research setting, ideally using randomized controlled trials (RCTs), based on prior preclinical evidence from animal studies regarding initial safety and efficacy (Deprest *et al.*, 2011). Connected to these developments is an important broadening of the scope of the field. Whereas fetal therapy was initially aimed at giving fetuses with lethal conditions 'a chance for life' (Noble & Rodeck, 2008: 227), interventions are now also being developed for non-lethal conditions, in cases where intervening as early as in utero would lead to better long-term health prospects.

From an ethical perspective, these changes should all be welcomed. The trend towards safer and evidence-based interventions partly comes in response to earlier concerns about exposing women to disproportionate risks of highly experimental interventions offered outside a proper research setting. The broadening of the scope to include non-lethal conditions serves the morally important aim of giving children better lives. At the same time, these developments change the landscape for the ethics of fetal therapy, in the sense of raising new issues, requiring new concepts and setting the stage for new debates. (Dondorp & De Wert, 2018).

For instance, as the chapters by Joanne Verweij and Angus Clarke in this volume make clear, recruiting pregnant women for clinical trials presents difficult challenges that defy easy answers. Moreover, on the conceptual level, the move towards fetal therapy for non-lethal conditions both allows and requires ethical reflection to leave the unhelpful notion of 'the fetus as a patient' behind. As is pointed out in several of the chapters in this volume, the problem with that notion is twofold: it lacks a clear foundation and it threatens the position of the pregnant woman as a patient in her own right. However, when the aim is to provide future children with better lives through earlier interventions, there is no need to even ask whether the fetus has a moral status that would give it a claim to such treatment. Consider the (experimental) treatment for 'brittle bones' as discussed by Verweij: this is not about treating the fetus for its own sake; it is about treating the fetus in order to serve the interests of the future child.

In this chapter, we will discuss a further example of fetal therapy with this aim: treatment of fetuses diagnosed with trisomy 21 through maternally administered food supplements. Hopes are that by raising the IQ of children with DS, it will improve their quality of life. We will 1) briefly set out the rationale for offering this treatment prenatally, 2) explore possible objections to the very idea of a treatment for DS, 3) discuss conditions for offering this treatment both in the context of trials and as established therapy, and 4) ask whether and to what extent its availability would change the moral weight of the choices open to pregnant women with a fetus affected by trisomy 21.

With regard to terminology, we find it important to make the following preliminary remarks. First, although neurocognitive treatment addresses a key aspect of the condition, 'treatment for DS' is in so far a misnomer in that the underlying syndrome remains unaffected. There is currently no realistic prospect of a comprehensive treatment for DS. As this would require taking out or silencing the third copy of chromosome 21 in all cells of the body, this is only conceivable through future forms of gene-editing of oocytes or early embryos. At present, the relevant research is still at the basic science stage (Jiang *et al.*, 2013; Mentis, 2016). Second, convenient terms, such as 'fetal treatment' or 'fetal therapy', should not let us forget that all interventions targeting the fetus will have to pass through the pregnant woman's body, thus making her the patient whose interests should come first and whose consent will always be needed.

This chapter expands upon the reasoning in our earlier paper on the ethics of fetal treatment for DS with Diana Bianchi (De Wert, Dondorp & Bianchi, 2017). The scientific background and state of the art (summarized in the next section) are more extensively described in that paper.

The rationale for fetal neurocognitive treatment for DS

Only a few decades ago, DS was still regarded as an untreatable condition. As a consequence of serious congenital heart or intestinal anomalies, many infants born with DS did not survive the neonatal period, and those who did were often institutionalized. This picture is no longer true for today. Children with DS are now offered routine treatment of abnormalities in almost all organ systems that may be affected by the syndrome. As a result, life expectancy has dramatically improved. Moreover, in many countries it has become normal for children with DS to be raised by their families and to attend public schools (Newton *et al.*, 2015).

In addition to tests and therapies for a broad range of somatic conditions that may come with the syndrome, there seems to be a growing interest in developing neurocognitive treatment targeting the intellectual disability that (in varying degrees) affects people with DS. In general, the goal is to raise a person's intellectual quotient (IQ) to facilitate improvement in independent living skills. To date, a whole range of different molecules have been tested in adult and adolescent clinical trials, as reviewed in Guedj *et al.* (2014). While some of these molecules have demonstrated limited clinical benefits, the majority has not shown statistically significant improvement in treated individuals. Part of the explanation may be that the treatments are being administered too late in life.

This is also the rationale for moving treatment to the prenatal period. As deviation from typical fetal development starts to occur by the second trimester, leading to neuronal progenitor cells dying in fetuses with DS, several groups have hypothesized that, if treatment is early enough to reverse this process, it may lead to more typical brain growth and intercellular wiring and possibly also to improved postnatal cognitive performance (Guedj & Bianchi, 2013; Stagni *et al.*, 2015).

A first clinical trial is reported to be underway at the University of Texas Southwestern Medical Center (USA), comparing maternal administration of fluoxetine (Prozac) to a placebo control (Rochman, 2016). Based on studies in DS-mouse models, the idea is that by increasing the availability of serotonin (a neurotransmitter), fluoxetine will improve the formation of neurons in the brains of fetuses with trisomy 21. Other researchers have expressed reservations about giving fluoxetine to pregnant women without a psychiatric indication (Rochman, 2016). In view of the need for adequate preclinical data from animal models regarding the safety of an efficacious dose, there is a concern that this trial may have started prematurely.

In searching for alternative substances, researchers at Tufts University Medical School (USA) have identified a range of candidate molecules that are both confirmed to be safe for administration as food supplements by the United States Food and Drug Administration (FDA) and expected to reverse abnormal embryonic brain phenotype on the basis of extensive preclinical research (Guedj *et al.*, 2016). Clinical trials with selected food supplements are expected to start in the next few years (De Wert, Dondorp & Bianchi, 2017).

Ethics of neurocognitive treatment for DS: parents' views

One may think that safe and effective neurocognitive treatment for DS is as obviously a good thing as safe and effective treatment for osteogenesis imperfecta (OI), the 'brittle bones' disorder for which fetal therapy is currently being developed (as discussed in the chapter by Verweij). Much as reducing the risk of fractures for persons born with OI can be expected to improve their quality of life by allowing them to maintain independent mobility, a similar benefit would seem to result from limiting the degree of intellectual disability for persons born with DS. Raising their IQ will enable people with DS to have more control over their own lives, thus also taking away what they may experience as a source of frustration (Solomon, 2012). In addition to serving as a highly useful 'general purpose means' necessary for all possible life plans that a person may have (Buchanan *et al.*, 2000: 167), the ability to reason tends to be regarded as an essential part of human flourishing in itself (Nussbaum, 2009). How would promoting this ability in persons with DS be anything else but a morally worthwhile aim? Moreover, parents of children with DS would benefit considerably by being freed from the responsibilities related to their child's lifelong dependence and the connected concerns about who will take care of the child when they themselves are old and frail or have died (Skotko *et al.*, 2011).

But whereas it will be difficult to find parents of children with OI rejecting the very idea of a cure for that condition, things are different with DS. In a survey among parents of children with DS, Canadian researchers explored how they would perceive the hypothetical availability of a treatment that would mitigate or completely reverse intellectual disability in their child (Inglis *et al.*, 2014). As reported by the researchers, parental attitudes toward a possible cure for DS-related intellectual disability were complex and affected by different and sometimes conflicting ethical considerations. Of note, this concerned a scenario of postnatal treatment; we are unaware of similar research addressing a possible prenatal treatment option. Although – as we will suggest below – the difference is ethically relevant, the possible concerns are overlapping.

Most parents supported the statement that reducing intellectual disability in individuals affected with DS would be a good thing (Inglis *et al.*, 2014). Their arguments referred to enhanced independence and improved quality of life both for the child and the family. However, only a smaller proportion would want to use this for their own child. Several parents objected to the fact that neurocognitive treatment would change their child's personality. Many of those rejecting the very idea of neurocognitive treatment argued that the real problem was the lack of societal acceptance of diversity rather than their child's level of functioning (Inglis *et al.*, 2014).

Is neurocognitive treatment for DS intrinsically problematic?

The view that neurocognitive treatment for DS is intrinsically problematic, is strongly held among parents who are actively involved in the Down Syndrome community. As quoted by Andrew Solomon (2012), some of these parents feel that even 'talk about a cure is to diminish the value of the people who are alive with Down syndrome.' (p. 219) This line of argument tunes in with the well-known 'disability-rights critique' of prenatal screening and diagnosis (Parens & Asch, 2003). Much as these practices, treatment for DS would send a discriminatory message of (parental and societal) non-acceptance. Following this view, if anything is in need of change it is not people with conditions such as DS, but society's failure to properly support them (Davis, 2010). Behind this, one may discern the so-called 'social model of disability', according to which sociocultural barriers turn what is really only diversity into disability (Shakespeare, 2014). Whereas the opposite 'medical model' is seen as focusing on selective reproduction and normalizing treatment in order to reduce diversity, the social model calls for societal change aimed at facilitating inclusion and embracing diversity.

We do not think that this way of framing things is really helpful. Although it is certainly true that society should be more inclusive of people with conditions such as DS, the social-model perspective is one-sided in that it reduces their difficulties to mere prejudice and exclusion (Glover, 2006; Shakespeare, 2014). It is problematic when prioritizing societal change leads to denying affected individuals the opportunity of profiting from treatment that would enhance their quality of life. We also do not think that the abstract notion of 'diversity' as a social good, or the perception of disability as providing parents or society with options for moral growth (Garland-Thomson, 2012), can possibly justify such denial. Whereas this is obvious with regard to conditions such as OI, the same line of reasoning should apply to treatment for DS. And when this is obvious for treating the whole range of somatic conditions associated with DS, why would things be different with regard to improving cognition? Is it not simply a matter of justice to remove barriers to equal opportunities caused by disorders or handicaps (Buchanan *et al.*, 2000)? Is it not ironic that disability-rights reasoning would require keeping those barriers in place?

Further ethical concerns

But not all of those parents in the Canadian attitude study who were critical of the idea of a cure for DS based their reasoning on categorical objections related to disability rights or maintaining diversity. Several were simply not convinced that, on balance, their child would indeed benefit from such treatment. More specifically, their concern was that such treatment would interfere with their child's personality (Inglis *et al.*, 2014). In this connection it is important to note that the hypothetical 'cure' in this study was postnatal neurocognitive treatment, where parents of DS children of a broad age-range were asked whether they would now consider this for their child. Clearly, the 'change of personality' objection would not seem to apply to the same treatment when administered prenatally. In fact, some of the parents who raised this concern said they might have considered treatment at or before birth, when their child's personality was still to be formed, but not later in its life (Inglis *et al.*, 2014).

Other possible psychosocial concerns apply to both pre- and postnatally administered treatment. These relate to the fact that even if such treatment is effective, a comprehensive cure for DS will not (yet) be within reach. For instance, it may be that a significant but partial improvement in cognitive functioning will make persons with Down Syndrome only more aware of not being able to fully participate in society, or to realize the professional and reproductive options open to others (Solomon, 2012). They may also be more aware of the threat of developing early onset dementia, something that neurocognitive fetal treatment may or may not be able to avert.

Moreover: to the extent that such treatment would bring the IQ of some people with DS into the typical range, they would still be physically recognizable. How would this affect their social functioning and acceptance (Inglis *et al.*, 2014)? It can be imagined that for those with a normalized IQ, those DS traits will be experienced as telling a story about them that is at odds with who they really are. It is not impossible that this leads to more requests for 'facial correction' cosmetic surgery. In the past debate about the ethics of such corrections as requested by parents of children with DS, these were criticized from a disability-rights perspective as involving failure on the part of those parents as well as of society to fully accept people with DS (Jones, 2000; Goeke, 2003). This debate may have to be reconsidered when neurocognitive therapy proves effective, as this would arguably change the moral meaning of such corrections.

We conclude that although categorical objections to neurocognitive treatment of DS are not convincing, and although such treatment would seem to be able to contribute to the quality of life of people living with that condition, there are also concerns in the light of which the precise balance of benefits and harms is still an open question. However, these concerns are all hypothetical and can only be addressed in the context of a post-implementation evaluation of neurocognitive treatment. Therefore, we regard them as a reason for careful monitoring and psychosocial follow-up research, rather than for questioning the development and introduction of this treatment.

Clinical trials: challenges of recruitment and timing

Given that fetal treatment trials are meant to find out if the intervention is safe and effective, participation should only be offered to pregnant women whose fetus has a confirmed diagnosis of the relevant disorder (Deprest *et al.*, 2011). This means that a positive screening test would not be sufficient for inclusion in trials investigating fetal treatment for DS. To be eligible for participation, women should have a confirmed diagnosis of carrying a trisomy 21 fetus based on amniocentesis or chorionic villus sampling (CVS). Moreover, both in view of the need to have sufficient postnatal follow-up without including more research subjects than necessary, and in order not to expose participating women to the connected risks of therapeutic misconception and decision regret (see the chapters by Verweij and Clarke), inclusion should further be limited to women who have already decided on independent grounds that they will not ask for a termination (Deprest *et al.*, 2011). Of course, the message should not be that trial participation would commit them to continuing the pregnancy. The loss of data that termination would entail is not a justification for any form of pressure in this regard (Noble & Rodeck, 2008). Importantly, the information provided to candidate-participants should include, quite explicitly, that even if the treatment under investigation proves effective, a comprehensive cure for DS should not be expected.

As neurodevelopmental considerations may require administering the intervention as early as possible (i.e., in the first trimester) (Stagni *et al.*, 2015), a tension emerges between these inclusion criteria on the one hand, and ethical concerns about time pressure that might interfere with well-considered reproductive choice on the other. Further challenges arising with a push for early diagnosis and decision-making relate to the relatively high spontaneous fetal loss rate in the first trimester (especially concerning aneuploid fetuses), meaning that women may be exposed to possible treatment-related risks 'for nothing', and to the fact that comorbidities (e.g., heart defects) that some women carrying a DS-fetus may regard as relevant for whether or not to choose to have a termination, may only come to light later in pregnancy. Clearly, these challenges need to be taken into account both when deciding about the optimal trial protocol and as part of balanced information and counselling.

Thin lines between therapy, prevention and enhancement

Should fetal neurocognitive treatment for DS prove to be effective (more so than postnatal treatment) and safe, it may become established therapy. For offering this, the reasons behind the requirement of a prior decision to keep the pregnancy no longer apply. After all, as we will discuss in the next section, the idea is precisely to provide women with a further option that may allow them to make a different choice than they would otherwise have done. But what about the requirement that fetal treatment can only be considered on the basis of a final diagnosis? A strong argument for keeping this as a general condition for the field is that fetal therapy usually comes with burdens and risks both for the woman and the child-to-be and should therefore only be considered on strict conditions, including the requirement of a confirmed diagnosis (Deprest *et al.*, 2011).

However, there may be reasons for considering exceptions. A notable exception is the administration of dexamethasone to women *at risk of* bearing a fetus with congenital adrenal hyperplasia (CAH), as discussed in the chapter by Mathias Wirth and Marc-Antoine Marquis. The reason for making this exception is that treatment (in order to avoid virilization of affected female fetuses) has to start early in pregnancy, at a time when it is still unclear if the fetus is male or female and, when female, if she is affected. As Wirth and Marquis explain, this practice is contested for several reasons including the charge of exposing unaffected fetuses to treatment that may come with certain risks. It is expected that, with the new cell-free DNA based non-invasive prenatal test, it will become possible to obtain a diagnosis early enough to treat only affected fetuses and thus avoid the need for making this exception (see the chapter by Wirth & Marquis).

In our discussion, it is understandable that women determined to keep the child (those using prenatal screening for preparation rather than termination) tend to be reluctant to expose the pregnancy to the risks (however small) of invasive testing for diagnostic certainty (Van Schendel *et al.*, 2014; Van Schendel *et al.*, 2016). In view of this, it may perhaps be argued that a positive non-invasive screening result should suffice to make them eligible for treatment for DS. This would also remove the time pressure still connected to the condition of a final diagnosis preceding the start of treatment. Clearly, making this exception for these reasons should only be considered if it has been established not only that fetal treatment for DS is indeed effective and safe, but also that it should be started in the first weeks of pregnancy for it to be as effective as possible.

While this would blur the line between treatment and prevention, a conceivable next step would be to offer this intervention to all women in early pregnancy as a 'pre-emptive prevention'. This might be regarded as on a par (to some extent) with folic acid supplementation to reduce the risk of neural tube defects. However, this raises a further question with regard to the aim of the intervention: as most pregnant women will not be carrying a trisomy 21 fetus (or a fetus with another condition leading to a child with a cognitive impairment), any effect on neurocognitive development would in those cases be a matter of enhancement rather than prevention. This raises a Pandora's box of ethical questions. Whereas some will object that this opens the gates towards problematic forms of eugenics, others may argue that, in principle, cognitive enhancement would fall under a moral duty of prospective parents to make sure that their children have the best possible lives (Savulescu & Kahane, 2009). A proactive ethical analysis of this scenario is certainly in place.

Fetal treatment and reproductive choice: two moral pitfalls

Fetal neurocognitive treatment for DS creates a further option for pregnant women found to be carrying a trisomy 21 fetus, in addition to the choice between terminating the pregnancy and preparing for a child with special needs. Women who without this new treatment option might have considered asking for a termination, may now decide to continue the pregnancy. However, the ethics of this development can be analysed in different ways that may each come with a moral pitfall.

From a 'pro-life' perspective, fetal treatment for DS may be welcomed as it has the potential to reduce the number of selective terminations of trisomy 21 pregnancies and thus to save the life of affected fetuses. In fact, this is in line with how the aim of prenatal diagnosis was understood by Jérôme Lejeune, the French pediatrician and geneticist traditionally credited with the discovery of the chromosomal basis of DS. Lejeune has always regarded the use of prenatal diagnosis for terminations as a morally problematic form of medicine that should ideally be replaced by facilitating treatment (Neri & Opitz, 2009). Others have also stated that the development of safe and effective fetal therapy belongs to the 'ultimate goals of prenatal diagnosis' (Epstein *et al.*, 1983: 76). As such, this seems an ideal that no one could reasonably criticize. That is to say: until it takes the form of a political agenda that denies women the right to abortion on the assumption that fetuses have a right to be treated. Whereas it should certainly be welcomed that safe and effective fetal therapy gives women a further choice, presenting this as the only acceptable (or even the morally preferred) option would be ethically problematic, given the contested nature of the underlying view of the status of the fetus.

From a liberal ('pro-choice') perspective, the development of this new option is to be regarded as in line with the very aim of prenatal testing, understood as serving reproductive autonomy by giving individual women or couples meaningful options for choice with regard to reproductive risks (Dondorp *et al.*, 2015). But with this liberal perspective, an opposite moral pitfall looms: the tendency to dismiss not termination, but the very option of fetal therapy as unnecessary. For instance, in a recent paper on the ethics of fetal surgery a clinician was quoted as saying that she did not understand 'why anyone would go to such lengths when they could simply abort and start over' (Antiel, 2016: 230). Although this is anecdotal and one would probably not find this view defended in the literature, it may be quite influential. Ethically this view is problematic, as it betrays a motivation that is either eugenic or paternalistic, or both. It fails to acknowledge that for a substantial number of women or couples, abortion is simply not acceptable, and that, for many of those couples who are not categorically opposed to termination, deciding to end a wanted pregnancy remains an extremely difficult choice that may have lifelong psychosocial consequences. Moreover, in many parts of the world, abortion is illegal.

Fetal treatment and parental responsibility

But this is only part of the story. For those intending or having decided to keep a trisomy-21 pregnancy, the option of neurocognitive treatment emerges as a choice in which the interests of the future child are at stake, so that their decision about fetal treatment (if indeed safe and effective) cannot be regarded as morally indifferent. As we have also argued in our chapter on the aims of prenatal screening elsewhere in this volume, this changes the moral landscape for decision-making and counselling. For unless the woman decides to terminate the pregnancy, there will be a child whose interests may be furthered or harmed by her choices including those with regard to treatment options.

As several authors have remarked, this is not something most pregnant women need to be reminded of. In fact, many go to great lengths in order to safeguard the healthy development of the fetus and to give their child an optimal start in life. The primary concern seems rather that they would accept any possible risks or burdens to themselves in order to benefit their unborn child (Smajdor, 2011; Sheppard, 2016). Although we agree that the risk of a hypertrophy of maternal responsibility should be taken seriously, we do not think it follows that professional counsellors should never try to convince women to have fetal treatment. For reasons given above, we agree they should refrain from directive counselling when the aim of the treatment is to save the fetus from a lethal disorder. However, when the health and wellbeing of the future child are at stake, we would argue that, under further conditions of proven effectiveness and proportionality of the intended treatment, professionals can be expected to, if necessary, remind women of their responsibility.

Of course, one should only think here of established and generally accessible forms of fetal treatment that would protect the future child from significant and irreversible harm more effectively than options for postnatal treatment and without exposing the pregnant woman to a serious risk (Health Council of the Netherlands, 2009). The classic example is intrauterine blood transfusion for fetal anemia. When left untreated, this condition may lead not only to fetal or neonatal death, but also to neurological damage leading to cerebral palsy and/or mental retardation in surviving children (Lindenburg *et al.*, 2013). Depending on the outcome of the impending clinical trials and follow-up research, it may well be that fetal neurocognitive treatment for DS would also fit this profile.

Conclusion

Our conclusions are, first, that categorical objections to neurocognitive treatment of DS are not convincing – on the contrary, there are strong ethical reasons supporting the development of this treatment. Second, as it is still to be established whether neurocognitive treatment for DS effectively raises IQ and does so more effectively when initiated during (early) pregnancy than after birth, rigorous clinical trials are needed; challenges regarding recruitment of pregnant women and timing of the intervention should be given due attention. Third, monitoring and follow-up studies will be needed to determine whether such treatment is indeed beneficial for those born with the syndrome. Fourth, if prenatal neurocognitive treatment of DS would become established therapy, further scenarios of prevention and cognitive enhancement require a proactive ethical analysis. Fifth, as established therapy, it will give pregnant women carrying a fetus with trisomy 21 an additional reproductive option that should neither be presented to them as a morally superior choice in comparison with termination, nor withheld from them as a redundant alternative to it. Finally, if the woman decides to continue the pregnancy, the new option changes the moral landscape, in so far as choices that affect the wellbeing of the future child are not morally indifferent and may allow health professionals to make recommendations for the benefit of the future child.

References

Antiel, R.M. (2016) Ethical challenges in the new world of maternal-fetal surgery. *Semin Perinatol*, 40 (4), 227–233.

Buchanan, A., Brock, D.W., Daniels, N. & Wikler, D. (2000) From chance to choice. *Genetics & Justice*. Cambridge: Cambridge University Press.

Davis, D.S. (2010). *Genetic Dilemmas: Reproductive Technology, Parental Choices, and Children's Futures*, 2nd edn. Oxford: Oxford University Press.

Deprest, J., Toelen, J., Debyser, Z., Rodrigues, C., Devlieger, R., De Catte, L., Lewi, L., Van Mieghem, T., Naulaers, G., Vandevelde, M., Claus, F. & Dierickx, K. (2011) The fetal patient – ethical aspects of fetal therapy, *Facts Views Vis Obgyn*. 3 (3), 221–227.

de Wert, G., Dondorp, W. & and Bianchi, D.W. (2017) Fetal therapy for Down syndrome: an ethical exploration. *Prenat Diagn*, 37 (3), 222–228.

Dondorp, W., de Wert, G., Bombard, Y., Bianchi, D.W., Bergmann, C., Borry, P., Chitty, L.S., Fellmann, F., Forzano, F., Hall, A., Henneman, L., Howard, H.C.,

Lucassen, A., Ormond, K., Peterlin, B., Radojkovic, D., Rogowski, W., Soller, M., Tibben, A., Tranebjærg, L., van El, C.G. & Cornel, M.C. (2015) Non-invasive prenatal testing for aneuploidy and beyond: challenges of responsible innovation in prenatal screening. *European Journal of Human Genetics*, 23 (11), 1438–50.

Dondorp, W. & de Wert, G. (2018) Ethical issues in maternal-fetal medicine. (in press) In: Rodeck, C.H. & Whittle, M.J. (eds). *Fetal medicine: basic science and clinical practice.* London, Elsevier, Chapter 15.

Epstein, C.J., Cox, D.R., Schonberg, S.A. & Hogge, W.A. (1983) Recent developments in the prenatal diagnosis of genetic diseases and birth defects. *Annu Rev Genet*, 17, 49–83.

Garland-Thomson, R. (2012) The case for conserving disability. *J Bioeth Inq*, 9 (3), 339–355.

Glover, J. (2006) *Choosing children. The ethical dilemmas of genetic intervention.* Oxford: Oxford University Press.

Goeke, J. (2003) Parents speak out: facial plastic surgery for children with Down syndrome. *Education and Training in Developmental Disabilities*, 38 (3), 323–333.

Guedj, F. & Bianchi, D.W. (2013) Noninvasive prenatal testing creates an opportunity for antenatal treatment of Down syndrome. *Prenat Diagn*, 33 (6), 614–618.

Guedj, F., Bianchi, D.W. & Delabar, J.M. (2014) Prenatal treatment of Down syndrome: a reality? *Curr Opin Obstet Gynecol*, 26 (2), 92–103.

Guedj, F., Pennings, J.L., Massingham, L.J., Wick, H.C., Siegel, A.E., Tantravahi U. & Bianchi, D.W. (2016) An integrated human/murine transcriptome and pathway approach to identify prenatal treatments for Down syndrome. *Sci Rep*, 6, 323–353.

Health Council of the Netherlands (2009) *Care for the unborn child. Ethical and legal aspects of fetal therapy.* The Hague: Health Council of the Netherlands.

Inglis, A., Lohn, Z., Austin J.C. & Hippman C. (2014) A 'cure' for Down syndrome: what do parents want? *Clin Genet*, 86 (4), 310–317.

Jiang, J., Jing, Y., Cost, G.J., Chiang, J.C., Kolpa, H.J., Cotton, A.M., Carone, D.M., Carone, B.R., Shivak, D.A., Guschin, D.Y., Pearl, J.R., Rebar, E.J., Byron, M., Gregory, P.D., Brown, C.J., Urnov, F.D., Hall L.L. & Lawrence. J.B. (2013) Translating dosage compensation to trisomy 21. *Nature.* 500 (7462), 296–300.

Jones, R.B. (2000) Parental consent to cosmetic facial surgery in Down's syndrome. *J Med Ethics*, 26 (2), 101–102.

Lindenburg, I.T., van Klink J.M., Smits-Wintjens, V.E., van Kamp, I.L., Oepkes, D. & Lopriore, E. (2013) Long-term neurodevelopmental and cardiovascular outcome after intrauterine transfusions for fetal anaemia: a review. *Prenat Diagn*, 33 (9), 815–822.

Mentis, A.F. (2016) Epigenomic engineering for Down syndrome. *Neurosci Biobehav Rev*,71, 323–327.

Neri, G. & Opitz, J.M. (2009) Down syndrome: comments and reflections on the 50th anniversary of Lejeune's discovery. *Am J Med Genet A.* 149A (12), 2647–2654.

Newton, R.W., Puri, S. & and Marder, L. (2015) *Down Syndrome. Current perspectives.* London, Mac Keith Press.

Noble, R. & Rodeck, C.H. (2008) Ethical considerations of fetal therapy. *Best Pract Res Clin Obstet Gynaecol.* 22 (1), 219–231.

Nussbaum, M. (2009) The capabilities of people with cognitive disabilities. *Metaphilosophy.* 40 (3–4), 331–351.

Parens, E. & Asch, A. (2003) Disability rights critique of prenatal genetic testing: reflections and recommendations. *Ment Retard Dev Disabil Res Rev*, 9 (1), 40–47.

Rochman, B. (2016) Parents turn to Prozac to treat Down syndrome. *MOT Technology Review*. Available at www.technologyreview.com/s/545191/parents-turn-to-prozac-to-treat-down-syndrome/

Savulescu, J. & Kahane, G. (2009) The moral obligation to create children with the best chance of the best life. *Bioethics*, 23 (5), 274–290.

Shakespeare, T. (2014) *Disability rights and wrongs revisited*, 2nd edn. London and New York: Routledge.

Sheppard, M.K. (2016) Vulnerability, therapeutic misconception and informed consent: is there a need for special treatment of pregnant women in fetus-regarding clinical trials? *J Med Ethics*, 42 (2), 127–131.

Skotko, B.G., Levine, S.P. & Goldstein, R. (2011) Having a son or daughter with Down syndrome: perspectives from mothers and fathers. *Am J Med Genet A*, 155A (10), 2335–2347.

Smajdor, A. (2011) Ethical challenges in fetal surgery. *J Med Ethics*, 37(2), 88–91.

Solomon, A. (2012). *Far from the tree. Parents, children and the search for identity.* New York: Scribner.

Stagni, F., Giacomini, A., Guidi, S., Ciani E. & Bartesaghi R. (2015) Timing of therapies for Down syndrome: the sooner, the better. *Front Behav Neurosci*, 9, 265.

van Schendel, R.V., Kleinveld, J.H., Dondorp, W.J., Pajkrt, E, Timmermans, D.R., Holtkamp, K.C., Karsten, M., Vlietstra, A.L., Lachmeijer A.M. & L. Henneman (2014). Attitudes of pregnant women and male partners towards non-invasive prenatal testing and widening the scope of prenatal screening. *Eur J Hum Genet*, 22 (12), 1345–1350.

van Schendel, R.V., Page-Christiaens, G.C., Beulen, L., Bilardo, C.M., de Boer, M.A., Coumans, A.B.C., Faas, B.H., van Langen, I.M., Lichtenbelt, K.D., van Maarle, M.C., Macville, M.V.E., Oepkes, D., Pajkrt, E. & Henneman L. (Dutch NIPT Consortium) (2016) Trial by Dutch laboratories for evaluation of non-invasive prenatal testing. Part II-women's perspectives. *Prenatal Diagnosis*, 36 (12), 1091–1098.

14 Prenatal therapy for differences of sexual development (DSD): fuzzy boundaries in the clinical discussion and the ethical debate

Mathias Wirth and Marc-Antoine Marquis

Is it morally permissible to administer a medication to fetuses in order to limit variations of sexual anatomy (e.g. virilization) and behavior (e.g. "tomboyism/lesbianism"), without convincing evidence of its innocuousness? If this practice aimed at guaranteeing a normal appearance of genital organs, would banning it do injustice to affected individuals? Arguably, a significant majority of our contemporary societies expect sexual and gender appearances to be concordant. Justification for administering drugs to fetuses or refusing to do so requires solid grounding; the debate surrounding the use of dexamethasone to prevent virilization and normalize atypical genitalia in cases of congenital adrenal hyperplasia is a striking illustration (Johnston 2012). The entire dispute, with its kaleidoscope of arguments, offers a relevant subject to analyze the status of the fetus as patient.

Since the 1980s, the corticosteroid dexamethasone (DEX) has been used to treat fetuses with congenital adrenal hyperplasia (CAH), a cluster of rare but serious genetic diseases that, if left untreated, can lead to death from severe hypoglycemia, electrolyte abnormalities or hemodynamic instability. Such dire complications have led many countries to include some forms of CAH in their neonatal screening programs (Dreger *et al.*, 2012; Falhammer *et al.*, 2014; Hirvikoski *et al.*, 2012; Pearce *et al.*, 2016). Furthermore, CAH is one of the most common causes of 'ambiguous genitalia', a clinical entity characterized by the difficulty in ascribing the "correct" sex to an infant based on anatomy alone. Fetal DEX therapy concerns exclusively female fetuses with CAH at risk for sexual ambiguity. Fetal DEX does not prevent illness, nor the lifelong dependence on medication, but reduces virilization of female external organs, potentially avoiding surgical correction after birth (Hirvikoski *et al.*, 2012). Not only can this prevent the pain and usual risks of any surgical intervention, it also prevents the complications related to genital transformation, including but not limited to decreased sensation after clitoroplasty (Wiesemann *et al.*, 2010).

Clinical and ethical discourse surrounding the use of DEX for CAH is characterized by a vagueness that will be discussed here. This will shed light on the issue of the fetus being seen as a patient, the importance of which is rapidly growing due to the increasing detection of hereditary diseases through non-invasive prenatal testing (NIPT), including the detection of CAH.

The following approach is intended: (1) After an introduction to differences of sexual differentiation and how this term relates to intersex and CAH, (2) the role of DEX in the treatment of fetuses will be clarified. Here, vagueness exists because of lack of considerable long-term studies on the side-effects of DEX. Overall, there is substantial uncertainty surrounding the use of DEX. (3) It will then be argued that the ethical discussion itself is nebulous, specifically because of scarce ethical conclusions in the face of unconvincing long-term safety data on DEX, inaccurate disease classification of ambiguous genitalia, and an implied assumption that girls with sexual ambiguity would have preferred DEX over surgery. (4) Under these circumstances, we conclude the use of DEX must be discouraged for ethical reasons. In this summative point, the moral status of the fetus as patient will be considered: on the whole, it is apparent that little protection is provided to fetuses at large, even more specifically to fetuses at risk of certain forms of differences of sexual development, because on the one hand it is agreed and accepted that a majority of the fetuses exposed to DEX will be exposed unnecessarily and, on the other, through exposure to DEX, the fetus is denied the right to accept its own innate identity, that may be an identity of sexual difference.

Intersex, differences of sexual development (DSD), and CAH

The term *disorders of sexual differentiation* was proposed in 2006 by the International Consensus Conference to describe "congenital conditions in which development of chromosomal, gonadal, or anatomical sex is atypical" (Hughes *et al.*, 2006). Although initially proposed as a descriptive alternative to perceived pejorative terms such as intersex, pseudohermaphroditism, hermaphroditism, and sex reversal, there remains significant controversy regarding its use and, indeed, its objective nature.[1] DSD form a very diverse set of entities. Some present with completely normal external genital organs, while others can manifest with significant sexual ambiguity. Concurrently, some DSD concern only the external appearance of the sexual organs, while others cause complex and severe disruptions of hormone synthesis and can lead to the death of a newborn in a matter of days without intervention. However, most DSD are not life-threatening, and do not necessarily reduce health-related quality of life (Rolston *et al.*, 2015).

Hence, ambiguous genitalia *per se* are not a medical emergency. It can however be the presenting sign of a serious underlying disease (Brain *et al.*, 2010), or itself the source of health problems, such as urinary incontinence or repeated urinary tract infections from a predisposing anatomy. In some cases, anomalies may impede urination altogether by disrupting the urinary outflow, in which case they require medical intervention to allow for proper organic functioning. Other cases will require monitoring for complications, such as malignant transformation of gonads or infertility. Operations of this kind can be distinguished from elective or cosmetic interventions aimed at imitating the average sexual anatomy (Arboleda, Sandberg, and Vilain, 2014).

Traditional practices of sex-reassignment surgeries for DSD in the Western world can be traced back to the *optimal gender policy* established in the 1950s by sexologist and psychologist John Money (1921–2006) and colleagues, according to which ambiguous genitalia had to be corrected as early as possible to allow for proper gender identification (Mieszczak, Houk, and Lee, 2009; Wiesemann *et al.*, 2010). Ethical justification for such interventions appealed to emotional and social harms predicted to be natural consequences of being sexually different. Within that framework, early surgeries were considered essential and urgent: "Gender assignment is a neonatal surgical emergency and must not be delayed until the child is older. Gender roles are learned: an infant can be satisfactorily raised as male or female regardless of genetic sex" (Canty, 1977: 279; a similar line of reasoning can be found in Sultan *et al.*, 2002).[2] Even nowadays, parents' wish to have a *normal child* – however culturally laden the term might be – is often the impetus animating the medical community into action (Sandberg, Gardner, and Cohen-Kettenis, 2012).

The decades separating our time and the era of the *optimal gender policy* have seen an important shift in perspective. Early sex-reassignment surgeries in cases of DSD are being more and more recognized as having potentially disastrous effects on children involved (Rolston *et al.*, 2015). Vivid accounts of traumatizing experiences and criticisms of a tradition of concealing information from patients run parallel to evolving ideas on patient consent. The dominant medical ethics discourse has endorsed a widened notion of patient consent over the last few decades (Worthington, 2002); children as patients also benefit now from a general appreciation of their autonomy, and an assumption that their consent, without being a *sine qua non* condition, merits careful attention – often sufficiently enough to postpone important medical decisions. As a result, the *optimal gender policy* contrasts with a *full-consent policy* which holds, in the case of DSD, that any genital surgery must be performed only when the person can fully consent to it (for differences between the two paradigms, see Wiesemann *et al.*, 2010). Although Joel Feinberg's concept of an "open future" (Feinberg, 1980; Millum, 2015), which grounds the *full-consent policy*, applies to many contexts in medicine, a full-consent model cannot be credibly applied to all non-urgent irrevocable decisions about children or fetuses. There will be decisions about a child that must be made before he or she can be seriously involved as it might be too late to decide when the child is finally competent to do so. Examples include compulsory immunizations, removal and relocation of a neglected child by state care, and important but non-urgent pharmacological or surgical interventions, such as treatment of an eyelid hemangioma to prevent amblyopia or surgical correction of intestinal malrotation. Some decisions must be made on behalf of a child if they are to be made at all. Similarly, while some cosmetic or medically unproblematic anatomical considerations in CAH are consistent with a full-consent policy, the decision to proceed with DEX therapy will often stem from other imperatives. The desire to protect a child from otherwise inevitable interventions at birth (surgically creating a urinary outflow tract, for instance), or from the psychological burden of social stigmatization, are both pertinent for fostering an *open future*.

Guidelines published in 2010 delineate important ethical principles pertaining to the wellbeing of the child and future adult, respect for self-determination and for family relationships, as well as clues for clinical practice (Wiesemann *et al.*, 2010). One aim of counselling parents is to stress children's potential to cope with gender differences, and that sublime ideas of "freaks" are unnecessary (Mieszczak, Houk, and Lee, 2009). In this vein, one could consider it a naturalistic fallacy to understand parents' and practitioners' usual reaction to sexual ambiguity as *natural*: also available are cultural and religious beliefs that welcome and reinforce diversity (Wirth, 2015). This is not to minimize the reality and power of stigmatization of DSD-children in contemporary life experiences (Rolston *et al.*, 2015). Indeed, failing to recognize the importance of social pressures might lead to sacrificing children's happiness in favor of pure political correctness. Multiple ramifications to this moral conundrum exist, notably that many adults with DSD have reported the negative effects that childhood sex-reassignment surgeries have had on them. It seems reasonable that feeling congruent with one's self without being mutilated weighs more than the possibility of being protected from bullying. The opposite, however, might also hold true.

CAH is a subset of DSD[3] characterized by defective synthesis of hormones by the adrenal glands. Through mutations affecting specific enzymes in the biochemical pathway, hormone synthesis is destabilized, resulting in the deficient production of some hormones (specifically cortisol) with excessive amounts of other hormones (particularly testosterone) in affected individuals. Variations in the clinical presentation depend notably on chromosomal sex, the specific enzyme involved, and the degree of enzymatic malfunction.

The most common form of CAH is caused by mutation in the CYP21A2 gene, resulting in defective 21-hydroxylase enzyme and leads to a variable clinical picture. Some infants of either sex present early in the neonatal period with a serious, life-threatening "salt-wasting" form causing hypoglycemia and severe electrolyte abnormalities. Affected females (with 46, XX chromosomes) may also present at birth with ambiguous genitalia: a virilized appearance of the external sexual organs (for instance, clitoromegaly, fusion of the labia, etc.). Masculinization of female fetuses with CAH[4] begins *in utero* by exposure to increased amounts of androgens (Ahmed *et al.*, 2011). Along with their impact on genital molding, evidence suggests that androgens influence psychosexual development as well (Hughes *et al.*, 2006).

Unsurprisingly, the debate surrounding early sex-reassignment surgery in CAH mirrors that which is seen with DSD (e.g. Ogilvy-Stuart and Brain, 2004); interventions are being performed early in the neonatal period in some medical centers (Sturm, Durbin-Johnsen, and Kurzrock, 2015 report critically on this issue). In this context, DEX is an appealing alternative for females with CAH, as it might avoid the need for surgery and, at first sight, elude the ethical conundrum of sex-reassignment surgeries. Prenatal DEX administration, however, generates intense moral questions, stirring up debates in the medical community since its introduction, while attracting scrutiny from intersex defense groups. We turn to these matters in the next section.

The medical debate on DEX and female fetuses

The use of DEX to prevent virilization of female fetuses with CAH was first reported by a group of French physicians in 1984 (David and Forest, 1984); other reports quickly followed, corroborating the efficacy of DEX for this matter.

One of the most significant biochemical disturbances caused by a defective 21-hydroxylase enzyme is low levels of cortisol. As a result, the anterior pituitary gland increases its secretion of adrenocortocotropic hormone (ACTH), which in turn drives the production of steroid hormones and cortisol. In healthy individuals, the increase in cortisol production by the adrenal gland provides retroactive feedback to the pituitary gland to decrease the production of ACTH. In CAH, the ineffective cortisol production impedes this feedback loop, leaving ACTH production essentially unopposed and driving the adrenal gland to produce an increasing amount of steroids, which are then diverted into the production of androgens. While increased androgens do not have notable effects on male fetuses, they can induce female fetuses to masculinize, both genitally (giving rise to sexual ambiguity) and neurodevelopmentally. DEX, thought to be the most efficient pharmacological treatment available, bypasses the ineffective cortisol production of the 21-hydroxylase enzyme, reestablishes the feedback mechanism to the pituitary gland, decreases the secretion of ACTH, and reduces the amounts of androgens produced by the adrenal glands, thereby hindering the masculinization process (Bachelot *et al.*, 2017; Nebesio *et al.*, 2016).

To be effective, DEX must be administered as soon as possible when a pregnancy is confirmed in a mother at risk of bearing a fetus with CAH. Because virilization of the sexual organs begins as early as six weeks after conception, administration of DEX precedes the earliest time when fetal sex can be determined. In addition, while the CYP21A2 mutation can be detected through genetic testing (Baxter and Vilain, 2013; Arboleda *et al.*, 2013), such procedures cannot be undertaken reliably before 12 weeks by chorionic villus sampling or around 10 weeks of gestation by NIPT. Indeed, this implies that, at present, DEX must be administered before all relevant information is known – implying that 7 out of 8 fetuses will be treated for at least a few weeks without being the desired target of intervention and with no potential to benefit from it (Hirvikoski *et al.*, 2012; Miller and Witchel, 2013).

Even as new techniques of prenatal testing and diagnosis become available and allow precise identification of fetuses that are candidates for DEX therapy (Lajic *et al.*, 2004; Bachelot *et al.*, 2017), controversy remains regarding the deleterious effects of exposing a developing being to exogenous hormones. Medical research has raised concerns on the behavioral development of children, emphasizing the need for caution and surveillance on long-term effects of DEX on brain development and human metabolism (Bachelot *et al.*, 2017; Hirvikoski *et al.*, 2012); some commentators however question the causative role of DEX for these findings. Finally, critics also stress that virilization is vague, culturally dependent, and difficult to measure, hence arguing that the exploration and critical analysis of such phenomena in medicine is a strenuous task (Miller and Witchel, 2013).

Scholarly work from a Swedish group of physicians has led them to formulate a strong critique against those holding that DEX treatment is safe, calling for a ban on its antenatal use in Sweden (Dreger, Feder, and Tamar-Mattis, 2012). The team recalled that "there are plenty of theoretical harmful effects of foetal glucocorticoid exposure" (Lajic *et al.*, 2004: 63). They also reported severe side-effects seemingly correlated with *in utero* exposure to DEX, including cardiac septal hypertrophy, hydrocephalus, intrauterine growth problems, metabolic disturbances and other "negative effects on behavioral and somatic development" (Hirvikoski *et al.*, 2012: 1881; see also Falhammer *et al.*, 2014). However, the authors stress these side-effects occur rarely or can have multiple, complex causal factors to the point that it is difficult to associate them decisively with DEX (Lajic *et al.*, 2004). Most commentators, either sympathetic or hostile to fetal DEX therapy and including the aforementioned Swedish group, call for long-term studies to document adverse effects, both physiological and psychological (Lajic *et al.*, 2004). US researchers from University of California and Pittsburgh University Medical Center have stressed the teratogenic effect of high-dose DEX in animal experiments. It is worth noting that no such effects have been found at doses used in women at risk of having a girl with CAH (Johnston, 2012). Guidelines from the US Endocrine Society suggest keeping its use in fetuses within the realm of clinical trials (Speiser *et al.*, 2010). Owing to the paucity of long-term, large, and conclusive studies, the Swedish endocrinology group does not "consider it ethical to initiate further treatment" of fetuses at risk for CAH (Hirvikoski *et al.*, 2012: 1882), a statement hinting to the fact that information is lacking regarding follow-up of many, if not most, patients. It would be best practice that every child receives as good a follow-up as possible, to monitor for somatic, psychological, and cognitive wellbeing. Follow-up should not only be clinical but also made available to the medical community: in other words, these patients, receiving extraordinary therapy, must also receive extraordinary follow-up so as to monitor for possible complications related to DEX. And evidence about these potential complications should be made available to the public in order to support the making of clinical decisions and policy.

Recognizing that a significant portion of existing studies does not address the threat of harmful side-effects, including adverse effects on pregnant women which can be severe and require discontinuation of DEX therapy, one must be even more careful. The Swedish group brings important arguments to the debate, but seems to be dealing essentially with considerations of safety, at least in their newest publication (Hirvikoski *et al.*, 2012). They do not doubt DEX would be a welcome treatment should side-effects be absent or manageable and could be administered exclusively to female fetuses with CAH. Nonetheless, gender ethics, or closely related matters such as the question of autonomy and self-determination, would remain.

A group of mostly German, but also Austrian, Belgian, Dutch, English, and Italian scientists and physicians hold a position contrary to the Swedish scholars' approach.[5] Proponents of the prenatal use of DEX within this group have published studies demonstrating positive effects (e.g. Van Mil, and Hiort, 2008). They have eloquently written about the high scores of satisfaction with care amongst adult women with CAH, notably regarding virilization (Thyen *et al.*, 2014). A careful read of these studies does not obliterate worries about the long-term effects of DEX on patients, especially cognitive and behavioral problems (Blankenstein, 2014), which we propose to discuss in the next section.

The ethical debate on DEX and female fetuses

Immediate worries accompany the use of DEX to prevent virilization, as Sandberg, Gardner and Cohen-Ketternis (2012) have summarized. One interrogation was mentioned earlier in this chapter. One can reasonably expect that current biotechnologies such as NIPT will allow determination of the chromosomal sex of a fetus very early on, and help distinguish between affected females and unaffected (including carrier) fetuses as early as 7 to 9 weeks of gestation. In this context, one might wonder whether the balance of argumentation might favor treating fetuses known to be both female and affected, rather than refraining from intervening. While this is a reasonable conclusion within a strict biomedical model of risks and benefits, especially when considering the unsolved issues of iatrogenic risks, it is not certain that medical interventions prioritizing genders within a wide spectrum of possibilities are legitimate. From a wider angle, the relationship DEX therapy has with a culture of normalization will be analyzed here. The aim of this section is to tackle this question from several perspectives: first, by describing the relation of DEX to gender eugenics; then, by presenting a point of view for decision-making by re-evaluating the experimental nature of DEX; and finally, by arguing how the principle of proportionality applies.

(1) Perhaps the strongest argument against the use of DEX is a rejection of what we call "gender eugenics", to borrow the term from grievous events of the modern era. Robert Sparrow analyzed whether preimplantation genetic diagnosis (PGD) for DSD happens to be within the realm of eugenics or not. While PGD differs from fetal pharmacological interventions because it targets a number of very early embryos that have not yet developed into a fetus, Sparrow explicitly refers to CAH as an example of medical treatment of intersex conditions. To stress the significance of such interventions, he recalls the emergent character they used to have when a newborn bearing atypical genitalia contradicted the assumption that sex is by nature binary. As he observes, some forms of PGD must be valued 'in the name of medicine', when they help identify serious diseases that happen to include atypical genitalia as one of their manifestations. Apart from the possibility to detect genes directly linked to such phenotypical expressions (Wirth, 2012), Sparrow casts some doubts on the legitimacy of PGD should its motives rest on guaranteeing normal sexual organs. He however concludes that selection against some DSD that are a manifestation of serious medical conditions may be justified. He remains generally hesitant to apply the term "eugenics" to PGD, even when it boils down to cosmetics in cases of DSD. He is not alone when stating that diversity would be at risk should intersex conditions be annihilated through PGD used "in the name of normalization" (Sparrow, 2013).

(2) An argument, midway between the *optimal gender* and *full-consent* policies on early treatment of DSD, holds that both paradigms infer the wish of a young child by referring to actual and common wishes of adults. Both policies ignore actual desires of minors: the *optimal gender policy* by pharmacologically or surgically altering their body and the *full-consent policy* by deferring decisions on a child's wishes to his future adult self. Claudia Wiesemann *et al.* have stressed this latter position may also do injustice to the child (Wiesemann *et al.*, 2010). Wiesemann *et al.* also make the point that neither allowing virilization nor intervening to correct it are unequivocally in a child's best interest. Beside calls to prioritize the wellbeing of an individual, understood as both a child and a future adult, Wiesemann *et al.* suggest shifting the focus on parent-child relationships. This, they argue, provides another useful lens through which one can address the DSD

treatment conundrum: they call it the "optimal emotional and social development" paradigm (ibid.: 675).

(3) Alice Dreger, Ellen K. Feder, and Anne Tamar-Mattis begin by classifying bodily and behavioral variations associated with CAH as "benign". They develop an ethical analysis around concerns for "high-risk medical research" that targets these so-called benign variations (Dreger, Feder, and Tamar-Mattis, 2012). Moreover, the authors find that while studies on the prenatal use of DEX are of low quality, these interventions are conceptualized as positive illustrations of pharmacological therapy in pregnancy. Dreger, Feder, and Tamar-Mattis are eager to point out that DEX should only be considered experimental, given the following hurdles:

> de facto experimentation on fetuses and pregnant women, largely outside of prospective long-term trials and without adequate informed consent; failure to appropriately collect and publish evidence when promoting and providing a high-risk intervention; use of medicine and public monies to prevent benign variations of sexual behaviour, including tomboyism and lesbianism.
> (ibid.: 278)[6]

The research group finds the principle 'do no harm' is disregarded through the usage of DEX for CAH and sees this as ignoring the recent history of medicine, where the prenatal use of another drug, diethylstilbestrol (DES), caused tragedy and remains a lesson to learn from (Dreger, Feder, and Tamar-Mattis, 2012). The three authors distinguish between the fact that DEX for CAH means involving fetuses and pregnant women in clinical trials and the fact that risky medicine in this case is used to avoid benign variations, including a lesbian orientation. These inherent morally problematic aspects lead them to reject the use of DEX for CAH. Dreger, Feder, and Tamar-Mattis's argument, however, does not convincingly provide grounds to reject the use of DEX for preventing medically problematic anatomical defects.

To echo the title of this chapter, fuzzy boundaries become apparent when evaluating the remarks above. Sparrow stresses that treatment of severe DSD-related health problems, which can be life-threatening as is sometimes the case in CAH, does not inform our approach to DEX therapy for other reasons. Furthermore, it is yet impossible to predict with certainty which fetuses will suffer from severe anatomical defects, and which will present at birth with benign variation of sexual anatomy – adding an additional layer of complexity in the decision-making process. Wiesemann *et al.* suggest evaluating DEX therapy by its impact on emotional and social development of a child – a proposition that grounds clinical decision-making in a normative framework that provides no solid guidance for parents who might still be struggling between fear of social stigmatization and desire for self-determination. Referring to a future emotional and social wellbeing puts much weight on the social surroundings of a child or future adult, splitting the focus between multiple individual needs and feelings (Clayton *et al.*, 2014; Harrison *et al.*, 1997). Perhaps fuzzy boundaries are problematic on the one hand, but on the other may teach a valuable lesson: that placing less weight within clinical practice on what is precisely right or wrong allows for "fewer right answers" (McCabe, 1996: 505).

As mentioned earlier in this chapter, some proponents of DEX find justification in its promise to prevent traumatizing postnatal sex-reassignment surgeries. This approach, however compassionate it means to be, gives insufficient attention to the ethical issues outlined above. Our opposition to this line of thought echoes the *Intersex Society of North America* (ISNA) opinion on the matter, according to which genital surgery on children with some form of DSD should only be performed in case this intervention is mandatory for health and comfort. Excluded are surgical practices that aim at harmonizing a child's anatomy with common male or female sexual organs. We consider this special treatment permissible only when the child can fully consent; this further reinforces recognition that uniqueness and diversity are positive and can be coherent with an individual's conception of gender. It is more and more common within clinical practice that, when caring for patients with DSD, priority is given to a child's developing autonomy, which arguably equates to maximizing future life possibilities and choices (Brain *et al.* 2010). As a result, a newborn female with CAH and significant virilization should not undergo surgery (Creighton, 2001), especially because a certain number of women with CAH will choose to forgo any sex normalizing procedure (Hines *et al.*, 2016). Physical and emotional angst accompanying newborn sex-reassignment surgeries are real, as groups like the ISNA, and other scholars, made clear.

This chapter, so far, attempted in a kaleidoscope of ways to draw attention to multiple critiques raised from various fronts: gender-based assumptions, respect for self-determination, clinical and scientific paradigms, and dignity. Before turning to the relevance of the CAH debate on the status of the fetus as a patient, we wish to add another ethical argument. Even within a rigid binary gender framework, as might be the case in clinical practice where individuals often struggle with fuzzy boundaries, and in the context where DEX use is not exempt from plausible justification, an appreciation and weighing of values could bring clarity to the debate. One method of weighing values is to apply the principle of proportionality to the issue. Here, we suggest the following conclusion might be drawn: the value of wanting an average child, with a typical body, for the sake of social acceptance is weaker than the value of autonomy and self-ownership. This is because in the first case (parents and physician initiate early prenatal treatment) a possibility exists that the treated individual regrets the therapy, either because of side-effects or because of the general outcome. Other people would be responsible for this resentment. In the second case (parents and physicians refrain from intervening), relevant principles are not based on an eventuality (hostility against the child due to sexual differences), but on a definite state of affairs: respect for the autonomy, be it current or future, of an individual, in this case concerning self-determination of gender. This is not supposed to down-play the issue of stigma, which children may indeed experience if they look in any way different. Such stigmatization and fear of stigmatization are both commonplace and, one could argue, much more concrete than concerns about insufficient respect for autonomy that may have been shown in the past, even before the child was born. Although this position has its value in stressing the likeliness of stigmatization and thus pinpoints special (psychological) needs of children with CAH, it can be accused of confusing cause and effect. Changing bodily or character traits that are likely to provoke bullying in a certain society implies that the problem is really within the object of bullying and not in its subjects (ethics of complicity) (Little, 1998). The origin of stigmatization is not the physical feature itself: having an atypical sexual anatomy could be viewed positively (Wirth, 2013). Stigma lies in the eyes of the beholder, and is influenced by our learned prejudices and social norms. For instance, few would argue that a homosexual individual should change his or her sexual orientation in order to avoid stigmatization. The responsibility for terminating discrimination against "queer" people lies within society. Whoever agrees with this must also agree that the cause of the stigmatization is not queerness of the victim but aggression from his peers. Since the cause-and-effect argument appears to be rather theoretical, parents who expect a child with CAH and fear stigmatization should learn about efficient support for themselves and their future children so they can give or refuse consent to a procedure that is problematic from medical and ethical perspectives. This is not to say, however, that prospective differences in a future child will not give rise to legitimate disagreements, and even conflict, about how to respond to this possibility. This is especially true because the severity of social suffering caused by this difference could indeed, in at least some circumstances, justify even the use of medical intervention (Little, 1998).

Differently put: grown-up children could blame their parents and physicians for having decided to act upon their body's appearance, be it for their fear of social prejudice or in an appeal to normality. Grown-up children could not so easily blame their parents for deferring an elective or cosmetic intervention, when this decision is based on respect for their self-determination. Since virilization is partly reversible even during adulthood (e.g. by giving hormones) and because prenatal pharmacological treatments, as well as surgical and pharmacological intervention against virilization during adulthood, also come with risks and limitations, nothing requires intervention prenatally or in early childhood. Attempting to anticipate the will of an individual who is still in the process of developing is a particularly strenuous task.[7] It might be true that a majority of patients would want a typical sexual anatomy; what is less evident is whether the preference of a majority is sufficient to justify prenatal therapy when a significant minority might be even worse off with prenatal DEX therapy.

As gender dichotomization is decreasing and paternalistic decision-making is marginalized, safe spaces begin to open for intersex to outgrow the *optimal gender policy* framework. To be very clear: without any medical or functional emergency, it is ethically unacceptable to administer prenatal DEX for DSD. Therapy with DEX devalues otherness and diversity, and through it the ethical grounding of human lives (Wirth, 2016).

Epilogue: fetuses as patients?

The fetus, becoming more open to inspection through high resolution ultrasound and other screening programs, turns out to be treatable (Deprest *et al.*, 2011). Technological advances enable a new awareness of the fetus, forging a concept of it as a possible patient (Chervenak and McCullough, 1993). Fetal laboratory medicine and surgery, targeting CAH and DSD, is a field of developing importance (Geaghan, 2012). The management of diseases, as illustrated by CAH, begins long before a baby is born (Sandberg, Gardner, and Cohen-Kettenis, 2012). From this arises the thorny question of how much of a patient a fetus is, and what this means for prenatal medical ethics.

There is ample room to argue that the fetus is a "patient sui generis" (Deprest *et al.*, 2011: 221), although some will prefer to see it and treat it like a typical patient (Chervenak and McCullough, 1993). One obvious difference in comparison to other patients' treatments lies in the fact that a fetus is an organism within another organism that is affected by all interventions as well (fetomaternal risks). Another obvious difference lies in the problem of possible fetal pain and stress responses (Deprest *et al.*, 2011). More generally, the moral status of the embryo and fetus remains controversial (Chervenak and McCullough, 1993). Again, fuzzy boundaries seem to be the norm, as the status of the fetus is often considered *ens compositum*: it might not be fully human, especially in the early stages, but is not completely denied human attributions. Doubts begin to dissipate when the fetus is considered viable – that is, having the capacity to survive extrauterine life (ibid.). Balancing between potential risks and benefits might be a special medical and ethical concern in the newer field of prenatal medicine (Deprest *et al.*, 2011) but does not appear categorically different, as consent of newborns or young children is also delegated to responsible adults.

The controversy surrounding the use of DEX for CAH illustrates the difficulty of positing the fetus in the role of a patient; at the center of this observation stand clinical uncertainties and ethical criticism. Not only are we missing high quality long-term data on individuals treated with DEX prenatally, but some proponents also tone down the experimental character of prenatal medicine (Miller and Witchel, 2013) and re-emphasize *via facti* the unnecessary prioritization of anatomic normality over bodily integrity and diversity.

Mirroring the transformations we observe in contemporary societies, a rising openness towards gender fluidity seems to have been accepted by the medical community. Prenatal medicine cannot be immune to this cultural change. As open attitudes towards non-binary gender identities grow, one can appreciate how the ethical ramifications around DEX therapy will deepen.

References

Ahmed, S. F., Achermann, J. C., Arl, W., Balen, A. H., Conway, G., Edwards, Z. L., Eldford, S., Hughes, I. A., Izatt, L., Krone, N., Milest, H. L., O'Toole, S., Perry, L., Sanders, C., Simmonds, M., Wallace, A. M., Watt, A., and Willis, D. (2011) UK guidance on the initial evaluation of an infant or an adolescent with a suspected disorder of sex development. *Clinical Endrocrinology*, 75, 12–26.

Arboleda, V. A., Lee, H., Sánchez, F. J., Délot, E. C., Sandberg, D. E., Grody, W. W., Nelson, S. F., and Vilain, E. (2013) Targeted massively parallel sequencing provides comprehensive genetic diagnosis for patients with disorders of sex development. *Clinical Genetics*, 83 (1), 35–43.

Arboleda, V. A., Sandberg, D. E., and Vilain, E. (2014) DSDs: genetics, underlying pathologies and psychosexual differentiation. *Nature Reviews Endocrinology*, 10, 603–615.

Bachelot, A., Grouthier, V., Courtillot, C., Dulon, J., and Touraine, P. (2017) Congenital adrenal hyperplasia due to 21-hydroxylase deficiency: update on the management of adult patients and prenatal treatment. *European Journal of Endocrinology*, 174 (4), 167–181.

Baxter, R. M. and Vilain, E. (2013) Translational genetics for diagnosis of sex development. *Annual Review of Genomics and Human Genetics*, 14, 371–392.

Blankenstein, O. (2014) Hydrocortisone replacement in disorders of sex development. In: Hiort, O. and Ahmed, S. F (eds.), *Understanding Differences and Disorders of Sex Development (DSD)*. Basel, Karger, pp. 160–171.

Brain, C. E., Creighton, S. M., Mushtaq, I., Carmichael, P. A., Barnicoat, A., Honour, J. W., Larcher, V., and Achermann, J. C. (2010) Holistic management of DSD. *Best Practice & Research Clinical Endocrinology & Metabolism*, 24, 335–354.

Canty, T. G. (1977) The child with ambiguous genitalia: a neonatal surgical emergency. *Annals of Surgery*, 186 (3), 272–279.

Chervenak, F. A. and McCullough, L. B. (1993) Ethical issues in recommending and offering fetal therapy. *The Western Journal of Medicine*, 159 (3), 396–399.

Clayton, E. W., McCullough, L. B., Biesecker, L. G., Joffe, S., Ross, L. F., and Wolf, S. M. (2014) Addressing the ethical challenges in genetic testing and sequencing of children. *The American Journal of Bioethics*, 14 (3), 3–9.

Cools, M., Simmonds, M., Elford, S., Gorter, J., Ahmed, S. F., D'Alberton, F., Springer, A., and Hiot, O. (2016) Response to the Council of European Rights Commissioner's Issue Paper on Human Rights and Intersex People. *European Urology*, 70, 407–409.

Creighton, S. (2001) Surgery for intersex. *Journal of the Royal Society of Medicine*, 94, 218–220.

Crismann, P. H., Warner, L., Gardner, M., Carr, M., Schast, A., Quittner, A. L., Kogan, B., and Sandberg, D. E. (2011) Children with disorders of sex development: a qualitative study of early parental experiences. *International Journal of Pediatric Endocrinology*, 10, 1–11.

David, M. and Forest, M. G. (1984) Prenataltreatment of congenitaladrenal hyperplasia resultingfrom 21-hydroxylase deficiency. *Journal of Pediatrics*, 105, 799–803.

Deprest, J., Toelen, Debyser, Z., Rodrigues, C., Devlieger, R., De Catte, L., Lewi, L., Miegham, T. van, Naulaers, G., Vandevelde, M., Claus, F. and Dierickx, K. (2011) The fetal patient – ethical aspects of fetal therapy. *Facts, Views and Visions. Issues in Obstetrics, Gynecology and Reproductive Health*, 3 (3), 221–227.

Dreger, A., Feder, E. K. and Tamar-Mattis, A. (2012) Prenatal Dexamethasone for congenital adrenal hyperplasia. An ethical canary in the modern medical mine. *Bioethical Inquiry*, 9, 277–294.

Falhammer, H., Frisén, L., Norrby, C., Lindén, A., Hirschberg, C. A., Nordenskjöld, A., and Nordenström, A. (2014) Increased mortality in patients with congenital adrenal hyperplasia due to 21-hydroxylase deficiency. *The Journal of Clinical Endocrinology and Metabolism*, 99 (12), 2751–2721.

Feinberg, J. (1980) The child's right to an open future. In: Aiken, W. and LaFollette, H., Totowa, NJ (eds.), *Whose Child?* Lanham, MD: Rowman & Littlefield, pp. 124–153.

Geaghan, S. M. (2012) Fetal laboratory medicine: on the frontier of maternal-fetal medicine. *Clinical Chemistry*, 58 (2), 337–352.

González, R. and Ludwikowski, B. M. (2016) Should CAH in females be classified as DSD? *Frontiers in Pediatrics*, 48 (4), 1–4.

Harrison, C., Kenny, N. P., Sidarous, M., and Rowell, M. (1997) Involving children in medical decisions. *Canadian Medical Association*, 156, 825–828.

Hines, M., Pasterski, V., Spencer, D., Neufeld, S., Patalay, P., Hindmarsh, P. C., Hughes, I. A., and Acerini, C. L. (2016) Prenatal androgen exposure alters girls' responses to information indicating gender-appropriate behavior. *Philosophical Transactions of the Royal Society*, 371. Available from: doi: http://dx.doi.org/10.1098/rstb.2015.0125. [Accessed 23 March 2017].

Hirvikoski, T., Nordenström, A., Wedell, A., Ritzén, M., and Lajic, S. (2012) Prenatal Dexamethasone treatment of children at risk for congenital adrenal hyperplasia: the Swedish experience and standpoint. *The Journal of Clinical Endocrinology & Metabolism*, 97 (6), 1881–1883.

Holterhus, P.-M. (2010) Störungen der Geschlechtsentwicklung. In: Hiort, O., Danne, T. and Wabitsch, M (eds.), *Pädiatrische Endokrinologie und Diabetologie.* Heidelberg: Springer, pp. 391–409.

Hughes, I. A., Houk, C., Ahmed, S. F., and Lee, P. A. (2006) Consensus statement on management of intersex disorders. *Archives of Disease in Childhood*, 91, 554–563.

Johnston, J. (2012) Normalizing atypical genitalia: how a heated debate went astray. *Hastings Cent Rep*, 42 (6), 32–44.

Jordan-Young, R. M. (2010) *Brain Storm: The Flaws in the Science of Sex Differences.* Cambridge, MA: Harvard University Press.

Lajic, S., Nordenström, A., Ritzén, E. M., and Wedell, A. (2004) Prenatal treatment of congenital adrenal hyperplasia. *European Journal of Endocrinology*, 151, 63–69.

Little, M. O. (1998) Cosmetic surgery, suspect norms and the ethics of complicity In: Parens, E. (ed.), *Enhancing Human Traits: Ethical and Social Implications.* Washington, DC: Georgetown University Press, pp. 162–176,

McCabe, M. A. (1996) Involving children and adolescents in medical decision making: developmental and clinical considerations. *Journal of Pediatric Psychology*, 21 (4), 505–516.

Mieszczak, J., Houk, C. P., and Lee, P. A. (2009) Assignment of the sex of rearing in the neonate with a disorder of sex development. *Current Opinion in Pediatrics*, 21 (4), 541–547.

Mil, E. G. H. van and Hiort, O. (2008) Three out of four: a case discussion on ambiguous genitalia. *European Journal of Endocrinology*, 159, 91–93.

Miller, W. L. and Witchel, S. F. (2013) Prenatal treatment of congenital adrenal hyperplasia: risks outweigh benefits. *American Journal of Obstetrics & Gynecology*, 208 (5), 354–359.

Millum, J. (2015) The foundation of the child's right to an open future. *Journal of Social Philosophy*, 45 (4), 522–538.

Nebesio, T. D., Renbarger, J. L., Nabhan, Z. M., Ross, S. E., Slaven, J. E., Li, L., Walvoord, E. C., and Eugster, E. A. (2016) Differential effects of hydrocortisone, prednisone, and dexamethasone on hormonal and pharmacokinetic profiles: a pilot study in children with congenital adrenal hyperplasia. *International Journal of Pediatric Endocrinology*, 17, 1–9.

Ogilvy-Stuart, A. L. and Brain, C. E. (2004) Early assessment of ambiguous genitalia. *Archives of Diseases in Childhood*, 89, 401–407.

Pearce, M., DeMartino, L., McMahon, R., Hamel, R., Maloney, B., Stansfield, D.-M., McGrath, E. C., Occhionero, A., Gearhart, A., Caggana, M., and Tavakoli, N. P.

(2016) Newborn screening for congenital adrenal hyperplasia in New York State. *Molecular Genetics and Metabolism Report*, 7, 1–7.

Rolston, A, M., Gardner, M., Vilain, E., and Sandberg, D. E. (2015) Parental reports of stigma associated with child's disorder of sex development. *International Journal of Endocrinology*. Available from: doi: 10.1155/2015/980121. [Accessed 10 December 2016].

Sandberg, D. E., Gardner, M., and Cohen-Kettenis, P. T. (2012) Psychological aspects of the treatment of patients with disorders of sexual development. *Seminars in Reproductive Medicine*, 30 (5), 443–452.

Sparrow, R. (2013) Gender eugenics? The ethics of PGD for intersex conditions. *The American Journal of Bioethics*, 13 (10), 29–38.

Speiser, P. W., Azziz, R., Baskin, L. S., Ghizzoni, L., Hensle, T. W., Merke, D. P., Meyer-Bahlburg, H. F., Miller, W. L., Montori, V. M., Oberfield, S. E., Ritzen, M., and White, P. C. (2010) Congenital adrenal hyperblasia due to steroid 21-hydroxylase deficiency: an Endocrine Society Clinical Practice Guideline. *The Journal of Clinical Endocrinology & Metabolism*, 95, 4133–4160.

Sturm, R. M., Durbin-Johnsen, B., and Kurzrock, E. A. (2015). Congenital adrenal hyperplasia: current surgical management at academic medical centers in the United States. *Journal of Urology*, 193, 1796–1801.

Sultan, C., Paris, F., Jeandel, C., Lumbroso, S., and Galifer Benoit, R. (2002) Ambiguous genitalia in the new born. *Seminars in Reproductive Medicine*, 20, 181–188.

Thyen, U., Lux, A., Jürgensen, M., Hiort, O., and Köhler, B. (2014) Utilization of health care services and satisfaction with care in adults affected by disorders of sex development (DSD). *Journal of General Internal Medicine*, 29 (Suppl 3), 752–759.

Wiesemann, C., Ude-Koeller, S., Sinnecker, G. H., and Thyen, U. (2010) Ethical principles and recommendations for the medical management of differences of sex development (DSD)/intersex in children and adolescents. *European Journal of Pediatrics*, 169, 671–679.

Wirth, M. (2012) Der (un)durchsichtige Mensch der life sciences. Wie valide ist Karl Rahners änigmatischer Mensch nach Gen-Sequenzierung und Neuro-Imaging? *Theologische Zeitschrift*, 68, 335–354.

Wirth, M. (2013) Psychiatrie und Freiheit. Geschichte und Ethik einer Menschenheitsfrage. *Kirche und Gesellschaft*, 398, 1–16.

Wirth, M. (2015) "Living in a shell of something I'm not": transsexuality, medical ethics and the Judeo-Christian culture. *Journal of Religion and Health*, 54 (5), 1584–1597.

Wirth, M. (2016) Was bedeutet: Unbedingte Anerkennung der Andersheit des Anderen? Intersexualität und Transidentität im Licht advokatorischer Ethik. In: Schochow, M., Gehrmann, S. and Steger, F. (eds.), *Inter* und Trans*identitäten. Ethische, soziale und juristische Aspekte*. Giessen: Psychosozial-Verlag, pp. 105–133.

Worthington, R. (2002) Clinical issues on consent: some philosophical concerns. *Journal of Medical Ethics*, 28, 377–380.

Notes

1 More precisely, some claim the term DSD focuses on disorders and malformations of inner and outer genital organs, or constitution of male and female gonads and their adequate functional readiness for reproduction, favoring an analytical model

based purely on biological normality (e.g. in Holterhus, 2010). Others have attempted to reformulate DSD as "differences of sexual development," notably, hoping to emphasize the fluidity of sexuality rather than its pathological aspects (Wiesemann *et al.*, 2010). Furthermore, the use of terms such as "variations" and "differences" might shift the focus from treatment of disorders to acceptance of difference. Interestingly, many human rights organizations continue to endorse and use the term "intersex" (e.g. European Union Agency for Fundamental Rights, Council of Europe Commissioner for Human Rights).

2 Setting aside the fact that gender development is very likely dependent on multiple variables, including genetics and environment, another central difficulty arising from this claim is its inconsistency. Stating that gender identification is exclusively learned does not necessarily entail surgical correction must be undertaken early to fit the patient within a dualistic gender framework. Quite the contrary, it can be interpreted as the psychological ability to live with a fluid understanding of one's own gender and sexual identity.

3 There has been some criticism at the inclusion of CAH within the DSD classification (Gonzáles and Ludwikowski, 2016). Holding that affected females usually "have the potential for a normal sexual and reproductive life" (ibid.: 1), however, lacks not only scholarly grounding (Ahmed *et al.*, 2011) but also plausibility and relevance amongst peer- and support groups, such as the *Intersex Society of North America* (ISNA) (see www.isna.org/faq/ambiguous [accessed 23 March 2017]). Furthermore, referring to sexual and reproductive normality does not necessarily do justice to females with CAH who under this prerogative of normality might feel pressured to undergo surgical modifications that are not in their interest. A significant proportion of patients with CAH develop an identity that does not benefit from any surgical or pharmacological interventions (Mieszczak, Houk, and Lee, 2009).

4 For the sake of clarity, female fetuses with CAH are taken here as equivalent to 21-hydroxylase deficient female fetuses. The medical community will pardon this oversimplification.

5 That of course does not reflect the entire field, there are, for instance, many proponents in the US as well (Dreger, Feder, and Tamar-Mattis, 2012).

6 It is unclear is whether there really is a significant number of homosexual women amongst people with CAH. Apart from the fact that there is no clear concept of homosexuality, it is dubious that a simplified concept of homosexuality applies to these women (Jordan-Young, 2010).

7 Virilization, as indicated, is not completely reversible in adulthood. Indeed, adult hormonal treatment will not erase clitoromegaly, or labial fusion, etc. Furthermore, surgery can help give a somewhat "better" appearance to genitals, but it is not for now effective enough so that surgical results are completely comparable to typical sexual organs. Hence, an argument could be raised that DEX gives better cosmetic results by *preventing* virilization, than any adult treatment (be it pharmacological or surgical).

15 Perinatal palliative care as an option in prenatally diagnosed severe, life-limiting conditions of the fetus

Kathrin Knochel, Franziska Flaig, Julia D. Lotz, and Monika Führer

> We had three meaningful days with our daughter: We had the opportunity to meet her and the time to realize that she is gone. We bedded her in her small coffin and buried her with joy and in peace. Despite pain and grief our daughter has brought light and love into our life.
>
> (Written by parents)

Introduction

Due to rapidly expanding prenatal diagnostics, more parents are faced with the diagnosis of a life-limiting disease (LLD) during pregnancy. This raises numerous ethical and legal issues about the moral status of the fetus as well as the autonomy and the well-being of the pregnant woman and the fetus:

- Shall the pregnancy be continued or not?
- Shall the pregnancy be continued with or without disease-directed treatment of the fetus, and the neonate or comfort care or an individualized approach with a combination of both?
- On which basis should decisions be made?
- How can the best interests of the fetus and the future child be evaluated prenatally?

In case of a prenatal diagnosis of a LLD, pregnant women and their partners have to deal with a wide range of medical and prognostic information, knowing they will have to make difficult and complex decisions. The therapeutic options range from fetal interventional therapy to palliative care plans. Facing immense uncertainty and fear caused by the prognostic difficulties, as well as by societal influences, these families can benefit enormously from extensive support and care.

To enhance the ethical discourse with information about the context we summarize in this chapter first clinical experiences of the pediatric palliative care team at the Ludwig-Maximilians-University of Munich and give an overview about the literature focusing on perinatal palliative care (PPC). We seek to delineate PPC as one of the care pathways for families facing a perinatally diagnosed severe LLD to extend the available options in fetal and neonatal therapy.

The definition of severe LLD in this chapter is adapted to criteria for palliative patients described by Van Mechelen *et al.*: incurable disease, fast progression despite therapy, significantly limited life expectancy, and potential benefit of symptom-oriented therapy focusing primary on the quality of life (Van Mechelen *et al.*, 2013).

Clinical experiences in perinatal palliative care at the University Children's Hospital of Munich

Recently, the pediatric palliative care team at the University Children's Hospital of Munich was requested for support by an increasing number of parents in case of prenatally diagnosed severe LLD. These families were seeking palliative care as an alternative option due to their wish to continue the pregnancy despite the diagnosis of severe LLD.

Between 2005 and 2013, perinatal palliative care was provided for 15 families. In all cases parents initiated the contact: approximately two-thirds during the prenatal period and the others within the first days after birth. All families were accompanied beyond the death of their child. In Figure 15.1, the diagnoses of these children are summarized: genetic syndromes (n=8, 6 of them with trisomy 18), severe malformations of the brain (n=5, 3 of them with anencephaly), and severe asphyxia (n=2). Key aspects in palliative counseling conversations with parents were:

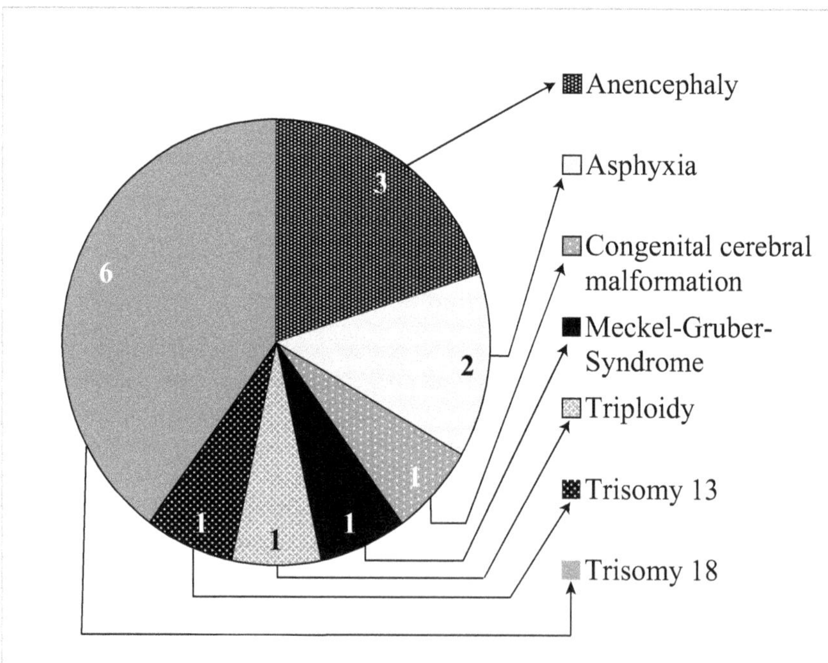

Figure 15.1 Diagnoses of patients with perinatal palliative care n=15, Pediatric Palliative Care Team at the Ludwig-Maximilians-University of Munich 2005–2013

- valuing the affected fetus, the neonate and the future child,
- searching for meaning,
- preparing siblings, and family members,
- making sure the fetus, the neonate, and the future child will not suffer,
- learning to cope with feelings of guilt, grief, loss, and bereavement.

Families who contacted the team during the prenatal period were already considering seriously how to manage the pregnancy. However, after receiving more information about the options of palliative care in their situation, all of them decided to continue the pregnancy.

More than half of the fetuses (8/15) died in utero or as neonates within the first week of their life. Only four lived longer than one month and one longer than one year. One child with severe asphyxia died in a neonatal intensive care unit after withdrawal of mechanical ventilation. The majority of the children who died were accompanied at home with support of our specialized pediatric palliative home care team (SPPHC). For parents, it was most important to feel supported and to know that everything would be done to keep the child comfortable before, during, and after birth.

Increasing clinical experience raised more questions about the needs of families and the structure of a PPC program, about the collaboration of different disciplines involved, and the parental outcome.

Perinatal palliative care – a literature overview

Background

In Germany, each year about 3500 children die from severe diseases. Sixty per cent of these children die within the first year of life and two-thirds of them (~40 per cent of the total) within the first four weeks of life. There are three major conditions causing death in neonates (Catlin and Carter, 2002):

1. preterm newborns at the limit of viability,
2. newborns with overwhelming illness who are deteriorating despite all appropriate intensive care intervention and
3. newborns with complex or multiple chronic conditions considered incompatible with prolonged survival, without benefit of neonatal intensive care.

Among neonates with complex chronic conditions (CCC) receiving palliative care, the group of congenital and genetic anomalies is the largest with about 33 per cent (Garten *et al.*, 2015).

Palliative care was defined by the World Health Organization (World Health Organization [WHO]) in 1998 and adapted for children by the IMPaCCT-group of the European Association of Palliative Care in 2007 as shown in Table 15.1 (Craig *et al.*, 2008).

Table 15.1 Definition of pediatric palliative care by IMPaCCT, (Craig *et al.*, 2007, 2008):

Palliative care for children is the active total care of the child‘s body, mind, and spirit and also involves giving support to the family.
It begins when illness is diagnosed and continues regardless of whether or not a child receives treatment directed at the disease.
Healthcare providers must evaluate and alleviate a child’s physical, psychological, and social distress.
Effective palliative care requires a broad multidisciplinary approach that includes the family and makes use of available community resources; it can be successfully implemented even if resources are limited. It can be provided in tertiary care facilities, in community health centers, and even in children’s homes.

Table 15.2 Perinatal palliative care and grief counseling

– Prenatal counseling
– Development of birth plans including type and location of delivery
– Care for mother and child after birth
– End-of-life care until death and care beyond
– Grief counseling

Palliative care started emerging in the late 1960s, fostered by hospice culture and by Cicely Saunders’s work with terminally ill adults. She emphasized helping people to live until they die. Palliative care for children was advocated by Saunders in 1969. She stressed, by citation of Green and Howel, the “importance of being able to say with truth that everything possible has been done” (Saunders, 1969: 551). She described co-operation, confidence, and communication as principles of care for the dying, in children as well as in adults (Saunders, 1969). The first adaptation for neonates was developed 1982 by Whitfield (Whitfield *et al.*, 1982).

Primarily in the US, UK, and Australia, frameworks for perinatal palliative care have been developed in the last decade, aiming at accompanying families and children during pregnancy, delivery, and after birth as summarized in Table 15.2. Perinatal palliative care is provided by an interdisciplinary team of obstetricians, pediatricians, palliative care physicians, nurses, social workers, psychologists, and chaplains to identify and respond to parents’ needs and concerns.

In neonatal and pediatric intensive care, it is often difficult to move from cure-oriented to palliative care goals. As outlined in the WHO-definition, palliative care can be offered from the moment of diagnosis and along with disease-directed therapy at the same time. If the diagnosis is made during the prenatal period, this approach involves the fetus, the mother, and the future child just like other options of fetal therapy. According to the American Academy of Pediatrics (2000),

Table 15.3 Newborns with complex or multiple congenital anomalies, incompatible with prolonged life, where neonatal intensive care will not affect long-term outcome. Adapted from (Catlin and Carter, 2002)

Genetic problems
Trisomy 13, 15, or 18
Triploidy
Thanatophoric dwarfism or lethal forms of osteogenesis imperfecta
Errors of metabolism that are expected to be lethal even with available therapy
Kidney problems:
Potter's syndrome/renal agenesis and severe lung hypoplasia
Some cases of polycystic kidney disease
Renal failure requiring dialysis
Central nervous system abnormalities
Anencephaly/acrania
Holoprosencephaly
Some complex or severe cases of meningomyelocele or large encephalocele
Hydranencephaly
Congenital severe hydrocephalus with absent or minimal brain growth
Neurodegenerative diseases requiring ventilation (e.g. spinal muscular atrophy)
Heart and lung problems
Acardia, inoperable heart anomalies
Some cases of hypoplastic left heart syndrome
Pentalogy of Cantrell (ectopia cordis)
Severe congenital diaphragmatic hernia with hypoplastic lungs

an integrative paradigm of curative and palliative care is favored with shifting from "doing to" to "being with" patients and families (Milstein, 2005: 563).

Thus, palliative care should be provided as an option for extremely premature newborns, for neonates with uncontrollable diseases as well as for fetuses, and newborns with prenatal diagnosis of complex congenital, and genetic disorders with a life-limiting prognosis (summarized in Table 15.3).

Perinatal, neonatal, and pediatric palliative care differ from each other in several respects. When palliative care starts prenatally, parents sometimes have to face parental decisions before they identify themselves as parents. Furthermore, prenatal decision-making is absolutely unique because it affects the pregnant woman and the fetus. Diagnosing a LLD right after birth leads to simultaneous experiences of bonding and losing within a very short period of time, sometimes at the same moment. Moreover, a newborn child does not have a place yet as a living infant in the family, and mostly, family members and others have not started to form strong bonds yet. Generally, fetal or neonatal loss is socially less recognized and parents feel lonely and abandoned (Guon *et al.*, 2014; Côté-Arsenault and Denney-Koelsch, 2011).

Perinatal palliative care aims at empowering parents who have to face a fetal or neonatal severe LLD to take some control of this challenging situation, and at reducing feelings of fear, isolation, and abandonment. It is a holistic approach covering physical, psychosocial, and spiritual needs, focusing on the quality of life and comfort of the child. It supports "time for bonding, loving and losing" (Hoeldtke and Calhoun, 2001: 527), recognizing that building memories is essential to the grieving process that already starts at the time of diagnosis.

In previous studies, approximately 40–85 per cent of parents to whom perinatal palliative care was offered decided to continue the pregnancy. Most of them did not regret their decision (Breeze *et al.*, 2007; Leuthner and Jones, 2007; Calhoun *et al.*, 2003). Parents reported an important and meaningful time despite deep grief. More than 90 per cent experienced the life of their children as positive: for their children and for their families (Guon *et al.*, 2014).

Prenatal counseling and decision-making in case of prenatal diagnosis of LLD

> Gray must be accepted as a respectable color. Issues of morbidity, family values, and quality of life are not black and white.... There is more than one good decision and any decision, whether to treat or not to treat, can be good as it is infant centered, best interests based, thoughtfully made, and abiding by the elements of full informed consent.
>
> (a statement by Peabody and Martin, in context of ethical issues at the limits of neonatal viability, (Peabody and Martin, 1996: 482))

The American College of Obstetricians and Gynecologists and the American Academy of Pediatrics strongly recommend non-directive prenatal counseling respecting the principles of informed consent. The "full range of options, including fetal intervention, postnatal therapy, palliative care, or pregnancy termination, should be discussed" (Steven J. Ralston *et al.*, 2011: e477).

Detailed counseling should include comprehensive information about diagnosis, prognosis, and the risks and benefits of all options for the pregnant woman and the fetus, as well as the psychological impact of termination or continuation of the pregnancy. Prenatal counseling should be as non-directive as possible to enable pregnant women and their partners to make an informed decision.

However, in several studies, most parents felt put under pressure to terminate the pregnancy, or felt that they were not offered all treatment options (Guon *et al.*, 2014; Walker *et al.*, 2008; Janvier *et al.*, 2016). In addition to the above mentioned guidelines, there are ongoing ethical debates about different approaches for counseling. Previously, e.g. for anencephaly, termination of pregnancy was counseled directively by the majority of obstetricians, but less often by clinical geneticists and least by genetics nurses (Marteau *et al.*, 1994). Nevertheless, recent results suggest that the provision of non-directive counseling becomes the norm, particularly in the case of morally controversial decisions (Yoon *et al.*, 2010).

The increasing number of new techniques in fetal therapy evokes further ethical issues. Decision-making and counseling are becoming more complex in balancing benefits and risks for the fetus, the woman, and the future child. Further research should accompany this tremendous progress and it seems inevitable to open up an individualized approach between doing "too much" and "too little" (Janvier *et al.*, 2016: 286).

In different qualitative studies, parents emphasized their desire for more information and stressed the value of honesty, truthfulness, and empathy (Guon *et al.*, 2014; Redlinger-Grosse *et al.*, 2002; Lathrop and Vandevusse, 2011). Allusions by health care professionals, suggesting that the affected child would be less important and less valuable were described by the mothers as most painful and evoked strong emotions even years later (Lathrop and Vandevusse, 2011). In contrast, families who experienced the positive valuing of the fetus and expressions of empathy by health care professionals reported higher mean satisfaction (Walker *et al.*, 2008).

Parents want to be involved throughout the multistage decision-making process. Further, they reported that they would have appreciated the honest acknowledgement by health care professionals of the prognostic uncertainty and their inability to predict exactly the individual disease trajectory (Redlinger-Grosse *et al.*, 2002). Parents need to reconsider their decisions repeatedly and develop different coping strategies. The participation in the decision-making process was linked with the feeling of control about the devastating situation. This led to more satisfaction (Walker *et al.*, 2008) and was appreciated by most parents (Caeymaex *et al.*, 2011).

To recognize hope as part of this process, and to ask for and listen to the parents' goals may enable health care professionals to better understand the parents' points of view. Remaining realistic and honest, the holistic approach of perinatal palliative care offers time for listening to parents and accepts hopes and other spiritual needs. This may open the door to build trust, to reduce fears, and to empower parents to make informed decisions.

Continuation of pregnancy in the case of severe LLD

In Germany, termination of pregnancy is unlawful, but not subject to punishment when termination is performed by a physician within the first 12 weeks of gestation after counseling pursuant to §219 section 2 at least three days before the operation (Criminal code StGB § 218a, section 1). Furthermore,

> the termination of pregnancy performed by a physician with the consent of the pregnant woman shall not be unlawful if, considering the present and future living conditions of the pregnant woman, the termination of the pregnancy is medically necessary to avert a danger to the life or the danger

> of grave injury to the physical or mental health of the pregnant woman and if the danger cannot reasonably be averted in another way from her point of view.
>
> (Termination of pregnancy on medical grounds, Criminal code StGB § 218a, section 2; chapter 1, page 9)

The international best practice standard for termination from the twenty-second week of pregnancy is that the termination should be preceded by feticide, unless neonatal death is inevitable due to severe LLD (Breeze *et al.*, 2007; Vadeyar *et al.*, 2005). The German Society of Gynecology and Obstetrics (2003) recommends that there should be discussion together with parents about whether or not a feticide should precede delivery in case of the possible viability of the fetus (Bender, 2003).

In many countries more than one-third of women ask for continuation of their pregnancy in case of severe fetal anomalies (Breeze *et al.*, 2007; Leuthner and Jones, 2007; Calhoun *et al.*, 2003). When being offered PPC, up to 85 per cent of women decided to continue their pregnancy and participated in the perinatal palliative program, but were not always supported by their health care providers (Calhoun *et al.*, 2003; Redlinger-Grosse *et al.*, 2002; Breeze *et al.*, 2007). Some of them described that even family members and friends did not understand their decision and did not respect it. Mothers reported experiencing the devaluation of their babies or their status as a mother compared to those of living children in their social environment (Lathrop and Vandevusse, 2011). This led to feelings of loneliness, doubts, and worries about the possible lack of support during the pregnancy and after birth (Walker *et al.*, 2008).

Parents report multiple reasons for continuation of the pregnancy:

- *Personal values, personal belief systems, and religious beliefs* are often expressed by parents to be important for the decision to carry the pregnancy to term. They expressed their feelings that the LLD in their fetus was a matter of fate and that they would anticipate feeling guilt and remorse if they chose to terminate their pregnancy (Breeze *et al.*, 2007; Redlinger-Grosse *et al.*, 2002; Janvier *et al.*, 2016).
- *Perceived prognostic uncertainty*, sometimes increased by lack of information, also led to the decision to continue pregnancy e.g. in parents with the fetal diagnosis of holoprosencephaly (Redlinger-Grosse *et al.*, 2002).
- *Previous personal experiences* with termination of pregnancy or with the diagnosis they are faced with were other important factors. Parents who found information about living children with the same so called "lethal" diagnosis reported they had never thought about termination (Redlinger-Grosse *et al.*, 2002).

The main goals for most parents were to meet their child (80 per cent), to be a family (72 per cent), and about 50 per cent wanted to bring their child home (Janvier *et al.*, 2016). Having time together and creating memories are invaluable, regarding mothers' greatest fear that their child would be forgotten (Capitulo, 2005).

Explanations for why women may choose to carry the pregnancy to term may be found in the concepts of prenatal parenting and attachment. It is described that ultrasound images may lead pregnant woman to view the fetus as a person (Lumley, 1990). Parents experienced the time during the pregnancy and after birth as meaningful and their baby as precious (Breeze *et al.*, 2007; Calhoun *et al.*, 2003; Janvier *et al.*, 2012). They tried to be the best parents for the short time they had together and they valued caring for and interacting with their baby (Côté-Arsenault and Denney-Koelsch, 2011). A current longitudinal study by Côté-Arsenault (2015) gives an overview of prenatal parenting behaviors and experiences of affected couples. All participants chose to continue their

Table 15.4 Categories of parenting behaviors after prenatal diagnosis of severe, life-limiting condition adapted from Côté-Arsenault (Côté-Arsenault, 2015)

Taking care	• Physical care of mother and fetus/ baby during pregnancy and after birth • Finding best health care for pregnancy management • Birth and death planning • Protecting the baby, even after death
Promoting baby's personhood	• Acknowledge the existence and value of their baby, as well as the uniqueness and purpose of their baby's life • Calling one's baby by name; referring to baby's gender • Creating mementoes to hold baby's place in the family
Interacting with baby	• Physical and audiovisual contact with the baby in utero or after birth where parents perceive or seek a reciprocal response from the baby • Parents' reciprocal responses to perceived interactions initiated by the baby
Being with baby	• To be as close to their infant as possible for seeking physical closeness and enjoying time together • Help parents to engage and bond with their baby • Physical closeness particularly important during time of their baby's death
Loving baby	• Having emotional ties to their unborn child and being proud of their child after birth • An affectional affinity and an unconditional emotional attachment to the baby

pregnancy, named their baby, identified themselves as parents and focused on what was positive about their baby. The following categories of parenting behaviors were described (Côté-Arsenault, 2015):

Increasing awareness that parenting behaviors already evolve prenatally may support health care professionals to thoughtfully recognize the needs and concerns of parents in this challenging situation.

Grief counseling

Regardless of their decision, many parents report experiencing strong grief (Wool, 2011). Parental grief after termination for reasons of congenital malformation is described as similar to postnatal loss of a child, and it may be experienced differently by the two parents, at their own pace and in their own manner (Lloyd and Laurence, 1985; Avelin *et al.*, 2013).

Parental grief is multidimensional, individual, and complex (Davies, 2004). It generally starts with the prenatal diagnosis of LLD and continues for parents lifelong (Arnold and Gemma, 2008). With the diagnosis of LLD, parental grief comprehends several losses: loss of "normal" pregnancy, loss of the healthy baby, and loss of future parenting (Côté-Arsenault and Denney-Koelsch, 2011).

Directed towards the grieving process, it is particularly important to recognize that the period of dying, the time immediately after death, and the days until the funeral will be remembered by parents with deep emotions. Caring for their baby: holding the baby in their arms, cuddling, talking, singing, comforting until death, and taking care after death help parents to cope better with the devastating emotions.

For health care professionals, it is important to know that anticipatory guidance helps parents to understand what emotions will come up throughout the process of grief. Parents appreciated this sense of "being prepared" for the outcome and the death of the baby (Breeze *et al.*, 2007).

Those parents who were offered support and chose continuation of the pregnancy described positive, extraordinary, and meaningful experiences (Calhoun *et al.*, 2003; Wool, 2011; Einaudi *et al.*, 2010). They treasured the time they had during pregnancy, after birth, and after the death of their child (Côté-Arsenault, 2015; Kavanaugh and Moro, 2006). Parental satisfaction was positively influenced by compassionate care (Wool *et al.*, 2016). The first quantitative results indicate a better psychological outcome for women after continuation of the pregnancy compared to women who chose termination (Cope *et al.*, 2015).

Conclusion and perspective

A prenatal diagnosis of LLD is almost always unexpected and devastating, leading to shock and followed by feelings like helplessness, anxiety and anguish, guilt, anger and intensive grief. Parents who are facing a prenatal diagnosis of severe LLD have to be informed non-directively about all options of care. The parental desires to meet their child and to be good parents, and the parental wish that the child will not suffer, require a broad multidisciplinary approach to provide individualized holistic care for these families.

Further research is needed to clarify the role of pediatric palliative care, to point out how the multidisciplinary approach should be structured and how the different disciplines could collaborate so that continuity of care can be ensured.

To learn more about the needs and concerns of parents and of the health care professionals involved, we planned a qualitative research project starting with an interview study with pregnancy counselors. Further, we plan interviews with other health care professionals involved and with parents, who have already experienced the process of decision-making in case of perinatal LLD.

Overall, we intend to improve the holistic support available to parents facing a prenatal diagnosis of severe LLD of their unborn child. We emphasize the need to empower these parents and to enable them to find their own best possible way through this devastating situation, and to value their journey regardless of their decision.

Based on our results, we aim at developing and implementing a perinatal palliative care program in close collaboration with the other disciplines involved in this field.

References

American Academy of Pediatrics. 2000. Committee on Bioethics and Committee on Hospital Care. Palliative care for children. *Pediatrics*, 106(2 Pt. 1), 351–7.

Arnold, J. and Gemma, P. B. 2008. The continuing process of parental grief. *Death Stud*, 32, 658–73.

Avelin, P., Radestad, I., Saflund, K., Wredling, R., and Erlandsson, K. 2013. Parental grief and relationships after the loss of a stillborn baby. *Midwifery*, 29, 668–73.

Bender 2003. Schwangerschaftsabbruch nach Pränataldiagnostik. www.aerzteblatt.de/down.asp?id=1136: Deutsche Gesellschaft für Gynäkologie und Geburtshilfe.

Breeze, A. C., Lees, C. C., Kumar, A., Missfelder-Lobos, H. H., and Murdoch, E. M. 2007. Palliative care for prenatally diagnosed lethal fetal abnormality. *Arch Dis Child Fetal Neonatal Ed*, 92, F56–8.

Caeymaex, L., Speranza, M., Vasilescu, C., Danan, C., Bourrat, M. M., Garel, M., and Jousselme, C. 2011. Living with a crucial decision: a qualitative study of parental narratives three years after the loss of their newborn in the NICU. *PLoS One*, 6, e28633.

Calhoun, B. C., Napolitano, P., Terry, M., Bussey, C., and Hoeldtke, N. J. 2003. Perinatal hospice. Comprehensive care for the family of the fetus with a lethal condition. *J Reprod Med*, 48, 343–8.

Capitulo, K. L. 2005. Evidence for healing interventions with perinatal bereavement. *MCN Am J Matern Child Nurs*, 30, 389–96.

Catlin, A. and Carter, B. 2002. Creation of a neonatal end-of-life palliative care protocol. *J Perinatol*, 22, 184–95.

Cope, H., Garrett, M. E., Gregory, S., and Ashley-Koch, A. 2015. Pregnancy continuation and organizational religious activity following prenatal diagnosis of a lethal fetal defect are associated with improved psychological outcome. *Prenat Diagn*, 35, 761–8.

Côté-Arsenault, D. and Denney-Koelsch, E. 2011. "My baby is a person": parents' experiences with life-threatening fetal diagnosis. *J Palliat Med*, 14, 1302–8.
Côté-Arsenault, D., Krowchuk, H., Hall, W. J., and Denney-Koelsch, E. 2015. We want what's best for our baby: prenatal parenting of babies
with lethal conditions. *J Prenat Perinat Psychol Health*, 29(3), 157–76.
Craig, F., Abu-Saad Huijer, H., Benini, F., Kuttner, L., Wood, C., Feraris, P. C., and Zernikow, B. 2007. IMPaCCT standards for pediatric palliative care. www.eapcnet.eu/?TabId=284: Steering Committee of the EAPC task force on palliative care for children and adolescents
Craig, F., Abu-Saad Huijer, H., Benini, F., Kuttner, L., Wood, C., Feraris, P. C., and Zernikow, B. 2008. [IMPaCCT: standards of paediatric palliative care]. *Schmerz*, 22, 401–8.
Davies, R. 2004. New understandings of parental grief: literature review. *J Adv Nurs*, 46, 506–13.
Deutsche Gesellschaft Für Gynäkologie Und Geburtshilfe (German Society of Gynaecology and Obstetrics) 2003. Schwangerschaftsabbruch nach Pränataldiagnostik. Available Available: www.aerzteblatt.de/down.asp?id=1136
Einaudi, M. A., LE Coz, P., Malzac, P., Michel, F., D'Ercole, C., and Gire, C. 2010. Parental experience following perinatal death: exploring the issues to make progress. *Eur J Obstet Gynecol Reprod Biol*, 151, 143–8.
Garten, L., Glockner, S., Siedentopf, J. P., and Buhrer, C. 2015. Primary palliative care in the delivery room: patients' and medical personnel's perspectives. *J Perinatol*, 35, 1000–5.
Guon, J., Wilfond, B. S., Farlow, B., Brazg, T., and Janvier, A. 2014. Our children are not a diagnosis: the experience of parents who continue their pregnancy after a prenatal diagnosis of trisomy 13 or 18. *Am J Med Genet A*, 164A, 308–18.
Hoeldtke, N. J. and Calhoun, B. C. 2001. Perinatal hospice. *Am J Obstet Gynecol*, 185, 525–9.
Janvier, A., Farlow, B. and Barrington, K. J. 2016. Parental hopes, interventions, and survival of neonates with trisomy 13 and trisomy 18. *Am J Med Genet C Semin Med Genet*, 172, 279–87.
Janvier, A., Farlow, B., and Wilfond, B. S. 2012. The experience of families with children with trisomy 13 and 18 in social networks. *Pediatrics*, 130, 293–8.
Kavanaugh, K. and Moro, T. 2006. Supporting parents after stillbirth or newborn death: There is much that nurses can do. *Am J Nurs*, 106, 74–9.
Lathrop, A. and Vandevusse, L. 2011. Affirming motherhood: validation and invalidation in women's perinatal hospice narratives. *Birth*, 38, 256–65.
Leuthner, S. and Jones, E. L. 2007. Fetal concerns program: a model for perinatal palliative care. *MCN Am J Matern Child Nurs*, 32, 272–8.
Lloyd, J. and Laurence, K. M. 1985. Sequelae and support after termination of pregnancy for fetal malformation. *Br Med J (Clin Res Ed)*, 290, 907–9.
Lumley, J. 1990. Through a glass darkly: ultrasound and prenatal bonding. *Birth*, 17, 214–7.
Marteau, T., Drake, H., and Bobrow, M. 1994. Counselling following diagnosis of a fetal abnormality: the differing approaches of obstetricians, clinical geneticists, and genetic nurses. *J Med Genet*, 31, 864–7.
Milstein, J. 2005. A paradigm of integrative care: healing with curing throughout life, "being with" and "doing to." *J Perinatol*, 25, 563–8.

Peabody, J. L. and Martin, G. I. 1996. From how small is too small to how much is too much. Ethical issues at the limits of neonatal viability. *Clin Perinatol*, 23, 473–89.

Redlinger-Grosse, K., Bernhardt, B. A., Berg, K., Muenke, M., and Biesecker, B. B. 2002. The decision to continue: the experiences and needs of parents who receive a prenatal diagnosis of holoprosencephaly. *Am J Med Genet*, 112, 369–78.

Saunders, C. 1969. The management of fatal illness in childhood. *Proc R Soc Med*, 62, 550–3.

Steven J. Ralston, M., Steven R., Leuthner, M., American College of Obstetricians, Gynecologists, C. O. E., and American Academy of Pediatrics, C. O. B. 2011. Maternal-fetal intervention and fetal care centers. *Pediatrics*, 128, e473–8.

Vadeyar, S., Johnston, T. A., Sidebotham, M., and Sands, J. 2005. Neonatal death following termination of pregnancy. *BJOG*, 112, 1159–62.

Van Mechelen, W., Aertgeerts, B., De Ceulaer, K., Thoonsen, B., Vermandere, M., Warmenhoven, F., Van Rijswijk, E., and De Lepeleire, J. 2013. Defining the palliative care patient: a systematic review. *Palliat Med*, 27, 197–208.

Walker, L. V., Miller, V. J., and Dalton, V. K. 2008. The health-care experiences of families given the prenatal diagnosis of trisomy 18. *J Perinatol*, 28, 12–9.

Whitfield, J. M., Siegel, R. E., Glicken, A. D., Harmon, R. J., Powers, L. K., and Goldson, E. J. 1982. The application of hospice concepts to neonatal care. *Am J Dis Child*, 136, 421–4.

Wool, C. 2011. Systematic review of the literature: parental outcomes after diagnosis of fetal anomaly. *Adv Neonatal Care*, 11, 182–92.

Wool, C., Repke, J. T., and Woods, A. B. 2016. Parent reported outcomes of quality care and satisfaction in the context of a life-limiting fetal diagnosis. *J Matern Fetal Neonatal Med*, 1–6.

World Health Organization [WHO]. *Definition of Palliative Care* [Online]. Available: www.who.int/cancer/palliative/definition/en/ [Accessed 10 January 2015.

Yoon, J. D., Rasinski, K. A., and Curlin, F. A. 2010. Moral controversy, directive counsel, and the doctor's role: findings from a national survey of obstetrician-gynecologists. *Acad Med*, 85, 1475–81.

Part V

The fetus as a patient: legal perspective

16 The legal status of the fetus as a patient in Europe

Atina Krajewska and Dimitrios Tsarapatsanis

Introduction

Our aim in this chapter is to provide a short analysis of the legal status of the human fetus in Europe in the context of fetal surgery, insofar as it pertains to the question of the treatment of the fetus as a patient. The majority of clinical procedures currently offered in Europe that aim to treat fetuses during pregnancy are minimally invasive. However, open fetal surgery,[1] which on occasion may involve a partial removal of the fetus from the uterus or a removal of the uterus from the mother's abdomen,[2] has been practised for some time now in the United States and elsewhere.[3] This raises specific legal questions with regard to civil and criminal liability of the medical professionals and the mother. First of all, the question arises whether the doctor is allowed to operate on the fetus and the mother without her consent. Does the doctor owe a duty of care towards the fetus even if the operation is in not in the best interest of the pregnant woman? If s/he decides to operate, will s/he be liable in criminal and/or civil law for violating the mother's bodily integrity? Second, can a mother who refuses treatment also become liable for not attempting to save her future child? These questions become relevant in light of a line of relatively recent legal and jurisprudential developments in the USA, where pregnant (and usually drug and/or alcohol-dependent) women have been sentenced or arrested for potentially causing harm to the fetus.[4] Other countries followed the attempts of the US courts to criminalize behaviour that does or can harm the fetus.[5] Similar attempts to use criminal law to restrict wom-

1 In open fetal surgery incisions are made through the mother's abdominal wall, which allows doctors to operate on the foetus.

2 BBC News (24 October 2016) Baby Lynlee 'born twice' after life-saving tumour surgery, *BBC*, available at: www.bbc.co.uk/news/world-us-canada-37750038

3 J. Deprest *et al.* (2011) The fetal patient – ethical aspects of fetal therapy 3(3), *Facts Views Vis Obgyn*, 221–227; C. Willyard (2008) Tinkering in the womb: the future of fetal surgery, *Nature Medicine* 14, 1176–1177. Avalable at: www.nature.com/nm/journal/v14/n11/full/nm1108-1176.html

4 C. Hackler (2011) Ethical, legal and policy issues in management of fetal alcohol spectrum disorder, *Journal of the Arkansas Medical Society*, 108 (6), 123–124. Available at: www.ncbi.nlm.nih.gov/pmc/articles/PMC4049518/

5 Z. Pringle 13 September 2013, Zoe's Law: will changing foetuses' legal status endanger abortion rights?, *The Conversation*. Available at: http://theconversation.com/

en's autonomy in Europe have been unsuccessful so far.[6] However, in some European countries, claims in *civil (tort)* law made against mothers who harm their children due to drug or alcohol use during pregnancy were successful.[7] Although a distinction should be drawn between an action that causes harm to a fetus (e.g. alcohol use) and a failure to act (refusal of treatment),[8] these developments may signify a shift in law towards recognition of some form of fetal personhood. Despite claims that the future of fetal surgery belongs to stem cell therapy,[9] some aspects of open fetal surgery could potentially become yet another battleground over women's reproductive autonomy and the fragile abortion compromise. It is thus important to clarify the law governing this area of clinical practice in Europe at this point in time.

At the time of writing, there have been no special laws regulating fetal surgery in Europe. In the absence of specific provisions, medical practice can be guided by general legal principles concerning consent to treatment and refusal thereof, both in criminal and civil law. These in turn stem from constitutional law determining the legal status of the fetus and the bodily integrity and reproductive autonomy of the mother, often further clarified in the courts' jurisprudence. It is constitutional law, understood as higher-level legal principles, that will be the focus of our discussion. In the absence of case law concerning fetal surgery, the jurisprudence concerned with the issue of abortion will be particularly useful.

Despite the heterogeneity of different national legal approaches, we submit that as a general rule, and with only a very limited number of exceptions, European legal orders do not recognize human embryos or fetuses before birth as distinctive legal entities, which can be bearers of rights or beneficiaries of duties in their own right. In Germany, where prenatal life seems to be protected both by the guarantee of human dignity and by the right to life, the fetus seems at best as a 'partial rights bearer'.[10] However, in most European states[11] there is only

---

zoes-law-will-changing-foetuses-legal-status-endanger-abortion-rights-18096; H. Anolak (2015) Our bodies, our choices: Australian law on fetal personhood, *Journal of the Australian College of Midwives*, 28(1), 60–64.

6 CP (A child) v. Criminal Injuries Compensation Authority [2014] EWCA Civ 1554.

7 J. Dorscheidt (2010) Developments in legal and medical practice regarding the unborn child and the need to expand prenatal legal protection, *European Journal of Health Law* 17, 433–454, at 436.

8 Moreover, the Dutch cases refer to women who suffer from mental health problems and the courts seem to also take into account the pregnant woman's best interests in deciding about the necessity to hospitalize pregnant women (the aim of hospitalization is to help the woman recover from mental illness). In this chapter we do not discuss the situation of mentally ill patients, who often lack mental capacity.

9 C. Willyard (2008) Tinkering in the womb: the future of fetal surgery, *Nature Medicine* 14, 1176–1177
www.nature.com/nm/journal/v14/n11/full/nm1108-1176.html

10 Becksche Kurz-Kommentare: Bürgerliches Gesetzbuch: BGB (2017) Buch. XXXIV, 3247 S. Beck.

11 Ireland and Malta being the most notable exceptions with a strong constitutional protection of the right to life of the unborn.

a limited form of acknowledgement that the life of the fetus has value, which increases as time passes and the fetus develops in utero. That value is not generally considered to override the autonomy or bodily integrity of the woman with the requisite capacity to consent to treatment. As a result, the medical treatment of fetuses, like any other medical intervention in the woman's body, legally necessitates her free and informed consent. Conversely, insofar as pregnant women have a legal right to refuse medical treatment, they cannot be forced to undergo medical treatment with regard to their fetuses.

We shall begin this chapter by examining the legal (constitutional) status of the fetus in three European countries. We have selected France, Germany and the UK as the focus of our study. These states are selected because they represent three different legal traditions. Yet, at the same time, they all belong to the same supranational organizations, i.e. the Council of Europe and the European Union, sharing similar political and ethico-legal values. Subsequently, we shall move on to examine the pertinent case law of the European Court of Human Rights with respect to prenatal human life, which will be followed by analysis of European Union law respectively. Our inquiry shows clearly that, contrary to the law in force in a number of states in the USA and some European exceptions, the human fetus generally is not considered to have a distinctive legal existence. Accordingly, we conclude that all medical interventions affecting the fetus necessitate the pregnant woman's free and informed consent. Moreover, we argue that, with the exception of Germany, competent pregnant women have a quasi-absolute right to refuse medical treatment, even if such treatment is absolutely necessary to save the life or promote the health of the fetus.

The legal status of the fetus in select European countries

The dominant legal position concerning fetal surgery in most European countries is determined by two broad sets of rules. On the one hand, the legal and constitutional status of the fetus remains normatively open and relatively undetermined. On the other hand, there is a robust recognition of bodily integrity and inviolability, and thus, the right to free and informed consent to medical treatment and medical experimentation. This leads to the conclusion that, in the vast majority of cases, any balancing exercise undertaken by courts or public authorities between these two constitutional values should result in a decision, which prioritizes the autonomy and dignity of the woman over the duty to protect the fetus. However, it is important to note that, as we will illustrate below, courts in different countries may arrive at this outcome through different reasoning.

France

The French Constitutional Council has made clear in unambiguous terms that, while the 1958 Constitution affords a certain level of protection to human life *in utero*, this protection, when balanced against a pregnant woman's right to autonomy and bodily integrity, is consistent with liberal access to various forms of abortion.[12] The Council's established case law is best understood against the background of its seminal 1975 judgment, in which it confirmed for the first time that the decriminalization of abortion through Law n. 75–17 of 17 January 1975 is compatible with the Constitution. The Council balanced the liberty of the pregnant woman, protected by Article 2 of the Declaration of Rights of Man and Citizen of 1789, against the principle of respect for fetal life, which was also afforded a degree of constitutional protection. The upshot of the Council's reasoning was that Parliament had balanced the competing constitutional values in a way compatible with the Constitution. This reasoning was repeated in all subsequent judgments, which involved deliberation concerning further liberalization of access to abortion.[13] Of particular interest for the purposes of this chapter, is the Council's ruling concerning a liberal reform of the regulatory regime for abortion in 2001. One of the amendments extended from 10 to 12 weeks the period of time during which access to abortion for reasons of 'distress' was allowed and created a novel criminal offence of 'hindering access to voluntary interruption of pregnancy'.[14] The Council ruled that the amendment did not violate the principle of human dignity for the fetus *in utero*, which was considered secondary to the rights of the pregnant woman.

The principle of free and informed consent of the woman is clearly set out in Article L. 1111–2 of the Code of Public Health. The Code guarantees the right of the patient to refuse medical treatment. It also imposes an obligation on the doctor to respect such a refusal, even when it endangers the patient's life or health (Article L. 1111–4 para. 2–3). The clarity of the law coupled with the established jurisprudence of the Constitutional Council explains the absence of any litigation on maternal-fetal conflicts in France and supports the idea that any treatment of the fetus necessarily requires the consent of the pregnant woman. Furthermore, it bears noting that the current legal position has been confirmed by the French National Advisory Ethics Committee, which stated in its Opinion no. 87[15] that, by virtue of the principle of free and informed consent to medical treatment, 'no one has the right to force an intrusion into the [pregnant woman's] own body' to save the life or health of the fetus (p. 12). According to the Committee, doctors may only try to convince the pregnant woman to receive medical treatment in cases in which fetal treatment is deemed necessary (ibid.), but they are under a strict duty to respect her wishes, whatever these may be.

The UK

The situation in the UK has important similarities with France, even though the case law suggests that the right to refuse medical treatment is sometimes set aside

12 Tsarapatsanis D (2010) Les fondements éthiques des discours juridiques sur le statut de la vie humaine anténatale, PU Paris Ouest, at 66–67.

13 Ibid., at 68–72.

14 Ibid., at 71–72.

15 Available at www.ccne-ethique.fr/en/publications/treatment-refusal-and-personal-autonomy#.WWc2I9PytAY (last accessed 13 July 2017).

if the medical intervention is considered necessary to save the life of the fetus. Interestingly, this is usually argued on the grounds of lack of mental capacity of the woman, rather than because of the legal status of the fetus.

First, despite persistent ambiguities in the absence of a comprehensive legislative framework, it is generally accepted by virtue of longstanding jurisprudence that the human fetus is not to be considered a 'person' within the meaning of the law. In the words of Lord Mustill, the fetus is a 'unique organism',[16] whose life is afforded a certain degree of legal protection, but not a bearer of legal rights.[17] The symbiotic relationship between the mother and the fetus is one of bond, not identity. This approach reflects a pragmatic and gradualist approach to the protection of human life. On the one hand, Sections 58 and 59 of the Offences Against the Person Act 1861 impose a maximum sanction of life imprisonment for procuring miscarriage, which includes the pregnant woman herself. In addition, the Infant Life (Preservation) Act 1929 criminalizes the intentional act of 'child destruction' of any child capable of being born alive, if the child dies before it has an existence independent of its mother.[18] On the other hand, however, the Abortion Act 1967 provides a defence against these charges under the conditions set out by its provisions. Among those, s 1(1) (d) of the 1967 Act permits abortion later in pregnancy in cases where there is a substantial risk that if the child were born it would suffer from serious physical or mental abnormalities. It is worth noting that in those cases a fetal surgery might be offered as an *alternative* to abortion. This leads to the conclusion that if abortion is considered lawful under s 1(1) (d), so must be the refusal to undergo surgery that might benefit the fetus.

Second, it is also well established that a competent pregnant woman has a right to refuse medical treatment. This has been reinforced in a series of cases of putative maternal-fetal conflict. Thus, in *Re MB* involving a refusal to undergo anaesthesia, it was pronounced that a competent woman may choose to forego medical intervention '*even though the consequence may be the death of the child she bears or her own death*' (emphasis added).[19] Treatment of a pregnant woman without her consent is a crime and a tort (of battery). Furthermore, in *St George's Healthcare NHS Trust v. S*, in which an emergency caesarean section performed

16 *Attorney-General's Reference (No. 3 of 1994)* [1997] 3 WLR 421; for criticism of the judgment see: J. Miola and S. Fovargue (1998) Policing pregnancy: implications of the Attorney-General's reference (No. 3 of 1994), *Medical Law Review*, 6(3), 1998, 265–296, in which the authors have argued that the ruling was a constraint to the facts of the case and thus left open the possibility of maternal liability for fetal welfare as a result of criminal or grossly negligent conduct of the mother.

17 Also earlier in Paton v. Trustees of the British Pregnancy Advisory Service [1979] QB 276.

18 Because the 1929 Act speaks of 'intentional' and 'wilful act' of child destruction, its relevance for fetal surgery will be limited, as the sole purposes of the treatment would be for the benefit of the foetus.

19 *Re MB (an adult: medical treatment)* [1997] 2 FCR 541, 38 BMLR 175.

on a pregnant woman despite her objections was deemed to be unlawful, Lord Judge famously stated that

> while pregnancy increases the personal responsibilities of a woman it does not diminish her entitlement to decide whether or not to undergo medical treatment. She is entitled not to be forced to submit to an invasion of her body against her will, whether her own life or that of her unborn child depends on it.[20]

However, it should be noted that in *Re MB* the Court of Appeal ultimately authorized the caesarean section against the expressed will of the woman on the grounds, first, that the woman lacked mental capacity and, second, that the treatment was in the woman's best interests. Likewise, the decision in *St George's* was issued by the Court of Appeal after the operation has been successfully carried out and a healthy child was delivered despite the mother's protests.[21] This line of judgments significantly obscures legal rules, since it suggests that English courts are deferential to health care professionals and sometimes willing to accept exceptions to the principle of free and informed consent of competent patients. If the decision to refuse treatment is not considered rational by the medical profession, pregnant women can be deemed to lack capacity.[22] Nevertheless, the growing recognition of reproductive autonomy (also by the medical profession) makes it difficult to imagine a situation in which the woman would be held liable for not consenting to fetal surgery.[23] Furthermore, as confirmed by the Nuffield Council in 2006,

> [i]n all but one exceptional circumstance, the mother is granted immunity from any civil liability for prenatal injury inflicted on her child by her conduct; this means that a child cannot sue his or her mother for compensation if her conduct while pregnant causes him or her harm.[24]

Germany

Among major European countries, Germany is the one of the main outliers when it comes to attributing constitutional and legal value to fetal human life. In the so-called First Abortion Decision the German Federal Constitutional Court (FCC)

20 St George's Healthcare NHS Trust v. S; R v. Collins and others, ex parte S [1998] 3 All ER 673, at 692.

21 Lord Justice Thorpe (1997) The caesarean section debate, *Family Law* 27(663), 663–664.

22 This approach to some extent resembles the justification of the Dutch courts about hospitalization of pregnant mothers in their best interest on the basis that they lack mental capacity due to mental illness.

23 Moreover, English law distinguishes between an act and an omission. The latter does not usually incur liability. It could be argued that, the woman's failure to act upon the doctor's advice to undergo fetal surgery constitutes an omission, rather than an act.

24 The Nuffield Council (2006), *Critical Care Decisions in Foetal and Neonatal Medicine*, London, 127–128; available at: https://nuffieldbioethics.org/wp-content/uploads/2014/07/CCD-Chapter-8-Decision-making-regulsation-and-resolution.pdf

struck down legislation passed in 1974, which permitted abortion in certain circumstances, on the grounds that the legislation was contrary to the constitutional principle of the inviolability of human dignity (Article 1(1) of the German Constitution).[25] The Court interpreted Article 2(2), the right to life, in conjunction with Article 1(1) to mean that an embryo is 'life' within the meaning of the Constitution, and that the state has a duty 'to protect and foster this life' even against the wishes of the pregnant woman. Finally, the Court defined abortion as 'an act of killing', which should be clearly condemned by the law. The duty to protect fetal life takes precedence as a matter of principle for the entire duration of the pregnancy over the right of the pregnant woman to self-determination.

However, this strong endorsement of the right to life by the FCC did not mean that fetal life must always prevail over claims of the pregnant woman. Based on its reading of Article 2(1), which confers upon everyone the 'right to the free development of ... personality in so far as... [one] does not violate the rights of others or offend against the constitutional order or the moral code', the Court concluded that abortion does not need to be punished, provided certain conditions are met. A continuation of the pregnancy cannot be enforced if the termination is necessary to protect the woman's life or prevent a serious risk to her health. The legislature is also at liberty to identify other 'extraordinary burdens of similar gravity', which would make the interruption of pregnancy justified.

Exceptions to the criminalization of abortion were further extended in the Second Abortion Decision, in which the FCC held that criminalization was not required in the first trimester of pregnancy.[26] The Court recognized that the 'obligation to protect life is not so absolute that it even takes priority, without exception, over every other legal value'. Accordingly, any decision about fetal surgery would require the courts to reconcile the right to life of the fetus with the woman's rights to life, physical integrity, personal autonomy and the protection of her dignity.

Constitutional requirements as interpreted by the FCC have shaped the content of German Law with regard to protection of *in utero* human life and the duties of doctors and pregnant women. Thus, dominant doctrinal interpretations of the criminal law framework pertaining to duties concerning the protection of human life include the fetus *in utero* and are generally considered to ground concomitant duties on the part both of the pregnant woman and of doctors as guarantors of fetal life. The German courts have not yet considered whether a woman should be forced to undergo obstetric intervention for the benefit of the fetus, or indeed whether she should be liable for a refusal of treatment resulting in the death of or harm to the fetus. Such liability cannot be inferred from the Abortion Decisions. We would, thus, concur with the opinion expressed by S. Halliday that prior to viability a woman will be under no obligation to accept treatment for the benefit of the fetus. Once the fetus achieves viability, courts (and doctors)

25 German Federal Constitutional Court (1975), Abortion I, BVerfGE, 39, 1.
26 German Federal Constitutional Court (1993), Abortion II, BVerfGE 88, 203.

will have to engage in a balancing exercise of the main constitutional values. However, in such cases

> account will need to be taken of a low probability of survival following treatment, and of whether the fetus will have suffered such harms as would justify the termination of pregnancy under §218 a II of the German Criminal Code. The existence of either factor will weigh heavily against it being considered reasonable to expect woman to undergo treatment'.[27]

In established forms of fetal therapy, where the chance of survival is significant or where the therapy aims to improve the life of the future child (e.g. laser surgery for twin to twin transfusion syndrome, in utero spina bifida repair, stem cell therapy for osteogenesis imperfecta), the court may in theory impose a legal duty on the mother to act in the best interests of the fetus. However, in practice, it is difficult to imagine that the court, applying the principle of proportionality, would give priority to the interest of the fetus, in this case improvement of life quality, over dignity and bodily inviolability of the mother, unless the intervention is minor and does not carry any risks to the mother's health. This position, although developed from a diametrically different starting point, appears surprisingly similar to that in the UK in its outcomes and deference to medical opinion. This convergence seems to be reflected in the courts' jurisprudence at the supranational level.

The position of the European Court of Human Rights (ECHR) and the Court of Justice of the European Union (CJEU)

The ECHR

The leading case by the European Court of Human Rights (ECtHR) on the status of the human fetus under the ECHR (ECHR), *Vo v. France*,[28] supports the idea that, whilst the fetus enjoys a certain degree of protection, this does not amount to a right to life. At the same time, and at least for the time being, the Court made clear in its *A, B and C v. Ireland*[29] case that it does not consider that the ECHR guarantees a right to abortion on request. As a result, state parties to the ECHR are free to afford varying degrees of protection to fetal human life.

In *Vo v. France* the main question was whether Article 2 of the Convention, which protects the right to life of 'everyone' applies to fetuses. The Court responded that, whilst there was some common ground between Member States in presuming that prenatal human life should be considered as belonging to the

27 S. Halliday (2016) Autonomy and Pregnancy: A Comparative Analysis of Compelled Obstetric Intervention, Routledge.

28 *Vo v. France* [2004] Application No. 53924/00.

29 *A, B and C v. Ireland* [2010] Application No. 25579/05.

human race and therefore requiring protection on grounds of human dignity, there was no European consensus as to whether it falls under Article 2. Accordingly, the Court refused to answer in the abstract the question whether the unborn child was a person for the purposes of Article 2 of the Convention. As a result, it concluded that states' parties to the Convention enjoyed a large margin of appreciation allowing them to decide freely the level of protection afforded to fetal life. Moreover, the Court held that there is no requirement that states use the apparatus of the criminal law for this purpose. The upshot is that there is no requirement under Article 2 ECHR to protect fetal life in the same way as human life after birth.

In comparison to the legal status of the fetus, the right of patients to free and informed consent in the context of medical treatment has been significantly developed. In an important line of cases the ECtHR has relied upon an expansive interpretation of Article 8 ECHR (the right to family and private life), with occasional recourse to Article 3 ECHR (banning of torture and inhuman and degrading treatment), in cases where the absence of respect for free and informed consent raises particularly serious concerns. Thus, in *Glass v. UK*,[30] the ECtHR found that the UK had violated the applicant's right to private life when a hospital treated the applicant without obtaining free and informed consent, or authorization from the courts. Moreover, the Court interestingly relied on *Glass* in Articles 5–9 of the European Convention on Human Rights and Biomedicine, despite the fact that the respondent state was not a party to it. In this way, it emphasized the importance of the norm of free and informed consent in contexts of medical treatment. Moreover, as demonstrated by the case of *VC v. Slovakia*,[31] where a woman of Roma origin had been sterilized without consent, there are instances where medical intervention constitutes an abuse so grave as to reach the threshold of 'inhuman or degrading treatment' within the meaning of Article 3 ECHR. Importantly, rights protected by Article 3 are absolute and non-derogable. This entails, among other things, that they may not be balanced against other rights or collective goods nor limited on the basis of proportionality considerations.

To sum up, first, in the absence of European consensus on the issue, Article 2 ECHR, does not apply to fetuses or, if it applies, it does not give rise to a stringent duty to protect fetal life. Second, Article 8 and, in cases of important abuses, Article 3 ECHR, are understood as protecting the right to free and informed consent to medical treatment, the corollary of which is the right to refuse such treatment. Importantly, Article 3 admits of no derogation or balancing, whilst Article 8, which sets out a qualified right, can be balanced against other rights and collective goals. As a result, Article 8 may be lawfully limited, provided that the limitation pursues a legitimate aim in a proportionate way. Last, at the time of writing, there is no case law by the Court on the specific issue of maternal/fetal conflict. However, on the basis of the ECtHR jurisprudence and the wide

30 *Glass v. UK* [2004] Application No. 61827/00.
31 *VC v. Slovakia* [2011] Application No. 18968/07.

margin of appreciation of states' signatories to the Convention we conclude that it would be difficult to argue that the protection of the fetus through the concept of human dignity could trump the right of the women to refuse medical treatment.

The CJEU

When it comes to the legal status of prenatal human life, it could be particularly important to contrast and compare the position of the ECtHR with the position that the CJEU took in the *Brüstle* case.[32] In *Brüstle* the CJEU relied on an expansive understanding of human dignity under the Charter of Fundamental Rights to afford a high level of protection to human embryos *in vitro*. The case concerned the validity of a national German patent regarding the processes for production of neural precursor cells from embryonic stem cells and the use of the former for therapeutic purposes granted to Professor Oliver Brüstle in 1998. The CJEU reasoned that exceptions to patentability pertaining to human embryos had to be interpreted in an expansive way, despite the fact that 'the definition of human embryo is a very sensitive social issue in many Member States, marked by their multiple traditions and value systems' (para. 30). It ruled that the concept of human embryo, for the purposes of the 'bio-patent' Directive 98/44/EC, must be interpreted broadly as covering any cell capable of commencing the process of development of a human being, including the human ovum as soon as fertilized.

A number of remarks are in order. First, the CJEU explicitly used the principle of human dignity to justify an expansive understanding of the protection that should be afforded to prenatal human life. Second, the ruling, which was connected with the treatment of embryonic human life *in vitro*, does not apply automatically to contexts where other values and rights are at play, such as the right to autonomy or bodily integrity of the pregnant woman. Third, it is important to stress that the expansive understanding of human dignity used to justify the protection of prenatal human life appears somewhat at odds with the reluctant case law of the ECtHR. Indeed, as we have seen previously, the ECtHR took a different approach, recognizing a wide margin of appreciation and thus leaving it open to state parties to the ECHR to adopt their own understandings and practices with regard to the appropriate treatment of prenatal human life (*in vitro* and *in vivo*).

Conclusion

In this chapter, we have claimed that satisfactory resolution of the practical and legal issues connected with the treatment of the fetus as a patient depends on balancing the value of the life and health of the fetus against the right to bodily integrity and self-determination of the pregnant woman, which is reflected in the

32 C-34/10, *Oliver Brüstle v. Greenpeace eV*, (Grand Chamber) of 18 October 2011.

principle of free and informed consent to medical treatment. A brief analysis of the positions adopted by select European states as well as by the ECtHR and the CJEU reveals a number of common points. First, the legal and constitutional status of fetal life is relatively indeterminate. Most states afford some protection to fetuses, but none equalizes their legal status with that of life after birth. Second, this is not the case with respect to the right of the competent pregnant woman to free and informed consent and, conversely, with her right to refuse medical treatment. Contrary to the principle of respect of fetal life, those rights are not only well established in and across European states, but also particularly stringent. As a result, they are only exceptionally overridden to protect fetal life. Concomitantly, the default legal position is that any treatment of the fetus as a distinctive patient necessarily passes through the free and informed consent of the woman that bears it.

References

Anolak H. (2015) Our bodies, our choices: Australian law on foetal personhood, *Journal of the Australian College of Midwives*, 28 (1), 60–64.

BBC News (24 October 2016) Baby Lynlee 'born twice' after life-saving tumour surgery, *BBC*. Available at: www.bbc.co.uk/news/world-us-canada-37750038.

Beck'sche Kurz-Kommentare: Bürgerliches Gesetzbuch: BGB (2017) Buch. XXXIV, 3247 S. Beck.

Deprest J., Toelen J, Debyser Z, Rodrigues C, Devlieger R, De Catte L, Lewi L, Van Mieghem T, Naulaers G, Vandevelde M, Claus F, Dierickx K. (2011) The fetal patient – ethical aspects of fetal therapy, *Facts Views Vis Obgyn* 3 (3), 221–227.

Dorscheidt J. (2010) Developments in legal and medical practice regarding the unborn child and the need to expand prenatal legal protection, *European Journal of Health Law* 17, 433–454, at 436.

Hackler C. (2011) Ethical, legal and policy issues in management of fetal alcohol spectrum disorder, *Journal of the Arkansas Medical Society*, 108 (6), 123–124. Available at: www.ncbi.nlm.nih.gov/pmc/articles/PMC4049518/

Halliday S. (2016) *Autonomy and Pregnancy: A Comparative Analysis of Compelled Obstetric Intervention*, Abingdon: Routledge.

Miola J. and Fovargue S. (1998) Policing pregnancy: implications of the attorney-general's reference (No. 3 of 1994), *Medical Law Review*, 6 (3), 1998, 265–296.

Pringle Z. (13 September 2013) Zoe's law: will changing foetuses' legal status endanger abortion rights? *The Conversation*. Available at: http://theconversation.com/zoes-law-will-changing-foetuses-legal-status-endanger-abortion-rights-18096

National Consultative Ethics Committee for Health and Life Sciences (2005) Opinion No. 87 on treatment refusal and personal autonomy, Paris. Available at: www.ccne-ethique.fr/en/publications/treatment-refusal-and-personal-autonomy#.WWc2I9PytAY

Nuffield Council (2006) *Critical Care Decisions in Foetal and Neonatal Medicine*, London: Nuffield Council, pp. 127–128. Available at: https://nuffieldbioethics.org/wp-content/uploads/2014/07/CCD-Chapter-8-Decision-making-regulsation-and-resolution.pdf

Thorpe L.J. (1997) The caesarean section debate, *Family Law*, 27 (663), 663–664.

Tsarapatsanis D (2010) *Les fondements éthiques des discours juridiques sur le statut de la vie humaine anténatale*, Paris: PU Paris Ouest.

Willyard C. (2008) Tinkering in the womb: the future of fetal surgery, *Nature Medicine*, 14, 1176–1177. Available at: www.nature.com/nm/journal/v14/n11/full/nm1108-1176.html

Case law

European Court of Human Rights

A, B and C v. Ireland [2010] Application No. 25579/05.
Glass v. UK [2004] App. No. 61827/00.
Vo v. France [2004] App. No. 53924/00.
VC v. Slovakia [2011] App. No. 18968/07.

Court of Justice of the European Union

Oliver Brüstle v. Greenpeace eV [2011] C-34/10, (Grand Chamber).

German courts

German Federal Constitutional Court [1975], Abortion I, BVerfGE, 39, 1.
German Federal Constitutional Court [1993], Abortion II, BVerfGE 88, 203.

English courts

Attorney-General's Reference (No. 3 of 1994) [1997] 3 WLR 421.
CP (A child) v. Criminal Injuries Compensation Authority [2014] EWCA Civ 1554.
Paton v. Trustees of the British Pregnancy Advisory Service [1979] QB 276.
Re MB (*an adult: medical treatment*) [1997] 2 FCR 541, 38 BMLR 175.
St George's Healthcare NHS Trust v. S; R v. Collins and others, ex parte S [1998] 3 All ER 673.

Index

Note: 'n' indicates chapter notes; bold indicates tables; italics indicate figures.

A, B and C v. Ireland (2010) 204
Abate, M. 20–1
abortion *see* termination of pregnancy
adrenocortocotropic hormone (ACTH) 170
Amnesty International 24
Appelbaum, P.S. 125, 126, 138
Association for Improvements in the Maternity Services (AIMS) 18
Australia, perinatal palliative care 184
autonomy of the pregnant woman: as cancer patient 107–9; in clinical trials 136–7, 141; discourse on 65, 74; ethical concepts of the fetus and 45–7; legal status of the fetus and 198–9, 202–3, 206; moral status of the fetus and 23–5, 52, 55–8; perinatal palliative care and 181; and prenatal screening 146–8, 150, 152; and therapy for DSD 168, 171, 174; and treatment for Down syndrome 162

BabyPod (speaker) 21
Bacon, Francis 42, 44
Beauchamp, T.L. 55
Bianchi, Diana 148, 149, 150, 155
Bild-Zeitung (German newspaper) 66–74, *70*, *72*, 77n8
Blackstone, William 17
body, female: legal status of the fetus and the 199–200, 202; metaphors of 67–8, 76n3
BOOSTB4 ('Boost Brittle Bones Before Birth') study 134–6, 155
Brogaard, Berit 30
Brown, S.D. 50, 55, 56
Brüstle v. Greenpeace eV (2011) 206

CAH *see* congenital adrenal hyperplasia (CAH)
Campbell, Stuart 18
cancer, pregnant women with 104–11; considerations of the fetus in treatment 106–9; during pregnancy 105–6; support services for 109–11
Casper, M.J. 133
Chervenak, Frank A. 10, 28, 39n9, 40–8, 50, 54–9, 107, 123, 138
Childress, J.F. 55
CJEU *see* Court of Justice of the European Union (CJEU)
Clarke, Angus 3–13, 117–30, 146, 154
clinical trials 133–41; current state of 133–5; for Down syndrome 156, 159–60; importance of 135–6; inclusion design 136–7; misconceptions 138–40; patient regret 137–8; prenatal screening and 148–9; *see also* experimental treatments
Cohen-Ketternis, P.T. 171–2
Cologne Manifesto, *The Right of Otherness* (1994) 51
congenital adrenal hyperplasia (CAH) 166, 169–76, 180n4, 180n5, 180n7
Conley, W.K. 150
consent for fetus intervention 11, 24, 33–4, 98, 100–1, 139, 200; full-consent policy 168, 172
Côté-Arsenault, D. 189
counseling, perinatal palliative care **184**, 186–7, 190; *see also* support services, patient
Court of Justice of the European Union (CJEU) 206

Dawkins, Richard 67
De Lia, J.E. 134
De Vries, M.C. 140
de Wert, Guido 12, 144–52, 154–63
DeGrazia, David 52
Dennet, Daniel 51–2
Dexamethasone (DEX) and female fetuses 166–7; ethical debate 171–5; medical debate 169–71, 180n9
diethylstilbestrol (DES) 173
disorders of sexual differentiation (DSD) 167–9
Donald, Ian 5, 18
Dondorp, Wybo 3–13, 144–52, 154–63
Donovan, S. 24
Dörries, A. 39n11
Down syndrome 24, 69, 80–1, 145, 154–63; classifying treatment 160–1; future ethical concerns 158–9; neurocognitive treatment for 155–8; parental responsibility and 162–3; reproductive choice and 161–2
Dreger, Alice 173
DSD *see* disorders of sexual differentiation (DSD)
Duchenne muscular dystrophy (DMD) 118–19
Duden, Barbara 24, 73

Eberl, Jason 57–8
ECHR *see* European Court of Human Rights (ECHR)
embodiment model 108
Epstein, J. 17, 21
Ettore, E. 18, 24
European Court of Human Rights (ECHR) 6, 204–6
experimental treatments 117–30; advocacy groups and 128–9; 'new, rational treatments' 118–20; outcomes 125–6; questions 118; scope and intensity of 123–4; for tuberous sclerosis (TS) 122–3; for X-linked hypohidrotic ectodermal dysplasia (XHED) 121–2, 126–8; *see also* clinical trials

Faden, R.R. 56
Feder, Ellen K. 173
Feinberg, Joel 23, 150, 168
fertility, media representations of 71–3, *72*
Fetal Anomaly Screening Programme (FASP), NHS 78, 144
'fetal medicine', as concept 9
'fetal personalized medicine' 90
fetal-maternal relationship 133, 141
'fetus, the' in clinical discourse 83–9
fetus as a patient, background 4–9; ethical concept of 45–7, 54; critique of the ethical concept of 55–8
'fetus fiction' genre 20–1
Flaig, Franziska 181–91
'Formula of Humanity' (FH; Kant) 95–102
Foucault, Michel 65
France, legal status of the fetus in 199–200
Fried, C. 138
Frith, Lucy 10, 17–25
Führer, Monika 181–91

Galilei, Galileo 76n7
Gardner, M. 171–2
gender and sexual development, prenatal therapy for 166–76, 180n1, 180n2; for anatomical differences 167–9; Dexamethasone (DEX) and female fetuses 166–7, 169–75, 180n9
genetic reproductive medicine 65–74; *Bild-Zeitung* (German newspaper) on 66–74, 77n8; discourse and metaphors on 65–6, 76n3, 76n7; *see also* experimental treatments
Germany, legal status of the fetus in 198, 202–4
Gilligan, Carol 35
Glass v. UK (2004) 205
Grady, C. 125
Gregory, John 43–4
Guedj, F. 156

Halliday, S. 203–4
Haraway, Donna 67–8, 74, 76n1
Hauskeller, M. 53
Häyry, Matti 99
Hays, S. 20
Hoffmann, Friedrich 43–4
hope 127, 137, 187
Horng, S. 125
Hume, David 42

Infant Life (Preservation) Act (1929; UK) 201, 201n18
'intensive motherhood narrative' 20
intersex 167–9
Intersex Society of North America (ISNA) 174
interventions, therapeutic 6–8, 94–102; consent 98; ethical principles for 34–6; 'Formula of Humanity' (Kant)

and 95–102; risk 99–100, 141; social pressure and 100–1

Jäger, Siegfried 66
James, William, pragmatism 42–3

Kant, Immanuel 23, 41–3; 'Formula of Humanity' 95–102
kidney donors (analogy) 97–100
Kim, S.Y. 126
Knochel, Kathrin 12, 181–91
Krajewska, Atina 12, 197–207
Krause, Janina 11, 65–74

legal status of the fetus 54, 197–207; Court of Justice of the European Union (CJEU) 206; European Court of Human Rights (ECHR) 204–6; France 199–200; Germany 198, 202–4; UK 200–2, 205; *see also* moral status of the fetus
Lejeune, Jérôme 161
life-limiting disease (LLD) *see* perinatal palliative care
Linkeviciute, Alma 11, 104–11
Little, M.O. 56
Lörch-Merkle, Katrin E. 10, 50–9
Lotz, Julia D. 181–91
Ludwig-Maximilians-University of Munich, perinatal palliative care at *182*, 182–3
Lupton, D. 21
Lyerly, A.D. 36, 56

McCollough, Laurence B. 10, 28, 40–8, 50, 54–9, 107, 123
McDougall, R. 125
Mackenzie, C. 23
McMahan, Jeff 22–3
McRobbie, Angela 66, 70, 73
Mahowald, M.B. 41, 46–7
Malich, Lisa 73
Marquis, D. 23
Marquis, Marc-Antoine 12, 160, 166–76
Martin, Emily 72
Martin, G.I. 186
'maternal patienthood' 83, 87–90
maternal-fetal relationship 133, 141
means, pregnant women as mere 95–102
Mills, C. 22
Money, John 168
moral status of the fetus 17–25, 50–9; clinical practice and 56–8; contradictions in 21–3; 'dependent moral status' 40–3, 47, 54–5; 'disposable fetus' concept 17–19; 'independent moral status' 40–3, 47, 54–5; pragmatic ethical concept 43, 54–6; 'protected fetus' concept 19–21; significance of physical individuation for 31–4; *see also* ethics; legal status of the fetus
mothering, fetal 19–21
Murray, Thomas 108, 150
Myles, M. 19

Netherlands 108, 144, 198n8, 202n22
Newman, Karen 39n4
Nilsson, Lennard 4–5, 31
non-invasive prenatal diagnosis (NIPD) 78–85, 89
non-invasive prenatal testing (NIPT) 7–8, 74, 78–90, 93n1, 129, 144, 147, 166, 172
Novas, C. 127
nutrition 6

'optimal gender policy' 167–8, 172, 175
osteogenesis imperfecta (OI) 134–5, 156, 204

palliative care *see* perinatal palliative care
Peabody, J. L. 186
perinatal palliative care 181–91, **184**; background 183–6, **185**; clinical experiences in *182*, 182–3; LLD and continuation of pregnancy 187–90, **189**; parental counseling, prenatal and grief **184**, 186–7, 190
personhood 51–3; fetal 'personhood movements' 19–20, 22
Petrie, Roy 50
physical individuation, significance of 31–4
pragmatic concept of 'being a patient' 43–7
pregnancy, medicalization of 3–5, 95–6
pregnant women 3–5; in clinical trials 133–41; ethics of the fetus as patient and 31–4, 45–7; fetal-maternal relationship 133, 141; legal status of fetus and 197–207, 198n8; as mere means 95–102; moral status of the fetus and 23–5; own discourse on 'the fetus' 83–9; popular media representations of 66–74, *70*, *72*, 77n8; reproductive choice and DS 161–2; social expectations/pressure on 6, 29, 100–1; wellbeing 109; *see also* autonomy of the pregnant woman; body, female; cancer;

pregnant women with; termination of pregnancy
preimplantation genetic diagnosis (PGD) 117, 120, 172
prenatal diagnosis (PND) 78–9, 81–4, 117, 120
'prenatal personalized medicine' (PPM) 149–51
pre-natal screening (PNS) 81–2
Prenatal Screening for Infectious diseases and erythrocyte immunization (PSIE), Netherlands 144
professional responsibility model 107
'protected fetus' status 19–23; fetal mothering 20–1; fetal personhood movements 19–20, 22

quickening, the (first fetal movement) 4, 17–18

Re MB case (1997) 201–2
Reason, human 42–3
reproductive medicine *see* genetic reproductive medicine
responsibility of care 35
risk in fetal interventions 99–100, 141
Robinson, Jean 18
Rose, N. 127
Rothman, Barbara Katz 19
Ruddick, William 45

S v. St George's NHS Trust (1997) 24, 201–2
Samerski, Silja 73
Sandberg, D.E. 171–2
Saunders, Cicely 184
Schmitz, Dagmar 3–13
screening, prenatal 7, 144–52; aims 145; autonomy paradigm 146–7; counselling challenges 151; double-purpose screening 147–9; ethics of 149; fetus or future child, focus on 150–1; lack of debate over 148–9; mixed messages in 147; moral status of the fetus and 18; 'prevention as beneficence' 149–50; in professional and patient discourse 79; termination of pregnancy as prevention 145–6; types of (PS1, PS2) 144
self-defence model 106
self-sacrifice model 106
sexual development *see* gender and sexual development
Sheppard, M.K. 128, 139
Smajdor, Anna 11, 39n11, 94–102
Smith, Barry 30
social expectations of maternal behaviour 6
social interests, gene-based treatments 118, 128
'social model of disability' 157–8
social pressure in pregnancy 100–1
Solomon, Andrew 157
Sparrow, Robert 172, 173
spina bifida 134, 204
Stein, Z. 145
Steinbock, B. 23
Strange, Heather 11, 78–90
Strathern, Marilyn 68
Strong, C. 41
support services, patient 109–11; *see also* counseling, perinatal palliative care
surgery: postnatal 9, 134; prenatal/'open fetal' 8, 29–32–33, 39n11, 133–4, 154, 197–8, 197n1
surveillance, fetal 6–8, 18

Tamar-Mattis, Ane 173
termination of pregnancy: ethics and 28–9; legal status of the fetus and 198, 200–1, 203–4; LLD and perinatal palliative care as alternative 187–90, **189**; media discourse on 68; moral status of the fetus and 17–19, 21–4, 54–5, 60n3; prenatal testing and 80–2
testing, prenatal 18–19, 78–81, 93n1, 93n2; discourse on 'the fetus' during 83–9; genetic 129; 'therapeutic gap' 81–2, 90
therapeutic misconception (ThM) 126–7
Thompson, Judith Jarvis 23, 39n8, 96
Tsarapatsanis, Dimitrios 12, 197–207
tuberous sclerosis (TS), treatments/trials for 122–3
twins, conjoined (ethical example) 32–6, 39n7
twin-to-twin transfusion syndrome (TTTS) 133–5, 204

ultrasound scans *see* screening, prenatal
'unborn child', as term 50, 51, 54–5, 59
United Kingdom (UK): legal status of the fetus in 200–2, 205; moral status of the fetus in 24–5; perinatal palliative care 184; prenatal testing in 78–9, 144
United States of America (USA): expectations for maternal behaviour

in 6; legal status of the fetus in 197, 199; moral status of the fetus in 17, 19–21; perinatal palliative care 184

Van Mechelen, W. 182
VC v. Slovakia (2011) 205
Verweij, E.J. (Joanne) 12, 133–41, 154–5
virilization *see* Dexamethasone (DEX)
Vo v. France (2004) 6, 204

wellbeing: child and future adult 168–9; pregnant woman 109
Whitfield, J. M. 184
whole genome sequencing (WGS) 146–8
Wiesemann, Claudia 10, 28–37, 172–3
Wilcox, William 45
Wilkinson, Stephen 98, 99
Williams, C. 139
Wirth, Mathias 12, 160, 166–76
women *see* pregnant women
Woods, S. 127, 139

X-linked hypohidrotic ectodermal dysplasia (XHED), treatments/trials for 121–2, 126–8

For Product Safety Concerns and Information please contact our EU
representative GPSR@taylorandfrancis.com
Taylor & Francis Verlag GmbH, Kaufingerstraße 24, 80331 München, Germany

www.ingramcontent.com/pod-product-compliance
Ingram Content Group UK Ltd.
Pitfield, Milton Keynes, MK11 3LW, UK
UKHW011009180926
475701UK00004B/637

* 9 7 8 0 3 6 7 5 9 1 3 7 3 *